A Doctor's Guide

WELCOME TO THE MIDDLE YEARS

A Doctor's Guide

WELCOME TO

HE MIDDLE YEARS

By Robert Taylor, M.D.

 PUBLISHED BY ACROPOLIS BOOKS LTD. • WASHINGTON, D.C. 20009

Library of Congress Catalog Card No: 77-46
ISBN: 87491-171-0

ACROPOLIS BOOKS LTD.
Colortone Building, 2400 17th St., N.W.
Washington, D.C. 20009

Printed in the United States of America by
COLORTONE PRESS, Creative Graphics Inc.
Washington, D.C. 20009

Library of Congress Cataloging in Public Data

Taylor, Robert B.
   Welcome to the middle years.

   Bibliography: p.
   Includes index.
   1. Middle age—Health and hygiene. 2. Middle age—Psychological aspects. 3. Adult-
   hood.
I. Title.
RA777.5.T39   613'.04'37   76-39649
ISBN 0-87491-171-0

CONTENTS

PREFACE

YOUNGSTERS, OLDSTERS, AND THE IN-BETWEEN generation all agree: the middle years are the prime of life. Here are the powerful, the beautiful, the knowledgeable and skillful. It's fun being on top—enjoying the highest income, exerting the greatest community influence, and standing proudly at life's apex.

And yet, with the attainments of the middle years often comes the feeling that "it's not enough." The fifty-year-old executive ponders what he or she lacks, not what has been achieved. The over-forty housewife broods about opportunities missed, forgetting all she has. The stage is set for the mid-life inventory, a time of reflection and reevaluation when assets are balanced against liabilities as the adult takes stock of his or her life. Painful as the introspection may be, the inventory helps define the challenges and guides the search for happiness in the middle years.

I'm a family physician (and in the middle years as well). We doctors think in terms of problems and solutions. While writing this preface, I stopped to see a patient with a throat infection. The remedy? A prescription for penicillin. The problems of the middle years are as common as sore throats, but the cures are rarely as straightforward. Some time after the thirty-fifth birthday, all adults face the awareness of aging, the mid-life financial squeeze, an erosion of personal prerogatives, losses large and small, plus perhaps even a whisper of failure. But we will make it through the middle years using the knowledge and experience gained during prior decades.

Modern people in the prime of life realize that we all encounter day-by-day challenges, constant as the spring rains and winter snows. There are no easy answers, just as there is no painless way to stop smoking. We adults—you and I—make our way as best we can.

ACKNOWLEDGEMENTS

APPLAUSE FOR CAROL OSTMARK who sorted references and typed the manuscript. And three cheers for artists Karin Blake, Dagmar Foerster, and Terry Dale. Without their enthusiasm, I might still be muddling through the first chapter.

Bouquets to my parents, Mr. and Mrs. O. C. Taylor, to my wife Anita, and to my daughters Sharon and Diana—with whom my middle years are never dull, and who make it all worthwhile.

Robert B. Taylor, M.D.

THE VITAL YEARS

> *Just think of all the things you can do after*
> *40! Professor Webster was 57 when he cut up*
> *Dr. Parkman and threw him into the furnace of the*
> *Harvard Medical School, and Dr. Parkman was 70*
> *himself! Nero was 52 when he set fire to Rome.*
> *Thomas Jukes was 54 when he married his own daughter*
> *to conceal the fact that he had killed her first*
> *husband. And I myself was 42 when I fell down a*
> *flight of steps and got water on the knee.*
> *Middle-age? Bosh!*
>
> *Robert Benchley (1889-1945)*
> *From Bed to Worse*

WELCOME TO THE MIDDLE YEARS—the adult generation, the productive decades, the time of promise and fulfillment. In the coming pages we'll examine the in-between years, with their trials and triumphs, and we'll turn the spotlight on you, Mr. and Mrs. America in the middle years.

Look in the mirror. What do you see? A few gray hairs. Some forehead lines that weren't there last year. A kind smile, a sense of concern, and perhaps a twinkle in the eye? You probably see a face that looks responsible, one that can be trusted. And the physique, well, perhaps you're slightly out of shape, but with a little practice you could show the young kids a thing or two.

What makes people in their middle years the way they are today? What has molded their character, shaped their thoughts, and charted their destiny?

Today's adult is the product of family and the world about him.

Tales of the Great Depression have made him frugal; World War II gave him a sense of omnipotence; he emerged from the Korean Conflict with a feeling of futility; and the Vietnam War eroded his confidence in our country's leaders. The rise of giant corporations and the super-giant federal bureaucracy have made him question the effectiveness of individual effort. Jet travel and the automobile have made him mobile, medical science has made him healthy, and changing morality has caused him to reexamine the old traditions.

The Diary of the Middle Years

The middle years: it's the forgotten generation—ignored by social planners, neglected by educators, and forsaken by the fashion industry. No mobs march on Washington demanding equal rights for those in their middle years. For the forty-year-old, there's no special interest congressional lobby, no federal health plan, and no tax relief. Bookstore shelves bulge with volumes telling how to feed, care for, and understand the younger generation, but literature about the mature has been in short supply.

With one exception. There's been a single constant chronicle of the middle years—the popular magazine sold at the corner newsstand. The magazine journalist has been the Boswell of people in their prime time. Let's jump into the middle years through the pages of some magazine articles from not too long ago.

In the 1960's, *Time* magazine presented a pioneering documentary of the middle years—it's joys and woes—and on the cover of that issue beamed Lauren Bacall. Remember her triumph in *Applause,* glorious in her role as a mature protagonist challenged by a postadolescent opportunist. Oh, how we cheered her victory. The title of the *Time* article was "The Command Years," and it pictured someone in their middle years in command of skills and experience, self-confident, and ready for adventure.

A few years later, in October, 1971, *McCall's* paid tribute to the middle generation in a special issue titled "The Underrated Joys of Being Over Thirty." It reminded youth worshippers that box office idol Ben Gazzara and "Say Hey" Willie Mays had both celebrated their fortieth birthdays, as had Angela Lansbury ("The girl who looked mature at nineteen has finally become that forty-five-year-old woman," the article said). Even the ubiquitous Dr. David Reuben offered his thoughts on "Sex and Middle Age," accompanied by a lithograph depicting a bacchanalian revel. Assured Dr. Reuben,

"There is no doubt that the second thirty years of a woman's life can be far and away the most satisfying sexually."

In the same 1971 issue of *McCall's*, Elizabeth Janeway expanded the concept of the middle years command: "We can act instead of wishing, and when we do, things happen. Not everything by any means and not always what we hope for. But more than the young, more than the old, we can intervene in events and change their course."

It was all heady stuff a few years ago. Then came the August, 1973 issue of *Harper's Bazaar*. The cover pulled no punches in announcing, "Good News About the Menopause" and "Sex Begins at Forty," and promising to tell "How You Can Feel and Look Sensational in Your Forties."

The cover girl was Dina Merrill—successful actress, razor-sharp businesswoman, warm mother of four children, loving wife of actor Cliff Robertson, and in her middle years just like you and me. Her formula for success at all ages: "My father always said, 'Smile and proceed as the road opens.' "

In the same 1973 *Harper's Bazaar* issue, Gloria Vanderbilt spoke of the middle years. "What matters is doing things that mean something to you," she said. "As you get into your forties, you see that if you are not doing what you want to, you'd better start."

"I've discovered that in the forties, you grow into your own strength," she concluded.

And strength we'll need to face the challenges ahead. For you and me, the road is not always open as it is for Dina Merrill. We can't always change the course of events as much as we and Elizabeth Janeway might wish. Yet how we prepare for and meet the challenges of the middle years—whether avoiding, confronting, or even yielding—will set the stage for life in the decades to follow.

Of course, there's more. The middle years are the age of rewards—when wishes come true. For most of us, the job's secure, there's money in the bank, and time to enjoy the good life. The middle years should be a joy, if you only dare to dream . . . and act.

The Middle Years Begin At . . .(fill in blank)

The first three decades are like shopping in a clothing store. You try on one outfit, then the next until you find the look you like. Finally, at about age thirty or forty, you've found an image that fits you comfortably, a personality you can feel at home with. And you settle into the middle years.

When does it happen? Pinpointing the middle years can be an evening's entertainment. Try it. Toss out the question at the next cocktail party. Some will say it begins at thirty, or thirty-five, or forty; and most people will agree that the middle years begin at least 5 years older than they are.

The truth is this: the middle years are a state of mind. You've reached them when:

Your son or daughter calls you The Establishment.

You can afford to dine in luxury and count calories instead of cost.

The gleam in your eye is the reflection from bifocals.

It's more fun to watch baseball than play.

The beauty you ogle on the street turns out to be your daughter's schoolmate.

The middle-years memory is a storehouse of facts from days gone by, and recollections can betray your age as surely as your birth certificate. You've reached the middle years if you can remember when:

Air was clean and sex was dirty.

Orson Welles' Martian invasion hoax caused panic in the streets.

A "going out of business" sign meant the shop was going out of business.

All movies were rated G.

Cars had running boards.

Wednesday was dish night at the local cinema.

A five dollar bill bought two bags of groceries . . . or more.

Today nostalgia is in fashion, and players search their memories for oddities of days gone by. Try the trivia test. Those in their middle years should remember most of these:

Comin' In On a Wing and a Prayer
Collier's
Nathan Detroit
Jeepers Creepers
The over-thirty-five who found romance

Win with Willkie
The man on the wedding cake
Fibber McGee's closet
Mairzy Doats
Captain Midnight
"Don't look back. Something may be gaining on you."

Perhaps I like Joan Rivers' comment best of all. In October, 1971, she wrote in *McCall's* " 'Where does middle age begin?', I asked myself this morning as I pulled on a new pair of orthopedic pantyhose."

"If you have to ask, my dear, you are obviously light years away from it."

Yet, trivia aside and witticisms notwithstanding, there's a more down-to-earth definition of the middle years. The middle years are when you can say, "I'm responsible."

The adult in the middle years has fought the battles of youth, and has the scars to prove it. He pays his own way, and perhaps supports a few who can't. He makes his own decisions based upon knowledge and experience, and takes responsibility for his actions.

The Age of Responsibility

It's being responsible that makes the juices flow during the middle years. Visitors of the late President Harry Truman chuckled at the sign on his desk: THE BUCK STOPS HERE. In our society, the buck stops at the middle years. The symbol of the adult in his middle years is Atlas holding the world on his shoulders. He is the builder that houses, the tailor that clothes, the farmer that feeds, the educator that teaches, and the banker that foots the bills for less productive generations.

WHO PAYS THE BILL

Each year the Internal Revenue Service extracts more than $200 billion from United States citizens, the money financing the all-but-overwhelming federal debt, the Armed Forces, and astronautical sojourns into space, not to mention congressional junkets to Paris and Rome. Do these funds flow from elderly affluent capitalists or bright young college graduates? Not a chance! The lion's share of revenue receipts comes from the middle-income wage earner in the middle years.

More than 60 million Americans are enrolled in schools and colleges, most of them dependent for support upon money from home, perhaps supplemented by Uncle Sam's largess or state scholarships. But whether it's from Daddy's wallet or governmental generosity, the source of most of these funds is the taxpayer in his or her middle years.

How about the aged, now enjoying property tax exemptions in many localities? Inflation has eroded the foundation of their savings and only the bulwark of social security payments saves many from inundation by debts. Also there's Medicare—the government's costly experiment in national health insurance. Despite federal claims that these programs are self-supporting, the bitter truth is this: each generation is paying for the last, and it is the people in their middle years who bankroll Social Security, Medicare benefits, and tax exemptions for today's senior citizen.

A LOOK IN THE MIRROR

It's men and women in their middle years, not the elders, that provide the driving force of government. During the middle years, the professional man finally hits his stride, the author masters verbs and participles, the housewife learns to cope with a clogged sink without tears, and the businessman rises to a post where his efforts pay off. He shoulders the responsibilities of supporting the family, perhaps financing a married son or daughter, and often supplementing the retirement income of aging parents.

Yet during the middle years, some duties diminish. Lessened is the emotional drain of childrearing, as offspring finally conclude college, perhaps marry, and first feel the thrill of paying their own way.

The executive can often plop his feet on the desk and say, "I've arrived. I've found my niche in the organization and don't need to compete any more." There's a stolen afternoon on the golf course, while the young comers still toil at their desks. With the children home less often or perhaps not at all, there are fewer housekeeping duties—more time for coffee, bridge, and painting. Here and there the idle hour gives a preview of retirement.

It's a time of change in many ways—in duties, in outlook, in opportunity, and even in physical appearance. Changing too are personal relationships, as married couples pass the tenth, twentieth, and thirtieth milestones.

The yoke of responsibility may chafe, one day seeming to drag tediously into another. And he sometimes surveys his image in the mirror and exclaims, "You've worked hard and sacrificed so much, what do you have to show for it? A frame house with a lawn that needs mowing again, two cars that gobble gas, and a pair of ungrateful children too busy to be home at Christmas. But most important, you've got a few years left. What are you going to do with them?"

The stage is set for the age of discontent, the abdication of responsibility: the rebellion of the middle years.

A Time of Discontent

> *Of all the barbarous middle ages, that which is most barbarous is the middle age of man.*
>
> *Byron*
> *Don Juan*

Last week, forty-eight-year-old Henry Smythe, trusted accountant with the same firm for two decades, suddenly tore up his balance sheet; deserted his wife, cocker spaniel, and garden tractor; and ran away with a twenty-two-year-old cocktail waitress.

The middle years is a time of life when, as in a hotel, most of the guests want to change their rooms. Few escape the urge. The comfortable life, once coveted, now seems trite; youthful fantasies cast their spell and the promise of new conquests beckons.

Some, like Henry, fall prey to the sweet siren song and their lives fall battered on the rocks of discontent. Others spurn the luring call and lash themselves to the mast of tranquility.

The discontent of the middle years is as a civil war—a barbarous conflict with duty pitted against desire, fantasy jousting with reality. Henry Smythe must have felt the battle rage; in one camp, the sexual reawakening whispered, "Henry, you've spent too many years with ledger books. Here's your chance for days of desire—and nights of fulfillment. Take this woman and escape!"

Opposing forces implored, "Henry, you can't desert your wife, the mortgage, the crabgrass. And how about your pension plan? You have obligations: There's the timeclock. Deadlines. The car payment is due. Stay! The bubble of folly will burst!"

Desire triumphed, and Henry bolted.

THE REBELLION OF THE MIDDLE YEARS

How does the civil war of the middle years begin?

New nations and young marriages are planned in love and cemented by determination. In those innocent days, what glorious deeds are done! In 1776, 13 youthful colonies linked their destinies as two young persons might wed their futures. By the 1860's independence was secure and prosperity reigned—yet civil war emerged, just as conflict marred the middle years of Mr. and Mrs. Henry Smythe.

By the middle years, most goals are reached. The joint quest for independence is past and the age of comfort has arrived. There is time to think about dreams.

"It's not what I hoped for at all—not good enough," the voices say. The years of struggle are banished to memory's archives, and the voices of discontent implore us to topple the towers of tradition. Banish the old ways. Revolt!

It's a second adolescence, this rebellion of the middle years. It's a regression to the days of youth—a fantasy of juvenescence and illusion of omnipotence. Yet the conflict is real and the wounds painful, as one revolts against his career, his spouse, and the life he has created.

The upheaval of the middle years, as certain as today and as vital as tomorrow, shapes the destiny of the nation and the man. It's the catharsis that purges the poisons, the bloodletting that drains the fever, the fire that tempers the mettle, the testing that discerns true value, and the turmoil that begets tranquility.

The self-examination, the discontent, the rebellion of the middle years—and their resolution, whether by anarchy or accord—are all pulse beats in life's rhythm. As babies must cry, young people protest, and elders denounce the current generation, so those in their middle years must suffer dissatisfaction with their lot. Eda LeShan called it the wonderful crisis of middle age. The wise person, in step with the cadence of life, resolves the crisis and emerges stronger for the battle.

In Step With The Rhythm of Life

What a paradox—that the age of responsibility should be the time when men and women suffer the urge to chuck everything. But it's part of the rhythm of life—the beat of the pulse, the tread of the footbeat, the rise and fall of joy and gloom. For Henry Smythe, it was the tick-tock-tick of the clock over the door and the click-click-clack of his Underwood . . . until he could bear it no longer.

The rhythm of the middle years brings trials and decisions, with victory or disaster hanging in the balance. The challenges we face would tax Odysseus, yet the rewards are fit for Zeus himself. It's the counterpoint of the in-between decades—duty locked in conflict with desertion, and accounting threatened by the promise of adventure. Adversity challenges and one person will falter and stumble, but the next will prevail and emerge victorious.

Who is the winner? It's the man or woman who recognizes his capabilities and limitations, who conserves his health, who is secure in his relationship with his family and others about him, and who is confident in his role as an adult. His step is sure, his goal in sight, and he marches in step with the cadence of life.

In the next chapters, we'll look at the miles to be marched, the pitfalls along the way, and the goals at journey's end—and how to make the most of those middle years.

2

A TIME OF CHANGE

> All things change; nothing perishes.
> Ovid
> Metamorphoses

CHANGING—GROWING, MATURING, then declining into oblivion—but always changing: that's what life is all about. Change is what separates the living from a speck of sand that remains inert from one eon to the next.

What physical changes challenge those in their middle years? The woman in her middle years sees menstrual flow cease, and the childbearing years draw to a close; these are blameless physical facts, but we'll see how the menopause is a scapegoat for a host of middle-age complaints.

The man in his middle years sees vitality, and sometimes potency, diminish—usually in inverse proportion to activity and self-esteem.

Pounds become a problem, sex sometimes a chore, and there's the housewife's headache, the executive's dyspepsia, and the blue-collar backache that shouts, "See! You thought you were indestructible, but you're just as mortal as all the rest."

Yet it's the changes and challenges, the rhythm of the middle years that can make the fingertips tingle, put zip in the step, and heighten awareness of existence. As Seneca wrote, we "begin at once to live, and count each day as a separate life."

Menopausal Facts and Fallacies

A pox on the man who coined the word menopause. And a man it must have been, who devised the ultimate weapon against the middle-aged woman: "Pay no attention to Mother. She's in the menopause."

There's a wealth of folklore about the menopause. Most are old wives' tales; they are inaccurate and they dramatize the universal contempt for the intellect of the aging female. Let's set the record straight, confirming the facts and exposing fallacies of the menopausal years.

FACT: Hormone levels fall during the menopause. During the middle years, the well of ovarian hormones flows more slowly, and eventually will dry completely. Circulating levels of estrogen and progesterone hormones dwindle, and the effects of this physiological fact become apparent.

Most noticeable is diminished menstrual flow. During the menopause, menstrual periods become lighter, shorter, and further apart, culminating in eventual absence of menstruation. For many, that's all there is to it. That's what menopause is—menses pause, forever.

Oh, how threads of facts concerning this biologic change have been woven into a rich tapestry of myth and mystery.

FALLACY: Heavy bleeding is normal during the menopause. False, false and a dangerous misconception! As the menopausal years begin, menstrual flow becomes irregular. Just as in the pubescent girl, menstrual flow can pop up like an unexpected guest. Gone is the reliable lunar rhythm of the childbearing years, and during the change of life the only constant may be irregularity.

At all ages, prolonged heavy menstrual bleeding is an important sentinel of disease. The same holds true for bleeding between periods or spotting following sexual relations. The dangers? Cancer of the female reproductive organs or perhaps the uterine fibroid tumor—noncancerous, but a prime threat to retention of the uterus, as we will see on Page 17. Fibroids often announce their presence by abnormal bleeding, a sign that alerts the patient to danger and guides the doctor to the diagnosis.

Heavy bleeding always carries the threat of uterine cancer, responsible for more than 13,000 deaths annually. Most uterine neoplasms occur in the cervix (the neck of the uterus), and thanks to the Papanicolaou smear screening test, the mortality rate due to this common tumor is declining.

Yet despite the publicity and ready availability of the Pap smear, some women accept heavy or intermittent bleeding during the menopause with a "why worry?" attitude. "It's normal during the change of life," they say, their delay dramatizing the dangers of this fallacy.

FACT: As ovarian function wanes, hot flushes begin. Here's the hallmark of the menopausal endocrine upheaval. Sometimes described as a heat flash or sense of suffocation, the hot flush assaults the anatomy like a torrid wave, chiefly affecting the upper half of the body, sometimes attending eating, exercise, or anxiety, or perhaps awakening the individual at night.

What causes hot flushes? The ebb and flow of ovarian hormones is controlled by regulatory substances produced by the pituitary gland at the base of the brain. These regulators are called gonadotropins, and during the reproductive years, they constantly adjust the body's levels of estrogen and progesterone. They also cause hot flushes. When aging ovaries no longer can manufacture estrogen and progesterone, the pituitary pours out huge quantities of gonadotropins, vainly attempting to coax more female hormones from the failing ovaries. But the high levels of gonadotropins succeed only in producing hot flushes. After a few months or years, the pituitary learns the futility of its efforts and production of gonadotropins drops . . . and hot flushes disappear.

Can anything stop the hot flushes? There's only one reliable cure. Replace ovarian hormones with tablets or injections, and pituitary gonadotropin levels promptly plummet, abolishing the hot flushes.

FALLACY: The menopausal woman will be mad as a hatter for a few years. Menopausal depression it's sometimes called, and refers to weepiness, sleeplessness, and despair that sometimes occurs at this age. Or perhaps it's anxiety—the incapacitating free-floating dread that afflicts some women and men during the middle years. Of course, if we can attach the handy label "menopausal" to the emotional disturbance, we all feel more comfortable . . . all except the middle-aged woman to whom the label is applied.

But the truth is this: we live in an anxious age. No age group has an option on emotional problems. How about young persons? It is reported that each year 1,000 United States students commit suicide, another 9,000 try but botch the attempt, while yet another 90,000 threaten but fail to act. Young adults? They crowd the offices of psychotherapists and marriage counselors. Then there are the elderly, waiting for beds in state hospitals and nursing homes as mentality fails to mesh with an overmechanized society. Sure, emotional problems may occur during the menopause, but are no more confined to this time of life than a broken leg or common cold.

FACT: During the menopause, the outlook on life often changes. Yes, indeed! Yet it is more a change in family structure and responsibility, rather than a mental alteration related to hormonal readjustment. The kids are off to college or in the service or perhaps married and struggling to establish a new household. The husband? He may be more engrossed in work than ever. The house seems so empty: the days as Girl Scout leader are over, there's no more chauffeuring the kids to basketball games, and there are only two places at the dinner table. During these years, almost incidentally, menstrual flow ceases.

Certainly, it's a time of readjustment for the middle-aged woman, who will eventually emerge from this period of her life a different, and hopefully more vital, individual.

FALLACY: After the menopause, sexual satisfaction goes down the drain. Not necessarily so! Of course, there's always the misguided adult who says to herself, "Well, I'm forty-five years old. It's all downhill from here, so it really doesn't matter any more." She spends her days nibbling Oreo cookies and sipping soft drinks until she has all the sex appeal of a giant marshmallow.

But for most, the menopausal years can be a time of sexual rejuvenation.

How about the hormone balance? Well, as we'll see later in this chapter, the ascent of androgenic hormones may stimulate the sexual desire, awakening urges dormant during the demanding child-rearing years. Finally, there's the quest for youth—the second adolescence when warm blood flows in the veins again. Out of hand, the youthful urges may cause revolt, but properly channeled, the surge of youthful sexuality that grips men and women during the middle years can spark the love affair between husband and wife.

FACT: You can get pregnant during the menopause. There's many a change-of-life baby that attests to this assertion. Prevention calls for continued contraception, probably by the same means that proved reliable during previous years.

What's available? Surgical contraception—including hysterectomy, tubal ligation, or vasectomy—boasts 100 percent reliability, but is not advised for menopausal women with rapidly departing fertility unless otherwise indicated by disease. Oral contraceptive pills are almost as effective, provided they are taken as directed. They have the added boon of controlling menstrual flow, but carry the disadvantage of sometimes prolonging menstrual periods beyond their natural time of cessation. Available are a dazzling variety of intrauterine devices, coils, shields, and whatnot, reasonably reliable as contraceptives, but associated with an increased incidence of irregular, prolonged menstrual bleeding which may cause confusion to the doctor and patient concerned about possible cancer during the middle years. Then there's the diaphragm and contraceptive jelly, absolutely effective if used properly; if you get pregnant, you didn't use them correctly. Contraceptive gels and foams offer limited protection, but may be all that is needed to augment the relative infertility of the menopausal years. Out the window goes the rhythm method during menopause, as irregularity causes ovulation at capricious times, if at all.

When are you really safe? When can contraceptive practices finally be discarded? Most doctors agree that once two years have passed since the last menstrual period, the threat of pregnancy has departed and contraceptive practices may be discontinued.

FALLACY: When the menopause arrives, the figure goes to pot. While there will be some loss of breast fullness as estrogen levels drop, the many svelte women in their middle years belie this fallacy. But it takes work. Gone are the days of potato salad and chocolate cake; in middle age, a trim figure calls for dietary discipline, and exercise will be needed to burn up excess calories and tighten muscles. Adequate rest, too, is vital, as well as avoiding harmful habits. We'll discuss this all in Chapter 4.

FACT: The menopausal years, far from the disaster that grandmother whispered about, can be a time of fulfillment. Childbearing and rearing is over, but so is the daily drudgery that attended this duty, not to mention the monthly nuisance. The woman who defines herself as "Mother" may face a crisis, but the middle-ager who sees herself as a diamond with many facets—homemaker, wife, mistress, career woman, and community leader—can only view the menopause as a physiologic landmark, an alteration in hormone balance, and perhaps a release from some of the obligations that nature and society have imposed upon her sex.

Hysterectomy Hysteria

During or following the menopause, many women require a

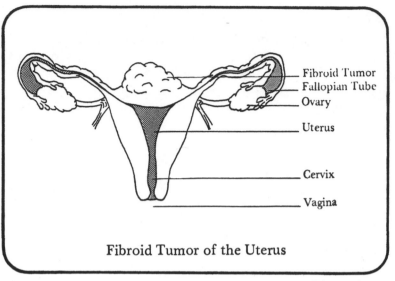

Fibroid Tumor of the Uterus

Figure 1

Figure 2

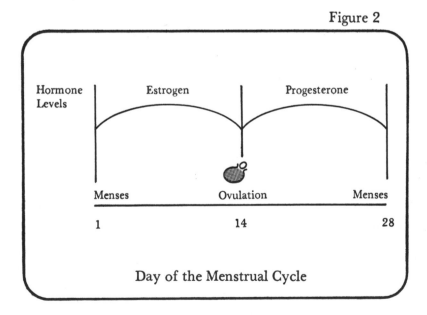

Day of the Menstrual Cycle

simple surgical operation called a hysterectomy, the third most frequently performed surgical procedure in the United States. Yet, like the menopause, this surgical operation is the subject of many misconceptions.

Let's make believe. Imagine you are Mrs. Nancy Brown, age forty-two. Nervously, you tug at a wayward curl of hair as you sit in the doctor's consultation room. Finally, after what seems like the whole afternoon, he enters and, with maddening self-control, peers at you over the desk.

"Nancy, my examination reveals a growth of considerable size on your uterus; it's causing troublesome bleeding, and the uterus must be removed. I'm talking about a hysterectomy."

What do you feel? Apprehension? Desperation? Terror? Or perhaps relief that he didn't mention cancer?

How about after the operation? Will you be left castrated, a female eunuch, with feminity only a memory? Will sex still be possible? What will your husband think? And will friends talk? What will you be like when it's all over?

Some of these questions, or perhaps others like them, pass through the mind of every woman who faces hysterectomy. With straightforward honest answers, she can usually face the operation with confidence. But, when the doctor is too busy to provide the answers, and well-meaning but thoughtless neighbors fill the void with misinformation, it's no wonder that many women suffer hysterectomy hysteria.

WHY HYSTERECTOMY?

Why is a hysterectomy needed? The most common cause is the uterine fibroid tumor—a noncancerous knot of tissue growing from the wall of the uterus (see Figure 1). Fibroids begin insidiously in young adult women and by the fourth and fifth decades may achieve troublesome proportions.

The trouble? Bleeding, often prolonged, profuse, and sometimes culminating in anemia (particularly if the woman subscribes to the fallacy that heavy bleeding is a normal menopausal phenomenon). Troublesome blood loss via the vagina brings her to the doctor, who diagnoses the fibroid tumor upon physical examination. The doctor will also perform a Papanicolaou smear and perhaps other tests to double check for cancer. Then he'll make his recommendation. Occasionally, all that is needed is a D & C—dilatation and curettage—

scraping away the lining cells of the womb. But more often, large uterine fibroid tumors causing troublesome bleeding demand hysterectomy.

Hysterectomy means surgical removal of the uterus (womb). Nothing more. Hysterectomy is a medical term joining the Greek words *hystero* meaning womb and *ektome* meaning excise. In a simple hysterectomy, the ovaries remain and continue producing estrogenic hormone. Because there's no change in female hormone levels following the procedure, feminity is preserved.

Sometimes the surgeon has a reason (such as cancer) for removal of the ovaries. The Greek word *oophoros* refers to bearing eggs and surgical removal of the egg-bearing ovaries is called an oophorectomy.

Other times the surgeon removes the Fallopian tubes. The Greek word *salpinx* means tube and surgical excision of the Fallopian tubes is called a salpingectomy.

The surgeon has all the options. He can remove the uterus, ovaries, tubes, or any combination. When all must go, it's called a hysterosalpingo-oophorectomy—a big mouthful to describe this major surgical procedure. Yet, if you sound out the individual Greek derivatives, the word is not nearly so formidable.

By examining the Greek roots of the word, we can see how hysterectomy involves the loss of only one organ—the uterus. Preserved intact is the remainder of the internal female anatomy.

AFTER SURGERY

The hysterectomy, whether performed through an abdominal incision or via the vaginal route, involves about ten days in the hospital, followed by a 1-month convalescence at home. There'll be skin stitches with the abdominal approach, with only internal stitches when the uterus is removed vaginally.

After surgery, Mrs. Middle-age should note little more than cessation of menstrual flow—no hot flushes, anxiety, loss of libido, or other of the real or fancied menopausal maladies. Why? Because the ovaries, not the uterus, produce the all-important female hormones, and in a simple hysterectomy, the ovaries function as before.

It's the same when the surgeon takes just one ovary—whether or not the uterus is removed. An airplane can fly on one wing, and the remaining ovary can provide more than adequate hormone support.

But what follows the clean sweep, the surgical removal of the uterus, tubes, and ovaries? The result is the surgical menopause, really due to sudden loss of ovarian hormones. Few if any symptoms can be blamed upon absence of uterus and tubes. It's the ovarian hormones, or rather absence of them, that causes the abrupt onset of menopausal symptoms following a hysterosalpingo-oophorectomy.

When a woman enjoys a normal menopause, ovarian function diminishes gradually and symptoms, if any, are few and spread over several years. Surgical removal of the ovaries at the time of hysterectomy, however, causes the abrupt onset of menopausal woes as the source of female hormones is removed with a slash of the surgeon's blade. When this happens, devastating hot flushes may follow abruptly, as well as accelerated aging of hormone-dependent tissues in the breasts and vagina.

It all has to do with hormones—those elusive chemical substances that control the lunar cycle and give girls their curves. Let's take a closer look at hormones, including how they function and how they can be replaced when needed.

How About Hormones?

The menstrual cycle sets the rhythm of life in the premenopausal woman, influencing her activities, weight, and sometimes mood. It's all controlled by female hormones and, as we have seen, alterations in hormone levels present one of the major challenges of the middle years. What are the female hormones, how do they work, and what follows their loss?

THE HORMONE SEESAW

The premenopausal woman has two types of hormones, female and male. Predominant are the female hormones—estrogen and progesterone—which maintain femininity. They give fullness to the breasts and hips, keep the face hair-free, set the pitch of the soprano voice, and soften skin. Both estrogen and progesterone are produced in the ovary, and their orderly rise and fall control the monthly menstrual cycle.

The menstrual cycle, perhaps obvious only as a once-a-month bloody nuisance, is actually an ever-changing process within the body (Figure 2). During the first half of the menstrual cycle, estrogen hormones predominate, causing growth of uterine lining tissue and priming the ovary for the second half of the cycle. By the end of the second week, estrogen levels have begun to decline, an egg is released from the ovary (ovulation), and progesterone levels rise. During the second half of the menstrual cycle, progesterone levels predominate, preparing the womb's lining cells for the fertilized egg which may follow. If pregnancy occurs, hormone levels remain high, sustaining the uterine lining cells that now carry a fertilized egg. However, if pregnancy fails to occur, the womb weeps for the pregnancy that might have been, seen as the monthly shedding of lining cells and blood.

Each woman has her own rhythm. In some individuals, menstrual flow occurs every 3 weeks, while others have a lunar rhythm of 5 to 6 weeks. In his medical text *Menstrual Disorders and Sterility,* S. Leon Israel writes that "the absolutely regular cycle is so rare as to be either a myth or a medical curiosity."

What about the male hormones? They're called androgens, and are primarily produced in the adrenal glands perched atop the kidneys. Available in much smaller quantities in women than in men, androgens give gusto, trim the hips, and sometimes influence hair growth in undesirable locations. They also stimulate the sexual urge.

The balance of hormones is a seesaw. When estrogenic hormones predominate, there's a full-bosomed, perhaps hippy figure, with lilting voice, and velvet skin. But if androgenic hormones have the upper hand, there'll be a boyish figure, husky voice, and the girl's best friend may be the cosmetician who treats her acne and removes her mustache.

How do oral contraceptives—birth control pills—influence hormone levels? They take control! Most oral contraceptives contain both estrogen and progesterone hormones, and produce stable hormone values throughout the month, eliminating the dip at 14 days that attends ovulation. With the egg sequestered in the ovary, fertilization cannot occur. The oral contraceptives also control menstrual flow, which can be hastened by stopping the pills a few days early or delayed by continuing to take a few extra pills at the end of the month.

THEN THE MENOPAUSE

Along comes the menopause. The swan song of the ovaries echoes through the endocrine system and, as levels of estrogen and progesterone drop, menstruation ceases. The gonadotropin hormones from the pituitary gland clamor for increased ovarian production, but elicit only the hot flushes of the menopause. With the passing years, the female hormone shortage may become apparent as breasts sag, skin wrinkles, and here and there a wayward hair emerges.

Then the androgen hormones rise to the fore. Remember, they're produced in the adrenal gland, not the ovaries, and their levels are diminished not a whit. Eventually, the postmenopausal woman loses her estrogen-dependent immunity to diseases that plague younger men (such as hardening of the arteries), perhaps balanced by an increased sexuality thanks to the androgenic hormones.

Through the ages, the postmenopausal woman has been defined as suffering a deficiency of female hormones. Oh, yes, biologic assays have demonstrated that more than half of all women secrete some estrogens as long as 10 years after the last menstrual period, but not enough to preserve the feminity of the younger woman. And when the menopause followed surgical removal of the ovaries, the changes were all the more traumatic and abrupt.

What to do?

Medical treatment of the menopause, like votes for women, is a twentieth century phenomenon. Three factors delayed development of this landmark medical therapy: in the nineteenth century and in the years before, medical science directed its energies toward conquest of the great plagues—diphtheria, yellow fever, smallpox, tuberculosis, and others; their defeat allowed physicians to focus on less life-threatening entities. Of course, prior to the nineteenth century, most women did not survive past the menopausal years and, in fact, in 1900 a woman's life expectancy was only 52 years; today's post-menopausal survival of 20 years or more was only a distant dream. Finally, the estrogenic hormones—the tool to treat menopausal deficiencies—became available only during our lifetimes.

What weapons do doctors and menopausal women now have in their arsenal? Available are natural estrogens, such as conjugated estrogens (Premarin or Menest) or ethinyl estradiol (Estinyl), found in the urine of horses and pregnant women, as well as in the human placenta. Or the doctor may prescribe artificial estrogens such as diethylstilbestrol, now widely used in both medical and veterinary practice. As well as being active components of birth control pills, the estrogens are the vanguard of attack against post-menopausal estrogen deficiency.

Available also is progesterone, the hormone that prepares the womb for arrival of the egg. One brand is the Provera tablet. Although a vital ingredient of birth control pills, progesterone is not routinely prescribed for symptoms of the menopause, although some doctors insist that a few tablets at the end of the cycle are beneficial.

Androgens play a minor role in treatment of the menopause; they are used infrequently, and almost always in combination with estrogen to treat the selected individual who needs a boost in vitality. As Doctor Israel writes, "The quantity of androgen required to alleviate the menopausal syndrome is too close to the masculinizing dose to warrant its widespread usage for this purpose."

WHO NEEDS HORMONES?

Why take hormones and meddle with the body's chemistry?

Taking estrogenic hormones after the menopause merely replaces a deficiency, just as the diabetic injects his dose of insulin each morning. In a sense, it's correcting one of nature's mistakes. If we could sum up the boons of estrogen therapy in one sentence, it's this: *estrogens help preserve youthful feminine tissues.* They delay softening of the bones that could result in shortened stature or even the classical dowager's hump of old age, and they help preserve breast fullness and prevent the vaginal irritation that plagues many aging women. Estrogens help combat the masculinizing changes of aging—the facial hair, the husky voice, and the slight balding at the temples. Last of all, and this is the reason that most often prompts doctors to recommend their use, they stop hot flushes dead in their tracks.

Other than the blessed absence of hot flushes, the postmenopausal woman may not see their benefits for years. But when she crosses that never-never line between the middle years and senior citizen status, the benefits of estrogen therapy become apparent as a more youthful appearance and enhanced integrity of vital organs, arteries, and bones.

"Well," you are probably thinking, "with all these wonderful advantages, shouldn't everyone take hormones?" Like bikinis, they're not for everyone. There are a few disadvantages, and even some hazards. The first problem often encountered is resumption of uterine bleeding, even after the menopause seemed to be past. As we mentioned earlier in this section, estrogenic hormones cause growth of the lining cells of the womb, just as in the first half of the menstrual cycle. If estrogens are taken continuously, growth may be colossal, eventually leading to persistent daily spotting. The cyclic use of estrogens, taking the tablets 21 or 25 days each calendar month or perhaps for 3 weeks out of every 4, lessens overgrowth of uterine lining cells, although the monthly rest period may be punctuated by episodes of spotting. Normal? Probably so, in a woman taking estrogens. But the doctor's never really sure, and must prove that the blood loss isn't due to cancer.

Of course, there's no such problem following a hysterectomy. Lacking lining cells that might bleed, the uterus-less woman seems the ideal candidate for estrogen replacement therapy.

But there are other dangers, too. Estrogens spur breast activity, restoring a youthful contour, but sometimes causing uncomfortable tenderness or even worrisome cysts. Dosage adjustment and monthly rest periods minimize these problems.

Although the controversy is as yet unresolved, the use of estrogens seems to be attended by an increased risk of blood clots in the leg, occasionally releasing a tiny particle that shoots through the veins to lodge in the lungs.

Then there's the cancer threat. Recent evidence has linked diethylstilbestrol to vaginal cancers in young women whose mothers took this apparently harmless compound while pregnant, and 1976 studies suggest that estrogens may contribute to uterine cancer. For these reasons, doctors continue to be cautious, avoiding estrogen therapy in women with known or suspected breast or pelvic tumors and in those individuals with a strong family history of cancer in these areas.

"How long should I take hormones?" My patients often ask.

"Indefinitely," is the best answer. If the effects continue to be beneficial and problems don't arise, there's no reason why hormone replacement can't continue for many years after menstrual flow has ceased.

The Frigidity Fable

"Doctor, I'm a little ashamed to tell you this, but I need help desperately. I think I'm frigid. My husband says I'm as cold as a TV dinner." Tearfully, Mrs. Harris told her story. She sweated shame from every pore, as though admitting robbing the poor box in church.

Married to the same man for 15 years, she had achieved sexual satisfaction a few times early in their marriage, but over the past decade her interest in sex had sunk to zero. "Sometimes I go through the motions, just to please my husband, or perhaps to keep him from chasing other women. But I haven't enjoyed sex in years. I complained of so many headaches that last year he bundled me off to a neurologist, and I sit through the Johnny Carson Show each night just so I won't have to go to bed. At times, I have even pretended to have an orgasm, just so he won't feel inadequate."

Frigidity. Even the word conjures up an icy lifeless image. Over the bridge table, matrons bandy gossip of indiscretion, infidelity, and divorce—but rarely female frigidity. Even the index of S. Leon Israel's text *Menstrual Disorders and Sterility* fails to list this seemingly common female problem. It's as though not discussing its existence will make it go away.

WHO'S FRIGID?

But the frigidity threat remains, and is far from exclusive to the middle years. It terrifies teenagers who fail to reach fulfillment in furtive liaisons. When the young bride finds the conjugal bed short of her expectations, she hastily concludes, "I'm frigid."

Even Mrs. Senior Citizen, perhaps really suffering an estrogen deficiency of the vaginal tissues or a partner of equivocal virility, may see herself a frigid failure as a female.

Let's define frigidity. *Dorland's Illustrated Medical Dictionary* describes it as sexual indifference. In common usage it means failure of the female to achieve full sexual satisfaction. But from these simple thoughts have evolved a cornucopia of misconceptions, and it's time to set the record straight.

There's a world of difference between "don't" and "can't." Rare indeed is the woman who can't achieve sexual satisfaction, yet there are millions who do so rarely, if ever. Why? Let's examine some of the causes of so-called frigidity.

One very common handicap is the inept husband. He comes in many sizes and shapes. One is Savage Sam who pounces on his wife as if she's a lamb at slaughter, satisfies his sexual hunger with all the tenderness of an angry grizzly, and bounds off to the refrigerator. Or there's All-Thumbs Arnold, who bungles the effort time after time. Most devastating of all is Speedy Gonzalez; a popular book once asserted that the sex act from beginning to end lasts an average of seven minutes. It's more like seven seconds with Speedy Gonzalez, who reaches the height of ardor in an instant and ejaculates before his partner begins to be aroused. Are these women frigid? We'll never know. They're denied the opportunity to find out.

Another cause is what's called performance anxiety and, as we'll see, it's the source of most male sexuality inadequacy. This woman tries too hard. Her lover may be skillful, and let's assume he is. But knowing she's failed before, she enters each sexual union with all the ardor of an experimental biologist. She analyzes each motion, waiting in vain for the orgasm that never comes. Next time she'll try harder.

But of all causes of frigidity, the most common is hostility. This woman is going to bed with a man who has spurned her intellect, demeaned the dinner she prepared, and failed to notice that she cut 6 inches off her hair. Or maybe he is a prince, yet she's angry that he can't provide a fatter pay check or ensconce her in the castle of her dreams. Her love-making is a chore, performed contemptuously. Reach satisfaction? Not a chance.

OVERCOMING FRIGIDITY

It's time these women were cured of their fancied affliction. Counseling is needed, but sad to say, most physicians are woefully inadequate sexual therapists, having received little or no formal instruction, and relying upon their fatherly image and personal experience (which may be no more enlightened than the patients').

What's needed is what I call the three T's—teaching, technique, and time. Teaching must involve both parties. Just as it takes two to tango, successful consummation of the sex act requires the cooperation of both partners. The counselor will discuss the more urgent sexual drives of the male, and the leisurely responses of the woman. Because sexual satisfaction is emotional as well as physical, the discussion will bring out repressed anger and hidden hostilities, dealing with these problems and channelling the energy into more constructive activities. Perhaps each partner will develop an enhanced self-image and a deeper understanding of his or her marital role.

Theoretical discussions rarely suffice. Music theory alone won't teach how to play the violin. Also needed is instruction in technique. The clitoris, the female equivalent of the male penis, plays a dominant role in sexual excitation. For example, Masters and Johnson reported that stimulation of this small knot of tissue lying at the forward junction of the vaginal lips could elicit an orgasm without vaginal penetration. Although it took twentieth-century studies of pioneering scientists to define its function, the significance of the clitoris has been known for centuries to primitive tribes in Africa, South America, and New Guinea. In these areas, ritual "circumcision" of pubertal females ensured that the adult woman wouldn't feel the thrill of her sexuality and, by so doing, helped guarantee that she would remain the docile servant of her husband. What's the significance of these facts for the supposedly frigid woman? Her partner's stimulation of this area by whatever mutually pleasurable means can help heighten her sexual responses and banish frigidity.

Proper technique includes exploration of other erogenous zones as well—breasts, ears, neck, even fingertips. The enlightened sexual counselor will suggest new techniques to banish the tedium that follows years of sexual congress with the same partner.

Time, too, is important in overcoming frigidity. The husband is encouraged to slow down, taking time to whet his wife's sexual appetite. Vital also is time to enjoy love-making without fear of interruption or worry that the roast in the oven may be burning. Finally, there must be time—weeks, months, and years—to give love a chance once again.

In almost all instances, sexual inadequacy is a fable—conceived in ignorance and nurtured by fear. Enlightened professional counseling can explode the myth and bring renewed sexual satisfaction to the middle years.

When Potency Wanes

Impotence is the male counterpart to frigidity, and the victim feels the same shame, perhaps more. His sword bent, his rifle jammed, and his baseball bat cracked; all phallic symbols seem to mock him. So shameful a sin is impotence that divorce laws often deny dissolution of the marriage for mental cruelty, yet permit a wife to rid herself of an impotent husband by the stroke of annulment.

THE FEAR OF FAILURE

Impotence differs from frigidity in one vital way. Cool sexual indifference characterizes most frigid women; the impotent male may be consumed with desire, yet he can't perform. He moans, groans, and makes excuses, but his manhood lies limp as a wet noodle.

Two types of impotence emerge. The first is Phil the Failure. He can't get it off the ground. Try as he might, each attempt at sexual intercourse meets with the same end—inability to achieve a satisfactory erection. Then there's Fast Fred, off to a speedy start but quickly petering out. He may ejaculate abruptly or simply lose the urge, in either case leaving his partner feeling gypped: "Is it all over already?"

What causes healthy men to lose their "nature?"

Just as the husband often shares the blame for female frigidity, the wife of the male who "can't cut the mustard" may be, in part, at fault. The castrating woman is her own worst enemy. "Why can't you get a better job like the other men around here? If you were more forceful, you could certainly get a raise. At least you could find some time to fix the car and paint the house. But you're just no good for anything, even in bed," is the constant refrain whenever he's at home. It's a wonder this man comes home at all, much less makes periodic abortive attempts at sex. No question about why this man lacks potency; his wife wouldn't allow it.

Even more often impotence begins with a combination of fatigue, anger, frustration, weariness, and perhaps even alcohol. The man who toils at an emotionally exhausting job often lacks the pep for sex at night; yet the wife may coax and, for reasons best known to him, he tries. When fatigue brings failure, he concludes the worst.

Anger and frustration dampen the fires of sexual ardor, as does preoccupation with business worries and financial woes. Add to these weariness—the tedium of mechanical caresses and predictable positions—and we'll see why Doctors Masters and Johnson wrote in their book *Human Sexual Response,* "Loss of coital interest engendered by monotony in a sexual relationship is probably the most constant factor in the loss of an aging male's interest in sexual performance with his partner."

Attempted sexual union often follows the use of alcohol, which William Shakespeare once described as increasing the desire but taking away the performance. It may be the before-dinner martini or an evening's spree, but alcohol takes its toll in potency.

Fatigue, anger, and the rest merely contribute to the periodic inadequacy that affects most, if not all, males from time to time. The severe potency problem arises when an occasional failure mushrooms into performance anxiety of monumental proportions.

"I'll try, but I know I'm going to fail. It didn't work last time or the time before, and why should things be any different now?" With the threat of failure foremost in his mind, our hero begins the clinical experiment. Little cares he about her emotional responses, nor is he sparked by the fires of passion. He remains a spectator, viewing his failure as though on a television screen. Predictably he fails as, frustrated rather than aroused, he sees the erection fail to materialize.

The speaker who freezes on stage and the athlete who blows his big chance must feel the same frustration. It's performance anxiety at its worst—the most common cause of male sexual inadequacy.

WHAT, HOW AND WHEN

What's the treatment? Therapy of impotence parallels that of frigidity, and includes the same three T's: teaching, technique, and timing. Counseling is needed, and a good start will be the family physician. A physical checkup confirms the absence of diabetes and the few obscure conditions, such as a blood clot in the lower aorta (Leriché syndrome), that causes a rare case. But unless he has more time than most family physicians I know, plus special training in the field, don't rely on good old Doc for sexual counseling. It's just not his line, but he can probably make an enlightened referral.

Counseling involves both partners, routing out sources of conflict and hopefully renewing the conjugal relationship. The whys of failure will come under scrutiny. Perhaps failure in bed is just a symptom of overwork at the office—a sign to slow down. Maybe alcohol has become a problem, with impotence merely another indication of the illness. Most important, the sexual counselor will examine the fear of failure, perhaps leading the couple for the first time into a discussion of their unhappy plight.

Proper technique can be as important in arousing the impotent male as in overcoming frigidity. Sometimes there's a relearning process. When potency goes plop or the onset of frigidity freezes sexual relations within a marriage, doctors often prohibit abortive coital attempts, and substitute graduated touching exercises. Call them sophisticated petting parties if you will, the touching exercises help stimulate sexual awareness without arousing performance anxiety, without interjecting the threat of failure. Handholding, back rubs, and fingertip explorations all help stir the interpersonal awareness buried beneath decades of marital ennui.

Next may come instruction in new techniques involving the erogenous zones, showing how creative tactile stimulation of the penis may arouse Phil the Failure while a quick squeeze may slow Fast Fred. Technique instruction may also include new coital positions, teaching the partners how to make the most of a less-than-optimum erection.

It all takes time. There must be time for counseling, touching, and getting to know one another again. Perhaps there's time to get away for a weekend, a few days each month, leaving children and cares behind. Nothing fancy. Check into a motel with instructions to be called only in case of fire. Then you'll have time to submerge the fear of failure in the act of love.

Sex in the Middle Years

Some people say, "I'm too old for sex. The urge leaves when you reach middle age."

Horsefeathers! What these people are really saying to their spouses is, "Our relationship has all the tenderness of cold oatmeal, and you haven't turned me on in years. Rather than do it badly, let's not attempt sex at all."

This union needs help. And quick! The middle years should be a time of sensitive sexuality. Androgenic hormones, spurring desire and drive, come to the fore and help heighten sexual responses. Then there's the lessening of some chores during the middle years, with the husband firmly settled in his job, the household functioning smoothly, and children off to school or on their own. As mundane duties lessen, there's time to savor personal relationships often neglected in the busy decades past.

Don't forget the youthful urges that beset adults of both sexes. When the in-between years bring the second adolescence and hot blood flows in the veins, libidinal energy will find an outlet. Marital strain is a danger, but the spouse who revels in his or her partner's sexuality will have little cause for worry. Perhaps if Mrs. Henry Smythe had kept her husband satisfied and happy, he would have said, "No, thanks" to the seductress.

More than ever before, sex during the mature years seals the union between a man and woman. The responses are deeper and more tender, strengthening bonds forged by decades of life together. Masters and Johnson said it all: "Those who can communicate in bed can usually communicate outside it."

Sex is the most fun you can have without laughing. And yet there's sometimes laughter too. A healthy sexual relationship is the celebration of mutual esteem, physical attractiveness, healthy bodies, self-confidence, and love. The middle years can be your sexual heyday. Enjoy!

3

THE LOOK OF MATURITY

A good face is a letter of recommendation,
as a good heart is a letter of credit.
            Edward George Bulwer-Lytton
            (1803-1873)

GONE IS THE DAY WHEN people in their middle years donned a frumpy housedress or perhaps a rumpled dark suit, and gave mere lip service to appearance and style. Magnificent describes the appearance of many over forty—trim waistlines, glowing skin, with-it hair styles, and the look of vitality.

Thanks to medical science, creative chemistry, and changing attitudes, the look of maturity can be your best ever. Here's how:

Saving Your Skin

Skin is the body's packaging, protecting vital organs against wind and weather, yet always on display. The slim, physically fit individual won't look his or her best if the skin looks like old shoe leather. She can't long rely on hot flushes to bring a rosy glow to the cheeks.

First the basics. There are three types of skin: dry skin, oily skin, and combination. The key is sebum—the ubiquitous skin oil that makes noses shiny.

Teenagers have abundant sebum, accounting for oil-clogged pimples and acne bumps. The typical teenage face is oily at its best, and sometimes the overproduction of skin oils persists into the middle years.

Dry skin is the other side of the coin, and is more common in middle age. As the teenage years become a memory, skin oil production dwindles and acne, like the old soldier, fades away. Next comes the golden age of skin—young adulthood—when facial tissues are ideal, not too dry and not too oily. But in time, there develops a crisis in skin oils, and the short supply brings dry skin.

Combination skin may plague the young adult or middle-ager. It's the paradox of oil production, with dry itching tissues of the temples, cheeks, and ears flanking a central oily panel with glistening nose and shiny forehead.

What's the importance of skin type? It's this: each skin texture requires special care, and while a super-fatted soap will merely fail to scrub away skin oils, a super-strong cleanser could devastate dry skin. Here's how to care for skin during middle age:

• Oily skin demands a thorough morning wash with soap and warm water. Then dry briskly and splash on an astringent. Wash again at noon if a fingertip drawn across the forehead shows oils, and if necessary reapply make-up. At bedtime, scrub well with soap and water and rinse thoroughly, perhaps adding a brisk splash of alcohol. For deep pore cleansing, once-a-week steaming or facial mask is recommended.

• Dry skin deserves gentle handling. Use a cleansing cream to wash the face each morning; soap is for youthful oily complexions. Gently blot dry before applying a moisture-saving make-up base. In the evening, wash again with a cleansing cream, followed by a nighttime moisturizer, perhaps a hormone cream, or even an eye cream left to work overnight.

• Combination skin requires dual care, with the peripheral dry areas handled delicately and the central oily panel scrubbed assiduously to remove excess sebum.

• Of course, there's the lucky individual with satin-smooth skin. Optimum care begins with a morning wash and brisk rinse, followed by a light moisture cream to preserve youthful texture. In the evening, remove make-up, wash again, and apply a night cream. The best cleanser? For normal skin, I recommend good old-fashioned Ivory soap. For individuals whose skin is exposed to urban grime, a weekly facial mask treatment will pry soot from pores.

PREVENTING PREMATURE AGING

Skin can grow old before its time. The changes occur at a turtle's pace, hardly noticeable, until one day you touch your cheek and it's dry, cracked, and has all the elasticity of cardboard. Itching in skin folds may occur, or perhaps there's advanced aging with keratoses in sun-damaged areas.

Skin, most exposed of all organs, suffers the assault of pollution, weather, and self-inflicted abuse—all contributing to premature aging. Sunlight can be the skin's worst enemy; small doses impart a healthy tan, but excessive sun-bathing can cause skin dry as the Sahara. Then there's wind, rain, and the nip of winter cold—all robbing skin of protective oils. City grime adds its insult, plugging pores and forming a dry dirty film. Skin oils also are lost in overheated rooms during winter and air-conditioned areas in hot summer months. Add to these factors the normal waning of skin oils with advancing age, not to mention departing hormone support as Mrs. Middle-age passes the menopause, and it's small wonder that aging skin can be a major problem of the middle years.

Help is at hand. Premature skin aging can be prevented or treated. Here's a seven-step program to preserve healthy skin during meridian years:

1.   Protect the skin from excessive sunlight, dampness, cold, and city air, as well as overheated rooms and relentless summer air-conditioning. This means effective use of gloves, hats, scarves, or even a skier's face mask, as well as moisturizing creams and lotions.

2.   Eat right, avoiding excessively rich, spicy, or acid foods which may trouble skin. Cake, chocolate, soft drinks, and large helpings of greasy foods are out.

3.   Exercise daily, stimulating blood flow to skin and vital organs.

4.   Get your share of rest, a full 8 hours of sleep each night, with time for relaxation on weekends. Burning the midnight oil drains vitality from skin cells, leaving the middle-aged epidermis looking pale and wan.

5.   Handle skin gently, using a light fingertip motion when applying soap, creams, or lotions. Always begin at the neck or chinline working upward—never down. Be kind; don't brutalize the skin.

6.   Choose skin care products rationally—no easy task considering the multitude of choices. There are moisturizing creams and lotions, some good, some better, and some containing exotic fruits and vegetables. Cleansing creams remove surface grime and open pores; astringents closes the pores. Finally, there are hormone

creams containing estrogenic substances—lifesavers for the estrogen-poor post-menopausal woman with skin beyond her years.

7.   Consult your physician if troublesome skin problems persist. There are a host of skin diseases, of far more import than complexion problems, that defy home-care efforts and require professional treatment. If in doubt, the doctor is only a telephone call away.

Better skin can be yours during the middle years. Facts are important, and a good reference source is my book, *Doctor Taylor's Guide to Healthy Skin for All Ages* (Arlington House Publishers, New Rochelle, N.Y., 1974). With the facts in mind, plan your skin care program and stick to it. The reward? Magnificent skin in the middle years.

Hair Today

Today, hair is in. It's been lauded in verse, immortalized in song, and raised to new heights over Broadway. Long hair is the badge of ritual nonconformity, short hair is for hardhats, and graying hair is a badge of distinction. For woman, it's her crown of glory; for man, it's an excuse to spend Saturday morning with cronies at the barber shop. Hair is to be enjoyed—tease it, fondle it, groom and caress it—while it lasts. Because what's hair today may be gone tomorrow.

HAIR AND CARE

The middle years can be hair's finest hour. It's when decades of proper hair care pay dividends. What are the hair care problems of the middle years and how can they be prevented?

Dry, flyaway hair, often brittle as October hay, may be the harvest of overtreatment—too many bleaches, tints, sets, dryings, and permanent waves. Or perhaps too many hours in the ocean or baking in the sun, not to mention wind whipping through the hair on the upper ski slopes. It's a classic hair problem in the middle years—protective oils in short supply and soon dissipated, leaving individual hair strands dessicated. The treatment? Dry hair shampoos and cream rinses, foreswearing overtreatment with bleaches and tints, as well as hiding hair from sun and surf.

Less common is the oily scalp in the middle years. But when present, luxuriously lubricated hair needs frequent shampooing, twice weekly or more often—or the set falls limp an hour after curlers are removed. Some wrap their hairbrushes with gauze to remove oils when brushing the hair each night. Vital is a strong shampoo, one specially formulated for oily hair or even a dandruff shampoo (since dandruff is nothing more than the caked residue of excessive scalp oils).

Hair with body has bounce. It's a natural for all hair styles and holds a set as though cast in bronze. Few are so lucky. The hair of many middle-agers is limp, lacking body and requiring a permanent wave to give fullness. Back combing (teasing) helps, at the risk of damaging hair fibers, and large-roller sets provide a cursory curl, but Mrs. America with limp baby-fine hair will find that most hair styles require a periodic permanent wave.

The permanent wave also helps hide thinning hair. By swelling the hair shaft, it adds needed body to the tresses. The permanent wave is a job for the beautician, who should test the waving solution on a sample curl before beginning.

Hair's vitality is safeguarded through proper care and handling. Here are the rules of hair care during middle age:

- Choose the shampoo that is right for your hair, and don't hesitate to seek professional advice. Then follow the package label directions and rinse thoroughly before drying.
- Avoid overdrying in the sun or under the dryer. Use heated curlers infrequently and the curling iron only for extra-oily hair. Excesive heat sucks vital oils from hair shafts, leaving them dry and brittle.
- Keep the ends well trimmed. Hair grows about 1/2 inch a month; the tip of a 4-inch hair strand is 8 months old. Sacrificing the terminal 1/2-inch helps avoid split frizzled ends.
- Tease gently, if at all.
- Curl carefully. Not too tight, or there's a tug at the hair roots. I discourage sleeping with curlers in place, or wearing tight headbands or hair styles that pull at the scalp.
- Shun excessive hair sprays which dull the hair's natural sheen. Use just enough to hold a hair style, and remove regularly by shampooing.

GRAYING HAIR

Each gray hair is a messenger of mortality; it seems to shout, "You're getting older, getting older!" We can accept silver hair as a badge of senior citizenship, but when premature graying colors middle age, it can be crisis time.

What to do? Tints can hide the gray, preserving the illusion of youthful hair color. Whether or not to tint depends upon your coloring; the fair complexion may look pallid with graying hair, while silver locks may complement olive skin tones. And, of course, there's the image. The middle-ager in an executive post beyond his years may welcome a few gray strands of dignity, while the individual whose career demands a youthful appearance may elect to dye. For generations, it was the ladies who hid gray hair, but during the past decade, men, too, have learned that removing gray can deduct years from their appearance.

Yet, perhaps the best solution to graying hair is equanimity. As George Bancroft observed, "By common consent, gray hairs are a crown of glory; the only object of respect that can never excite envy."

HAIR DEPARTING

During middle age, hair often says farewell and departs. First there are little hints of leave-taking—drains clogged with hairballs and brushes loaded with snarled strands. Then there's the receding hairline, the widow's peak, and rising forehead. Then one day there's the sudden realization, "Good grief! I'm losing my hair!"

Male pattern baldness often reaches its pinnacle in the middle years. Heredity is the key, and the man with departing hair probably has a family tree populated by bald eagles. For him, there's naught to do but accept the fate of male pattern baldness.

Therapy with males hormones enjoyed a brief flurry of popularity, until doctors discovered that absorption impaired hormone production by the testicles and might stimulate cancer of the prostate. Then there are hair transplants—leapfrogging plugs of tissue to the balding area—popular with entertainers and politicians, those in the public eye. But most accept the mirror pate with a sigh, if not with pride. As my father said, "It's just less hair to comb, more face to wash."

How about hair loss in the female? Sometimes it occurs following childbirth, and your neighborhood beautician can tell tales of women whose hair departed by the handful 3 months following delivery. Patience is the most prudent therapy, and almost all regain their full complement of curls after a few months of anxiety.

Occasionally female hair loss accompanies a thyroid deficiency, usually linked with weight gain, mental sluggishness, and coarse skin.

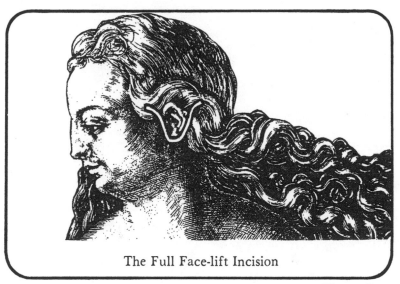

The Full Face-lift Incision

Figure 3

Figure 4

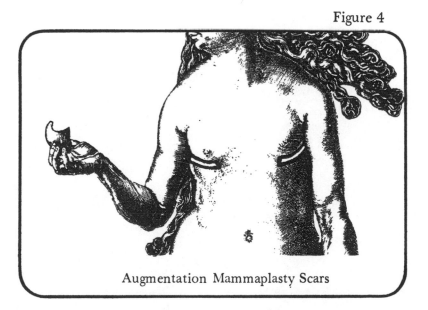

Augmentation Mammaplasty Scars

The doctor is the best source of advice, and if a thyroid hormone shortage is confirmed by blood tests, the prescription for thyroid replacement should restore lost hair before too many months have passed.

A few women suffer hair loss following the menopause, as estrogenic hormone production fails. The most rational treatment? Hormone replacement to stimulate hair growth and relieve other manifestations of estrogen hormone poverty.

With a Little Help From the Plastic Surgeon

Nature sometimes makes mistakes, and errors are often most distressing during the middle years, when sagging tissues accentuate defects and when it's most important to look your best in business and among friends. At times like this, many middle-agers seek a little help from the plastic surgeon.

Plastic surgery is not cutting up one's credit cards, nor has it much to do with synthetic chemical compounds, although a bit of silicone or an inert appliance may be used from time to time. The adjective plastic refers to the pliable, pullable, rearrangeable properties of skin, allowing the improvement in what nature has provided. Practitioners of this art should better be called cosmetic or aesthetic surgeons.

Mother may say, "Don't meddle with nature." But the middle-aged individual with a half dozen chins, or breasts that swing like pendulums, may fail to heed maternal advice, and in selected cases, creative cosmetic surgery can boost self-esteem and confidence.

ON THE OPERATING TABLE

There are six major plastic surgical procedures performed. Costs vary according to the area of the country, but a ballpark figure is $1,000 to $5,000, including the surgeon's fee and hospital bill. The results? These vary with the skill of the surgeon and the quality of the tissues with which he works.

The full face-lift tightens the jawline, eliminates jowls, and banishes built-in frowns. An incision is made as shown in Figure 3, sagging tissue is removed, and tiny sutures close the wound. Altogether, the operation takes about 4 hours, and up to 1 week in the hospital. After a decade, a major face-lift may sag, perhaps necessitating a small tuck on each side or even eventually a second full face-lift.

Rhinoplasty lets you pick your nose—pert bob, ski jump, or aquiline. The procedure takes about 2 hours and is capped by a postoperative nose splint. Seldom performed on middle-agers, the rhinoplasty is more favored by teenage girls and boys, whose appearance may show a striking change postoperatively.

Blepharoplasty tightens drooping eyelids, a common problem of middle-aged and older individuals. Two hours under local anesthesia and the surgeon is usually finished. Sometimes blepharoplasty is performed at the time of a full face-lift. Bleeding into the orbital tissues leave black eyes that may last for weeks, a small price to pay for the dramatic improvement in appearance afforded by this simple procedure. How long do results last? They're relatively permanent, usually outlasting the major face-lift.

Hair transplants leapfrog tufts of hair from hirsute areas to barren pates. Once the transplanted plugs have matured, the recipient seems transformed from a balding prematurely old individual to a more youthful person with a full complement of hair.

Mammaplasty may enlarge, equalize, or reduce breast size. Don't underestimate the extent of this procedure, which takes several hours under general anesthesia, and may involve a week or more in the hospital. Reduction mammaplasty is indicated for the middle-ager whose superabundant breasts cause sagging posture, while augmentation mammaplasty (making small breasts larger) is performed for more aesthetic reasons. Natural skin folds hide the scars (see Figure 4), and yes, it's true that the surgically reconstructed breast remains firm and youthful longer than those not having undergone surgery. For further information about augmentation mammaplasty, request a copy of the pamphlet *Facts You Should Know About Your New Look* from Dow Corning Medical Products, Midland, Mich. 48640.

Abdominal reduction removes redundant tummy tissues that often follows a dramatic weight loss. Horizontal incisions are the rule, partially masked by skin folds later. There are several types of operations performed, all major, and none to be undertaken lightly.

PLASTIC SURGERY: WHO AND WHY

Who has plastic surgery? For the most part, patients are middle-aged men and women filling vital roles in society and sharing one common defect: they look older than their years. And they share a single attitude—they're unwilling to accept premature aging when surgery is available. A random survey of plastic surgeons in New York City revealed that many of their patients (particularly those requesting face-lifts or hair transplants) were professional individuals, executives, entertainment personalities; curiously, labor leaders accounted for more than their share of surgery.

The "Why" is important, and middle-aged hysteria should never be the prime force behind plastic surgery. The ethical surgeon always asks the patient, "What do you expect from this operation?" If miracles are anticipated, the doctor probably will decline—politely. But if the operative candidate describes realistic goals and has a surgically correctable defect, then it's full speed ahead.

Plastic surgery is a logical extension of looking fit in middle age. If we encourage dieting, calisthenics, and jogging, and condone facial masks, hair dye, and strategically padded foundation garments, then why not a surgical tuck here and there?

Looking Your Best

In this all-important discussion of appearance, I've saved the key ingredient for last.

It's the smile that makes the difference. The toast of Europe in the mid-1800's, Lola Montez capped her brilliant dancing career with lectures on love and beauty. She once said of the mouth and lips, "It is the sentiment or emotion that lingers about the mouth that constitutes much of its beauty. A mouth perpetually contracted as though it were about to say no, or curled up with the passions of sarcasm and ill-nature, cannot be beautiful, even though its lips were chiseled like Diana's, or stained with the red of the ripest cherries."

All the skin creams, cosmetics, hair coloring, and plastic surgery in the world cannot mask a dismal countenance. A cheery smile and pleasant word for all—these are the secrets of looking magnificent in the adult generation.

Smile! And watch the road open.

KEEPING THE DOCTOR AWAY

It's a wise man's part, rather to avoid sickness,
than to wish for medicines.
            Sir Thomas More (1478-1535)
            Utopia

THE MIDDLE YEARS ARE A TIME of decisions about health: an expanding waistline demands dietary determination and puffing after one flight of steps may force a resolution to get in shape again. Tobacco, alcohol, the half dozen cups of coffee a day, and working till midnight all take their toll. Kids can survive these vices (although, of course, they shouldn't), but those in the middle years can't.

It's time to take the Fitness Pledge:

> I'm going to live to enjoy retirement in good health. There's no reason to spend my days with a spare tire around the middle, the foul morning taste of tobacco, and sitting on the sidelines while others enjoy the active life. Middle age doesn't mean over the hill. I've made my decision. I'm going to get in shape, and stay fit from now on.

Fitness Counts

Our forefathers followed the wagon trails West and cleared fields where great forests once grew. Our grandfathers and fathers plowed the fields, harvested the crops, and chopped wood for the long winter months. Today we guide our automobiles by power steering, harvest convenience foods at the corner grocery store, and chase winter's chill with a fingertip adjustment of the thermostat. During each day, we use electrical power, horsepower, and battery power—but very little muscle power. Our push-button world has banished physical labor for all but few, and most middle-agers must look to exercise and sports to maintain tone in seldom-used muscles.

It's the rare middle-ager who doesn't need exercise. Our bodies developed for the rigors of the stone age, when man battled nature and fierce predators. We live in the leisure age, and our greatest enemy is inactivity.

Physicians often disagree with one another; any three specialists in consultation will quibble about a diagnosis and quarrel about therapy, and often leave their patient in a quandary. But there's one topic upon which all physicians agree: properly graded exercise is essential for physical fitness at all ages.

Doctors know that exercise helps prevent and treat illness. Women used to languish in bed for several weeks following childbirth, as muscles wasted and tiny blood clots accumulated in the legs. No more! Today's new mother is up and walking the morning after childbirth. As early as 1955, Dr. Janet Travell recommended that young Senator John F. Kennedy of Massachusetts, then convalescing from back surgery, exercise the muscles of the lower extremities by rocking in a rocking chair.

The President's Council on Physical Fitness tells of a study covering 120,000 American railroad employees, showing the incidence of heart attacks among desk-bound office workers to be almost double that of men engaged in hard physical labor in the yards. The report continues: "The evidence is conclusive: individuals who consistently engage in proper physical activity have better job performance records, fewer degenerative diseases, and probably a longer life expectancy than the population at large. By delaying aging, proper exercise also prolongs your active years." (This quote and a first-rate fitness program are found in *Adult Physical Fitness*, a booklet prepared by the President's Council on Physical Fitness and available from the Superintendent of Documents, U.S. Government Printing Office, Washington, D.C. 20402.)

What does physical fitness mean to the middle-ager?

● Greater strength and endurance—the extra 50 yards on the drive down the fairway, or finishing the morning housework without feeling pooped.

● Better posture—shoulders back and head high as you take pride in your new physique.

● Fewer minor aches and pains—as unused muscles are called into action and creaky joints are limbered.

● A relaxed attitude—there's nothing like a brisk workout to banish the day's cares.

● More restful sleep—well earned following an active day.

● Greater vitality—as you bounce from bed eager to greet the morning sun.

How about you? How much did you exercise today? Did you ride when you could have walked a few blocks? Did you climb a flight of stairs once or twice? Did you swim, golf, or ride a bicycle, or perform any activity to exercise the 600-odd muscle systems in the body?

Probably not. "I don't know how to get started," you might say.

Here's how:

Three types of activity set muscles in motion. There's some exercise each minute of the day whether it's sitting, writing, thinking, or mowing the lawn. A conditioning program is more vigorous, helping tone muscles and increase vitality. And lastly there are sports, from badminton to skiing, each with its own rules and energy requirements.

EXERCISE IN DAILY LIFE

Muscle tissue makes up more than half of our body weight, and each movement of the body exercises some of these tissues. Take walking, which Thomas Jefferson called "the best of all exercises." Walking is readily available wherever you are, takes no special apparel, and it's free. In fact, it's been said that unless the human race begins to walk more, our legs, like the appendix, may become vestigial organs.

Perhaps women outlive men because of the exercise of housework—making beds, sweeping the floor, hanging laundry, and pulling the shopping cart. For Mr. Middle-age, there's mowing the lawn, changing the screens, or hammering and sawing in the workshop.

The number of calories burned during an activity is a fair measure of the value of the exercise. For example, peeling carrots or potatoes while standing at the sink burns almost twice as many calories as performing the same activity sitting at the kitchen table.

Here's a list of common daily activities and the calories burned each minute:

Activity	Calories burned per minute
Lying in bed	1.2
Sitting in a chair reading	1.4
Sitting doing desk work	1.6
Standing working at the kitchen sink	2.8
Carrying a bag of groceries	3.2
Taking a brisk shower	3.7
Ironing clothes	4.2
Chopping wood	4.9
Mopping the floor	5.3
Walking briskly outdoors	6.0
Shoveling snow	9.0

Each day offers endless opportunities to exercise, without donning tennis togs or toting skis to the slopes. Tomorrow when you take the subway to work, get off one stop early and walk the last few blocks. Or walk to the third floor and take the elevator the rest of the way. Don't lunch at your desk or at the kitchen table; walk several blocks, perhaps to a restaurant you've never tried before or even to a sandwich in the park. With more minute-to-minute exercise during the day, you'll lose that worn-out evening feeling.

PHYSICAL CONDITIONING

Conditioning means calisthenics; there's no other way to say it. A graded exercise program, beginning with warm-up drills and progressing to more strenuous efforts can tone the muscles, trim the waistline, and put pep in the step.

Actually, exercises can be fun. Pick the time that's right for you. Perhaps during a favorite radio or television program, maybe during the afternoon lull or before going to bed at night. Music helps, and you'll soon pick up the rhythm of the beat; perhaps pop your favorite disc on the stereo, something with a lively rhythm. For the sedentary executive or tired housewife, exercise can be more fun than a coffee break. Try it! The next time fatigue seems overwhelming, instead of a nap, take an exercise break.

Now's a good time for the obligatory word of warning. Regular physical exercise builds endurance, helps lower fats in the blood stream, pumps oxygen to vital tissues, and helps improve vitality.

kipping or running
n the spot for one
minute. Rest for half
minute. Then a new
eriod of work for
ne minute.

6
Stand on one leg,
supporting yourself
with one hand. Do
about 24 leg and arm
swings, changing
side every fourth
swing. Try to raise
up on your toes in the
extreme positions.

t on the floor with
ended knees and
pport for the feet.
e down and sit up
gain. The exercise is
peated up to 16
mes.

7
Standing with your
feet apart, hands on
hips, slowly rotate
the hips.

e on your stomach,
eferably with a
shion under your
vis. Lift your legs
d upper trunk so
t your body rests
the cushion. Keep
ur arms extended at
ur sides or stretch-
outward. The
ercise is repeated
to 16 times.

8
Easy skipping in
place or jogging for
half a minute.

nd with your feet
rt. Do about 24
ulder rolls.
nge the direction
rotation every rev-
tion or every fourth
olution.

9
Lie on the floor. Ex-
tend your arms with
your hands against
the floor (strong and
healthy persons) or
against a sofa or
chair. Do 1-15 push-
ups with the body
straight.

d with your feet
rt. Do about 24
swings across
front of your body
n exercise 4.

10
Skipping or running
on the spot or "step
test" 1—5 min.

Drawings by Claes Folcher
From *Health and Fitness*
by Professor Per-Olof Astrand, M.D.
Skandia Insurance Company Ltd., Stockholm
and the Swedish Information Service. 1972.

Total time for the training program: 8—15 min.

Infrequent bursts of frantic physical exertion, on the other hand, carry the risk of muscular strain, backache, or possibly a heart attack. As we'll discuss later in this chapter, each middle-ager should have a thorough physical examination each year. At that time, ask the doctor, "How about exercise, Doctor? Am I physically fit to start a conditioning program, and can you recommend a specific regimen?"

When starting, begin gradually. First come warm-up exercises to limber muscles and joints. Then conditioning exercises can begin, but each one should be repeated only a few times the first few days, gradually adding repetitions as endurance and strength grow.

There's a first-rate guide available from the President's Council on Physical Fitness and Sports, Washington, D.C. 20201: Ask for *An Introduction to Physical Fitness—Self-Testing Activities, Graded Exercises and a Jogging Program.*

Figure 5 shows an exercise program described by Per-Olof Åstrand, M.D. in *Health and Fitness* and reprinted with permission of the publisher, the Skandia Insurance Co. Ltd. of Stockholm.

Jogging deserves special mention. It's an excellent conditioning activity that has enjoyed recent public favor. A few minutes the first day is probably plenty, adding several minutes each subsequent outing. Plan a regular schedule; a once-a-week hour-long jog is not nearly as beneficial as a 10-minute run each morning.

Companionship helps. Some businessmen meet at the high school track or Y.M.C.A. each morning before work, to jog in concert. Take along your spouse, the children, or even Rover.

The right shoes are important. Cheap sneakers or ill-fitting footwear can quickly produce painful blisters. Better are firm tennis shoes with sturdy arch supports and tops that flex as the foot bends. For the true devotee, there are special shoes for distance running. The choice of footwear varies with the terrain: hard surfaces call for crepe or ripple soles, while tennis shoes are best for grass fields or running track.

Jog correctly, keeping the head and shoulders high; leaning forward strains the back and prevents full lung expansion. Use short steps, with the foot striking the ground beneath the knee instead of far in advance of the body. Land on the heel, then rock forward and push off on the ball of the foot. Deep breaths carry oxygen to the lungs. Jog until comfortably tired, then walk briskly until the urge to jog again strikes. It will, and daily jogging will soon become as routine as brushing your teeth in the morning.

SPORTS

Sports are the truly fun way to keep fit. Which sport? That's up to you and varies with your age, present physical condition, personal inclination, season of the year, and region of the country.

"I'm too old for sports!" you might say. Not true! There are sports to fit every individual, whether bicycling, swimming, golf, or skiing. As with conditioning exercises, it's a good idea to begin gradually; don't attempt too much the first day or the second. Vigorous sports should be attempted only after a program of physical conditioning. The best skiers spend autumn doing squats and sit-ups, limbering the hip and thigh muscles that will carry them schussing down the slopes in months to come.

Regular exercise builds stamina. An evening swim 4 or 5 days a week, a half hour on the tennis court each morning before work, or three afternoons each week on the golf course can all help keep you feeling fit.

Like the activities of daily living, each sport has its own quota of calories burned per minute. The following list can help you decide which sport is best for you:

Activity	Calories burned per minute
Sailing	2.6
Badminton	2.8
Golf	4.2
Bowling	4.5
Swimming	5.0
Tennis	7.0
Bicycling	8.0
Skiing	10.0
Squash	10.0
Handball	10.0
Jogging	15.0

Once you can say, "I'm as physically fit as I was at twenty-five," don't quit. Exercise, like weight control, should be a lifelong habit. A few minutes each day is all it takes to keep in trim. If the fitness program is interrupted by illness (or just plain laziness), start again. Begin at the beginning, slowly building strength and endurance to the peak of physical fitness that can keep you feeling alive in the middle years.

Eating Your Way to Health

In *Poor Richard's Almanack,* Benjamin Franklin wrote, "In general, mankind, since the improvement of cookery, eats twice as much as nature requires." It's still true. Furthermore, the middle-ager often selects foods of borderline nutritional value, consumed in unbalanced quantities and eaten at the wrong time of day. Few middle-agers are wasting away from malnutrition, but fewer still earn bonus points for creative nutritional programs.

Food has two functions in the body: it provides vital building blocks to maintain tissues and is burned as fuel to supply energy. Although most foods contain a little of each, they are classified as proteins, fats, or carbohydrates, according to the chief nutrient provided.

Proteins are the bricks and mortar of muscles, skin, and most other tissues. Each gram of protein provides 4 calories, and protein-derived fuel is burned slowly in the body. The best source of protein? Meats, fish, dairy products, and some vegetables.

Fats contain the most energy per ounce of all foods in the diet and are a prime source of calories. Flavor improves with the fat content of food—the marbled steak or the juicy rib roast—and a fat-free diet is as dull as dishwater. Yet, because fats contain a whopping 9 calories per gram, not to mention their contribution to arteriosclerosis, they must be curtailed in the sensible adult diet.

Carbohydrates are fuel foods, vital for the brain and nervous system, and providing energy to sustain the day's labors. Four calories per gram are provided, with more rapid metabolism than proteins. That's why a pancake-and-syrup breakfast leaves you hungry at 11 A.M., while a bacon-and-egg morning meal with the same total calories can fuel the body until lunchtime.

VITAMINS

How about vitamins? They're a mixed bag of chemicals, vital for proper nutrition and classified together because each aids the metabolism of proteins, fats, and carbohydrates. A vitamin shortage causes specific symptoms, but because a vitamin-poor diet may cause multiple deficiencies, the clinical findings are often not clear-cut.

Let's take a closer look at vitamins, examining classical deficiency states and how they might occur during the middle years.

Vitamin A, closely linked in nature to chlorophyll, occurs in abundant quantities in green leafy vegetables as well as in dairy products and eggs (thanks to the high chlorophyll consumption of chickens and cattle). Some fish, particularly the halibut, hoard vitamin A in the liver making fish liver oils the prime natural source of this vitamin. When vitamin A is in short supply, an early symptom may be poor adaptation to the dark, commonly called "night blindness."

Thiamine (vitamin B_1) deficiency has plagued mankind since the beginning of time. By removing the vitamin-rich outer coat of rice, inhabitants of Southeast Asia consuming a high-rice diet often suffered nerve pain and perhaps a wrist drop, mental changes, and occasionally heart failure. Does thiamine deficiency affect only those who consume a high-rice diet? We know now that the neuritis and mental aberrations of the alcoholic go hand in hand with thiamine deficiency and can sometimes be dramatically improved with administration of the vitamin. Eggs, green peas, Lima beans, wheat germ, liver, and pork are the best sources of this vital nutrient.

Riboflavin (vitamin B_2) is found in spinach, liver, milk, cheese, eggs, ham, and beef. A magenta-colored tongue, sores at the corner of the lips, and sometimes a scaly skin rash are the penalties for deficient intake of this vitamin.

Nicotinic acid (niacin) deficiency was known to eighteenth century Spaniards and Italians, who described *pelle agro* (meaning rough skin) which gives us the word pellagra. Doctors use the mnemonic device of 3-D's: pellagra causes dermatitis, diarrhea, and dementia. In the early 1900's, the disease was rampant in the southern United States, where corn and molasses were the dietary staples. Dr. Joseph Goldberger of the United States Public Health Service demonstrated in 1915 that pellagra could be cured—and prevented—simply by eating lean meat, yeast, milk, and fresh vegetables.

Vitamin C (ascorbic acid) is a vitamin with a history. Scurvy, the result of vitamin C deficiency, was described in the records of the crusades, and later became an occupational hazard of sailors on long voyages. A naval surgeon named James Lind in 1747 described "the putrid gums, the spots and lassitude with weakness of their knees" of afflicted mariners and prescribed for them "two oranges and one lemon given every day." Citrus fruits are our best natural vitamin C source, and a daily portion of fresh fruit or juice provides more than adequate amounts of the vitamin. How about vitamin C and the common cold? The chief proponent of this therapy is Dr. Linus Pauling, a two-time Nobel prize-winning chemist. Many physicians scoff at Dr. Pauling's claim and, at present, we can only say that the results aren't all in yet. In any case, the patient with a cold or flu is never harmed by taking substantial quantities of orange juice, and an extra one or two vitamin C tablets is unlikely to affect body chemistry adversely.

Vitamin D, found in fish oil and fortified milk and extracted from sunlight, is the catalyst in calcium metabolism. While youngsters deficient in vitamin D develop rickets, the middle-ager may suffer osteomalacia—softening of the bones, causing backaches and sometimes vertebral collapse. Vitamin D shortage usually results from poor absorption of the vitamin, such as the "malabsorption syndrome" or abuse of mineral oil laxatives which whisk vitamin D (and also vitamins A, K, and E) through the intestinal tract before absorption occurs.

Vitamin E (tocopherol) has sparked the fancy of food faddists and creative chemists, who have attributed to this simple molecule a host of mystical properties. Partisans claim that vitamin E reduces arterial blood clots, lowers the oxygen needs of muscle, prevents excessive scar tissue formation, and opens damaged blood vessels. On the fringe are reports that vitamin E can alleviate Mongolism, leprosy, and sterility. Most American physicians say, "Humbug." Who's right? Time will tell.

Vitamin B_6 (pyridoxine) is found in liver and yeast, and deficiency states are characterized by sores at the corner of the mouth, anemia, and weakness. Curiously, individuals receiving isoniazid treatment for tuberculosis sometimes develop a neuritis which can be prevented or treated with pyridoxine.

Vitamin K, extracted from food by bacteria in the intestinal tract, is vital for normal blood clotting, and anticoagulants of the warfarin family act by blocking vitamin K activity. A natural deficiency state is rare, but shortages may occur in middle-agers with liver disease or prolonged diarrhea, and following long-term antibiotic therapy that wipes out bacteria vital for vitamin K production.

Vitamin B_{12} (cyanocobalamin) helps bring red blood cells to maturity, and a shortage produces pernicious anemia. Yet, like vitamin E, vitamin B_{12} has been ascribed metaphysical properties far beyond its known role in red blood cell maturation. Many fatigued middle-agers report that a once-a-month B_{12} injection abolishes lassitude, and doctors have used the compound to treat neuritis, psoriasis, hair loss, and a welter of other ill-defined maladies.

A balanced diet containing meat, vegetables, fruit, and dairy products almost always provides more than abundant vitamins. Dieting may be a different story, and if there's a question about vitamin intake while on a weight reduction program, it's often advisable to take a supplementary multivitamin tablet such as Clusivol or Dayalet tablets once daily.

CHOLESTEROL AND FATS

During the middle years, sensible dieting calls for attention to cholesterol and fat consumption. Called atherogenic substances because they accelerate hardening of the arteries, cholesterol and fats abound in our lush American diet, combining with emotional tension and dwindling exercise to give Americans an awesome incidence of arteriosclerotic vascular disease. A daily cholesterol intake of only 300 milligrams (mg) is advised to help prevent cardiovascular disease. Fats should provide about one-third of calorics, with 2 mg unsaturated fats with each mg of saturated fats.

Here's a list of cholesterol and fats in each ounce of selected foods:

Food (uncooked)	Mg of cholesterol	Mg of unsaturated fats	Mg of saturated fats
Egg yolk	500	6	4
Whole egg	190	2	1.4
Beef liver	110	0.5	0.5
Butter	90	10	17
Lobster & oysters	75	0.4	0.2
Lard	36	20	13
Cheddar cheese	34	5	7
Bacon	31	11	6
Lean beef	25	0.8	0.8
Chicken	21	0.8	0.4
Corn oil	0	29	4

Individuals who shun saturated fats (lard, butter, and animal fats) and instead consume unsaturated fats (corn, cottonseed, soybean, or safflower oil) will enjoy reduced levels of atherogenic substances. Specific dietary recommendations include using skimmed milk rather than whole milk, liquid vegetable oil rather than solid shortening, fish rather than marbled beef, broiled food rather than fried, sherbet or ice milk rather than ice cream, and skimmed milk cheese rather than cheese made with whole milk or cream.

Detractors assert, "Diet isn't the whole answer. Many factors influence hardening of the arteries." True enough! But when all other factors are equal, the individual limiting dietary cholesterol and fats has the edge on avoiding coronary heart disease during the middle years.

BALANCING THE DIET

Let's put it all together. What's the proper diet for the adult years?

When calculating a diet, the doctor first considers the allocation by calories to proteins, fats, and carbohydrates. In cultures less affluent than ours, carbohydrates (such as rice) may provide up to 80 percent of the day's calories, and the protein content may be as low as 5 percent. In the United States, the dietary breakdown by percent of calories is about as follows:

Proteins . . . . 25 percent
Fats . . . . 30 percent
Carbohydrates . . . . 45 percent

Translated into foods, the recommended diet for the healthy middle-ager is as follows:

Daily Diet for Middle Age

2 servings of fresh fruit or fruit juice
2 servings of green or yellow vegetables
2 servings of meat, fish, egg, or cheese
3 servings of cereal, bread, or potato
6 glasses of water, which may include tea or coffee

Weight control within the framework of sensible nutrition is an ever-present problem for many adults, sometimes leading to ill-advised deviations from sound dietary principles. Fad diets give doctors gray hair and occasionally contribute to ulcers, gout, kidney

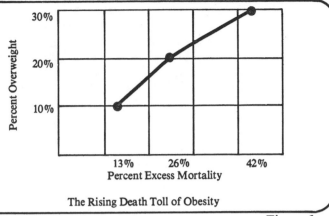

The Rising Death Toll of Obesity

Figure 6

CALORIE VALUES IN WEIGHT CONTROL FOR WOMEN WEIGHING 130 POUNDS:

Age		Daily Calories needed	
---	To maintain present weight	To lose 1 pound weekly	To lose 2 pounds weekly
30	2100	1600	1100
40	2000	1500	1000
50	1900	1400	900
60	1800	1300	800

Figure 7

CALORIE VALUES IN WEIGHT CONTROL FOR MEN WEIGHING 160 POUNDS

Age		Daily calories needed	
---	To maintain present weight	To lose 1 pound weekly	To lose 2 pounds weekly
30	3000	2500	2000
40	2900	2400	1900
50	2700	2200	1700
60	2500	2000	1500

Figure 8

stones, acidosis, and malnutrition of various sorts. Let's take a closer look at sensible weight control during the middle years.

A SLIMMER YOU

We'll start with the scales and tape measure. If your weight and measurements are the same as they were when you were twenty-five, and you can look in the mirror and say, "Even past thirty, you are still slim and fit," then you've got the fats under control. But many middle-agers could profitably shed a few pounds, and if your bottom bulges and a ripple of flab hangs over the belt, or if you've gained more pounds than you'd like to admit since age twenty-five, now is the time to take stock.

It's called obesity! Even the word has a dissonant ring. It's a spare tire around the middle; it's lugging a 20- or 30-pound load of excess weight all day long; it's feeling like a piano player in a marching band. Obesity is puffing after one flight of stairs, gussets in last year's clothes, and a salesclerk who tactfully guides you to the half-size dresses. From within comes the faint cry of the fabled thin man, "Help me escape from this load of lard."

Statistics round out the obesity picture: there are 30 million overweight Americans. And more to the point for middle-agers, the United States Public Health Service studies reveal that half of all adult males and 40 percent of adult women are significantly above their ideal weight.

The implications of obesity are ominous, and this section might well appear in the next chapter where we'll discuss the diseases of middle age. Four hundred years before the birth of Christ, Hippocrates observed, "Persons who are naturally very fat are apt to die earlier than those who are slender." Life insurance companies call it excess mortality—the likelihood of early death. Figure 6 tells the tale. The middle-ager who is 10 percent overweight (and half of all individuals aged thirty to thirty-nine carry at least 10 percent excess baggage) has a 13 percent greater risk of death than his or her slimmer counterpart, and the risk of excess mortality rises to 42 percent when the middle-ager is 30 percent overweight.

WHY FAT

Writing in the July-August, 1973 issue of *Medical Insight,* Carl C. Seltzer, Ph.D and Frederick J. Stare, M.D., discuss five factors contributing to obesity:

● There is certainly a **genetic or constitutional predisposition** to obesity. Pudgy parents beget chubby children, and the individual with the foresight to choose slim forebears begins life with a clear-cut advantage.

● **Impaired metabolism** plays a mysterious role, linking obesity to diabetes, atherosclerosis, and thyroid disorders. Stated almost too simply, the overweight middle-ager fails to consume his food as fuel and stores the residue as flabby fat.

● An **abnormal setting of the appetite thermostat** urges eating for its own sake. Food is consumed in prodigious quantities, long after satisfying hunger.

● The **psychosomatic** factor, eating to allay anxiety, adds pounds to individuals of all ages. The problem begins in infancy and childhood: "If you love Mommy you'll finish all your dinner." The message becomes clear—love equals food. The anxious adolescent snacks while under stress, the tense teenager turns to the refrigeratoɩ for solace, and the middle-ager nibbles when nervous.

● **Physical inactivity**, the failure to use the calories consumed, is the chief villain. Authors Seltzer and Stare assert, "Of these five causal factors, we think that the last, physical inactivity, is by far the commonest cause of obesity."

Other theories abound, and many diet specialists promulgate their hypotheses to justify their diet programs (and sometimes to sell their books), but there is no escaping basic principles, the most important of which is the fuel or fat potential of each food—its caloric content.

CALORIES COUNT

The weight-conscious adults (and aren't we all?) must learn to count calories. Let's start with a definition. The calorie is a unit of energy, and to convert it into measurable units, 1 calorie is defined as the amount of heat needed to raise the temperature of 1 gram of water 1 degree C.

That doesn't tell us much. Let's consider calories from another standpoint. One pound of weight is the penalty for 3,500 calories of excess food. This means that to lose 1 pound a week, 500 calories daily must be eliminated from the diet. If you cut your daily intake of calories by 100, you'll lose 1 pound every 5 weeks, while a 1,000-calorie daily reduction will shed 1 pound every 3½ days.

Caloric requirements change with each year of age, as metabolism slows and the adult acquires sedentary habits. After age twenty-five, the body requires about 1 percent fewer calories each year, and continuing to consume the same diet as an active teenager or even a twenty-five-year-old can quickly add inches to the waistline.

I advise my dieting patients to keep a diary, listing the foods eaten at each meal and noting the calorie content as found in standard dietary references. Breakfast and lunch should each contain about 30 percent of the day's calories, and about 40 percent should be consumed at supper, with the day's total calculated from Tables 7 and 8 according to age, weight, and desired rate of weight loss.

Planning the diet takes research—learning the calorie content of foods, including the low calorie good guys and high calorie villains. For example, butter at 200 calories per ounce has 40 times as many calories as lettuce, which weighs in at 5 calories per ounce.

Computing the diet also requires attention to fuel consumption. Many diligent dieters study the reference sources, visit the doctor, and keep careful diaries, yet the scale fails to budge. Why? Because the calorie intake, while theoretically correct for their age and weight, is not balanced by exercise. When planning a weight reduction program, be sure to review Page 44 showing the minutes of activity needed to balance mealtime calories.

Snack foods deserve special mention; they're the downfall of many middle-aged dieters. Let's consider a modest 100-calorie snack—an orange, large apple, or ten potato chips. To burn up the 100 calories, it takes seven minutes of running, 20 minutes of swimming, or 33 minutes of housework. And how about a 400-calorie strawberry shortcake splurge? You'll have to run 27 minutes, swim for 80 minutes, or do housework for more than 2 hours to consume the excess calories.

Don't, please don't diet faithfully all week and go down to defeat at the Saturday evening cocktail party. An 8-ounce glass of beer has 115 calories. One jigger of 86-proof whiskey has 100 calories, while a martini, Manhattan, or highball has about 150 calories. Even wine can be the dieter's downfall, containing 100 calories per 4-ounce glass of dry wine and a whopping 175 calories if the wine is sweet.

D-DAY BEGINS THE DIET

Controlling overeating is like stopping smoking. It takes planning, resolution, and determination to see it through. It means picking a D-day to begin dieting, hopefully during a time of minimal emotional turmoil. Tell your friends you are dieting; you'll be as embarrassed to reach for potato chips as the ex-smoker would be to mooch a cigarette. Keep tempting treats at arm's reach, preferably out of the house. And once you've begun, don't weaken. The stakes are too high.

Here are some helpful hints to help control weight during middle age:

● Eat your calories early in the day. A hearty breakfast helps ally hunger, and most food consumed after 7 P.M. ends up on the hips.

● Don't skip a meal, or you'll be super-hungry when mealtime next rolls around.

● Finish your salad (with a low-calorie dressing) before attacking the remainder of the meal. It helps control the urge to overeat.

● Try beginning dinner (and perhaps lunch) with a stomach-filling cup of beef or chicken broth, then top the light meal with a satisfying dish of low-calorie gelatin.

● Don't make thin foods into fat by cooking; a medium sized potato has 100 calories; French fried, it's up to 250 calories, and made into yummy home-cooked hash browns it can top 400 calories.

● Make it hard to cheat by banishing high-calorie snacks from the household.

● Form the habit of "just a small serving, please." Cutting each serving by one-third can drop the weight by 1 or 2 pounds each week.

How about diet pills? They're widely used, and have many ardent supporters among both doctors and dieters. Two general types are available. Bulk producers, usually containing methylcellulose (low-calorie fibers not unlike celery), are taken before the meal with a glass of water. "They absorb water and expand to fill the stomach," claim the manufacturers, although as I write this page, I'm watching one such tablet in a glass of water. It seems to crumble and bubble just a little, but its expansion is short of spectacular.

Then there are the anorexigenic agents—related to the amphetamines. These million-dollar darlings of the pharmaceutical industry reportedly provide a "lift," relieving the urge to overeat. Certainly, they increase metabolism, but much of their effect must accrue to the psychological value of consuming daily medication. Not insignificant are their possible side effects—nervousness, sleeplessness, increased heart rate, elevated blood pressure, and more. Use appetite suppressants only if prescribed by the physician. They supplement, rather than replace, dietary diligence and exercise.

Overweight individuals suffer the compulsion to put things in their mouths. I recall one teenage chubby who exclaimed, "I can't understand why I'm not losing weight. During the past month, I've eaten pounds of celery and lettuce, and consumed gallons of diet soda." Remember this: we lose weight by eating less and exercising more, not by increasing our consumption of pills or food. Substituting low-calorie items for fattening foods helps; adding low-calorie foods to an overly-rich diet doesn't.

Sometimes the urge to eat is overpowering and the yearning cavity in the stomach must be filled. At times like this, it's reassuring to have available low-calorie crisis foods that won't devastate the diet. Here's a list of diet-sparing treats that help halt hunger pains:

> Celery
> Coffee or tea, without cream or sugar
> Lemon juice, in water or on salad
> Pickles
> Radishes
> Bouillon or broth
> Gelatin

ON TO VICTORY

Weight control is a marathon race. We've all tried the short sprint—the crash diet guaranteed to lose a potful of unsightly pounds in an astonishingly short time. Sometimes it even works—for a while—but the metabolic turmoil created can be a high price, and once the diet is abandoned, pounds reaccumulate with monotonous predictability. We're beginning a long-distance weight control program. The goal is to attain the ideal weight for your age and height and keep it there. Begin with a trip to the doctor, including a thorough physical examination. He'll help choose the daily caloric allowance and assist in diet planning, and he'll prescribe exercise appropriate for your lungs, heart, waistline, and years.

Then follow the diet. No cheating. No days off. Set realistic objectives, both short-ranged and long. Plan perhaps to shed 1 or 2 pounds weekly, until the ideal weight determined with your doctor is attained. Don't forget follow-up visits at the physician's office; they help keep the dieter on course. The goal of successful dieting is not only a trim silhouette and increased vitality, but a reeducation of eating habits so that pounds shed remain off.

Eating your way to health during middle age calls for day-by-day determination and planning. Fad diets do little more than upset the metabolic apple cart. Sound nutrition is the answer, shunning unnecessary calories, trimming excessive dietary fats and cholesterol, and balancing the nutrients vital for continued good health during middle age and beyond.

When Alcohol Rules Your Life

More than two-thirds of all adults drink alcoholic beverages. For most it is an occasional cocktail or a glass of beer before bed, but for some, alcohol becomes a demon that can rule—and wreck—lives.

Whiskey is the catalyst of the modern social reaction, wine is for toasting, and beer the champagne of the working man. Curious it is, indeed, that the potentially toxic chemical alcohol exerts a major influence on our lives today.

From the ancient Celtic tongue comes the word whiskey, meaning water of life. Yet the "water of life" is really a depressant drug and might better be called the water of perdition, as it contributes to disease, property damage, and the perils of motoring on the highway.

Virtually any vegetable or fruit can be fermented to produce an alcoholic beverage. The resulting distillate is filtered, flavored, blended, and aged to create Spanish brandy, Scandinavian aquavit, Yugoslavian slivovitz, Japanese sake, Russian vodka, French wine, German beer, or good old-fashioned rye whiskey.

The quantities produced? They're gargantuan. For example, in the first 2 months of 1973, American swilled nearly 7 million gallons of Scotch whiskey.

With the public consuming a consciousness-altering drug in prodigious proportions, it's not unlikely that the middle-aged imbiber will suffer an occasional alcohol-related problem.

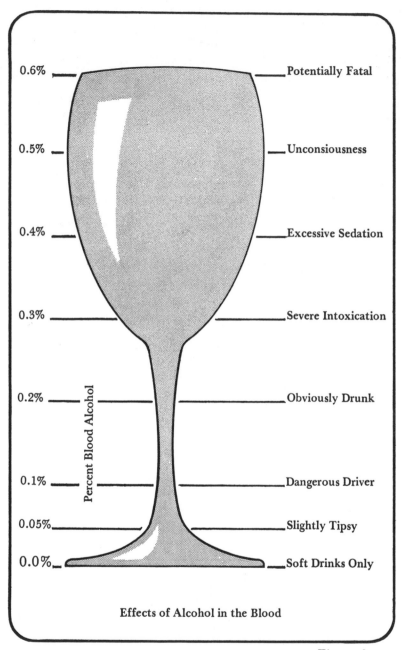

0.6%	Potentially Fatal
0.5%	Unconsiousness
0.4%	Excessive Sedation
0.3%	Severe Intoxication
0.2%	Obviously Drunk
0.1%	Dangerous Driver
0.05%	Slightly Tipsy
0.0%	Soft Drinks Only

Percent Blood Alcohol

Effects of Alcohol in the Blood

Figure 9

More than 200 years before the birth of Christ, Hammurabi in Babylon devised the first system of codified law; notable were sections devoted to alcohol abuse. The problem has skyrocketed with alcohol's increasing presence in the business and social world. In the next year, alcohol will be involved in 7,000 suicides, 25,000 traffic fatalities, more than 2 million arrests, and a national drain of more than $15 billion dollars in medical care, time lost from work, and damage to property.

THE PROBLEM DRINKER

Drinking problems come in two flavors: first there's the spree drinker. Sober, he is the paragon of respectability, trusted employee, community leader, dutiful parent. But give him a few drinks at a party to loosen inhibitions, and he doesn't know when to say, "when." Sometimes he regales the guests with witless tales and little harm is done, or perhaps he passes out under the mistletoe at the Christmas party. But place him behind the steering wheel of a car and he's an accident looking for a place to happen.

How much alcohol is too much? Figure 9 tells the tale. Two cocktails or two bottles of beer produce a blood alcohol of 0.05 percent, clouding judgment and confounding coordination in many individuals. Twice that amount, a blood alcohol of 0.1 percent, follows four 1-ounce cocktails, a level that may impair functioning in even heavy drinkers and described by the National Safety Council as indicative of a dangerous driver. When the blood alcohol level reaches 0.15 percent, acute intoxication is present. Unconsciousness comes at about 0.5 percent blood alcohol and death may occur if the 0.6 percent level is reached.

While we think of the spree drinker as a problem to his family and himself, the second type of drinker, the chronic alcoholic, blights far more lives.

There are 9 million American alcoholics. Stop a minute and think; that figure is astounding. One of every 20 to 25 Americans suffers the curse of alcoholism, and one of every six Americans faces the challenge of an alcoholic family member.

Traditionally, American Indians, Irish-Americans, and Eskimos have been particularly prone to alcoholism, as have been the offspring of alcoholic parents. But as the melting pot blurs ethnic distinctions, alcohol abuse has become a problem for middle-agers with scant regard for race, creed, or national origin.

Pity the alcoholic. If he has an ounce, he must have the whole quart. Once he starts drinking, his self-control goes down the drain. He'll beg, lie, or steal to get liquor, and often hides emergency bottles around the house for fear that the family will confiscate his hoard.

Most alcoholics consume a pint to a quart of liquor daily, and the 1,000-2,000 calories generated by metabolism of the liquor drown the appetite. In time, the alcoholic exists on a snack here and there, washed down by glass after glass of whiskey, wine, or beer. Little wonder that he is subject to vitamin deficiencies, malnutrition, liver disease, and all their complications, and has a life expectancy 10 years less than the nonalcoholic person.

ATTACKING ALCOHOLISM

How to treat the middle-aged problem drinker? There's no easy answer, as doctors are quick to admit. Unavailability is a good start—getting all liquor out of the house, even the hidden reserves. Counseling is an important next step, as the alcoholic forms a close relationship with a trusted family physician or psychotherapist trained in the management of the problem drinker.

Drugs are sometimes used. Tranquilizers may be substituted for alcohol during the early weeks of withdrawal, but there is a possibility of habituation to their use.

Sometimes the doctor will prescribe disulfiram (Antabuse) for the alcoholic who desperately desires enforced sobriety. After Antabuse is taken, even a small amount of alcohol will promptly cause palpitations, flushing, sweating, shortness of breath, and dizziness. A huge dose of alcohol could be fatal. Despite warnings, most alcoholics test the drug's effect once—but only once. For the well motivated alcoholic, Antabuse can be a beneficial aid, but the drug must never be given surreptitiously to an unsuspecting drinker.

The accolades in alcohol control go to Alcoholics Anonymous. Several factors explain their success. Group therapy is the keynote, with support offered by others who have endured the same misfortune, who praise success, and disapprovingly tolerate backsliding. When he joins Alcoholics Anonymous, the problem drinker must admit, "I am an alcoholic!" It's a big step forward and one that must be repeated daily.

The long-term member defines his status, "I am an alcoholic, and I have not had a drink for 15 years."

Alcoholics Anonymous, combined with family support and medical guidance, offers the best hope for controlling alcoholism. In most communities, the organization is listed in the phone book, or a note to Alcoholics Anonymous, Inc., P.O. Box 459, Grand Central Station, New York, N.Y. 10017, will bring a reply telling the time and place of the local branch meeting.

Do you have a drinking problem? Many do, deluding themselves about their alcohol consumption, yet often failing to fool family and friends. Information, educational services, and community action programs are available from the National Council on Alcoholism, Inc., 733 Third Avenue, New York, N.Y. 10016.

The after-work cocktail, or the nighttime toddy, can be a warm friend; but if the friend threatens to become master and rule your life, it's time to say, "I quit."

Foul Tobacco

I could deal with tobacco in one word: DON'T! Let's see why, and how.

Like the alcoholic, the tobacco addict should take the pledge and quit. An addiction? You better believe it! Doctors tell us that addiction occurs when habituation to a substance causes psychological dependence and when withdrawal results in physical symptoms. Smokers, read that sentence again and see if it doesn't describe you.

Why quit? Certainly, over the years tobacco has had some articulate spokesmen: Edmund Spenser in *The Faerie Queene* called it "divine tobacco." Molière said, "He who lives without tobacco isn't worthy of living." And Oscar Wilde called the cigarette "the perfect type of a perfect pleasure. It is exquisite, and leaves one unsatisfied. What more can one want?"

Yet all were habituated and, like tobacco addicts of today, sought to justify their continued use of the loathesome weed.

Now the Surgeon General has the last word: hazardous to your health. Yet, private doctors warned their smoking patients decades before the Surgeon General stole their thunder.

THE FACTS

More than 100 years before the Surgeon General grabbed the headlines, an 1859 study revealed the 68 patients in a French hospital at Montpellier suffered oral cancer—a huge incidence of an uncommon disease in a sparcely populated area. The cause? All were smokers, and a startling 66 of the 68 patients were habituated to short-stemmed clay pipes. Following the history-making report of these cases, the use of clay pipes plummeted, but tobacco use in other ways has flourished.

Here are some fascinating facts about tobacco consumption. The pack-a-day cigarette smoker:

Inhales cigarette smoke 60,000 times in one year,

Absorbs 90 percent of nicotine in inhaled smoke (puffing without inhaling cuts nicotine absorption to 10 percent),

Is hospitalized 50 percent more often than the nonsmoker,

Has a death rate from heart attack 70 percent greater than the nonsmoker,

Has a six times greater chance of premature death due to bronchitis and emphysema, and

Increases his chance of developing fatal lung cancer by ten.

And what of the two-pack-a-day smoker? The figures are much worse. His risk of a heart attack increases by 141 percent, and his likelihood of developing fatal lung cancer is 64 times that of the nonsmoker.

QUITTING

If you don't believe that cigarette smoking is an addiction, you will once you try to quit. It's tough, but it can be done. Here are some tips that may be helpful.

The next time the urge for a cigarette strikes, try to hold off for just 2 minutes. That doesn't sound too hard. By the end of 2 minutes, the urge will often have departed; you simply forget about the cigarette that seemed all-important a short time before. Sure, the urge returns, and when it does, try to hold out for 2 minutes again. By the day's end, there will be a· sizeable drop in cigarette consumption.

Some reluctant puffers keep a smoking diary. It may be a piece of paper taped to the cigarette pack recording each smoke, the time of day, the hour of day, and the activity at this time. A scorecard is available from the Public Health Service, showing the cigarettes not smoked each day and week (plus how much money has been saved). Write to Scorecard, Box A.R., Rockville, Md. 20852.

After a few days of keeping score, examine the pattern and resolve to eliminate the most vulnerable cigarettes—the smoke on the way to work or during midafternoon. After the easiest have been banished, go after the recalcitrants—the smoke after breakfast or during coffee break.

Try the 1-day cigarette fast. Promise yourself, "No smokes for one whole day." Then keep the promise! For 24 whole hours, you'll give your heart and lungs a break from toxic nicotine. After you have made it through the toughest 24 hours, why not go on to day two?

Cold turkey quitting sometimes works when you plan a countdown. Choose Q day—a date in the near future when stresses are likely to be least.

Get used to the idea; tell your friends you plan to quit. Reduce cigarette purchases so that you run out on the target date.

Then when the day arrives—QUIT! Announce to your family and all your friends, "I don't smoke any more!" The shame of failure helps keep you from lighting up. Burn your bridges behind you, giving away ashtrays, cigarette lighters, and other smoking paraphernalia; you don't need them any longer.

Tell friends, "Don't give me a cigarette even if I beg."

Make time in your schedule for long walks, and how about a few sit-ups or a quick jog around the house. After the first few days, you'll feel alive and fit, wondering why you ever were addicted to tobacco.

Most ex-smokers failed the first few times they tried to quit. After a few days of abstinence, they succumbed, wallowing in self-contempt after the first few puffs and saying to themselves, "I'd gone almost a week without cigarettes; now all that sacrifice has gone up in smoke."

So, Mr. and Mrs. America, if you're habituated to tobacco, take heed. Reread these statistics, send for a Scorecard, and perhaps request The Smoker's Self-Testing Kit and further information from The National Clearinghouse for Smoking and Health, Department of Health, Education, and Welfare, Bureau of Health Education, Center for Disease Control, Atlanta, Ga. 30333.

When you know the facts, you'll have the final word on smoking: DON'T!

But Only the Kids Take Drugs

"I don't know why the kids today take drugs. I'm sure my

children wouldn't, because we've tried to set a good example in the home. I've brought home pamphlets and books, and we've told them about the dangers of drug abuse. As parents we've done everything possible," laments the righteous mother or father.

But the advice given Mary and Johnny doesn't often jibe with the example set by the parents. The parents' actions, more eloquent than preaching, tell the tale. Parents can be heard to say, "The kids' drugs—marijuana and the rest—are loathsome and dangerous. They're not at all like the medication adults need to help lose weight, combat anxiety, and get some rest on sleepless nights."

Yes, Mr. and Mrs. America, take a look in your medicine cabinet. Check the pills that alter consciousness: tranquilizers, perhaps an antidepressant, certainly a sleeping pill to use in "emergencies," maybe diet pills left over from last summer's take-off-weight program, some codeine from the dentist, not to mention antihistamines, blood pressure depressants, and other worthwhile medication that could cause drowziness.

The physician-philosopher, Sir William Olser, once said, "A desire to take medicine is, perhaps, the great feature which distinguishes man from other animals." The follies of young people notwithstanding, the urge to consume drugs often reaches a pinnacle during the middle years.

It's nothing new. History and literature trace the adult urge to alter the state of consciousness. In Shakespeare's *Anthony and Cleopatra,* the Queen of the Nile pleaded, "Give me to drink mandragora . . . that I might sleep." Thomas DeQuincey in the nineteenth century wrote in *Confessions of an English Opium-Eater,* "Thou hast the keys of Paradise, oh, just, subtle, and mighty opium!" And even the intrepid Sherlock Holmes once said, "For me, there still remains the cocaine bottle."

As poetry and prose chronicled days gone by, life is seen through the omnipresent television eye. Tonight, pay attention to TV fare, not just the insipid sitcoms, but the blaring commercial messages. Count the advertisements for pills. Into our living rooms come exhortations for pills to subdue the pounding headache, calm jangled nerves, neutralize mother's cooking, and nudge us all to sleep. There is a pill for practically everything, or so it seems.

Doctors must share the blame. All too often, the busy practitioner succumbs to the temptation to jot a quick prescription, rather than root out the source of the patient's anxious symptoms.

Doctor Osler called it "nickel-in-the-slot, press-the-button therapeutics." At best, it offers relief of symptoms, without discovering the cause. The alternative? Uncovering the emotional origins of anxiety, depression, overeating, and sleeplessness—and uprooting them through counseling or psychotherapy.

Yet until the number of American physicians and psychotherapists is increased manyfold, adults will continue to take drugs. What are the problem pills?

DRUGS ADULTS ABUSE

Here's a partial list of potential problems in the medicine cabinets of most:

● The **antianxiety agents**, often called the minor tranquilizers, come in all colors and shapes. The long list includes chlordiazepoxide (Librium), diazepam (Valium), meprobamate (Equanil or Miltown), hydroxyzine (Vistaril), and many, many more. All help control the symptoms of mild emotional upsets, with a minimal loss of alertness. While true addiction is rare, millions of middle-agers are habituated to their use, dependent upon popping a "happy pill" whenever anxiety threatens. Although called minor tranquilizers, the side effects may be of major proportions; an overdosage may cause drowziness, slurred speech, and even coma. At risk particularly is the individual who takes an alcohol chaser after his pill; he may lose count, resulting in accidental overdosage and even death, accounting for many apparent suicides.

● The **antipsychotic agents**, also known as the major tranquilizers, include chlorpromazine (Thorazine), promazine (Sparine), thioridazine (Mellaril), trifluoperazine (Stelazine), and more. They are the doctors' big guns, indispensable in the treatment of schizophrenia and other psychoses. These potent medications are not for simple anxiety. When properly prescribed and the dosage carefully regulated, they decrease hostile and antisocial behavior, often allowing mentally ill patients to escape hospital confinement; their inappropriate use can cause tremors, jaundice, and low blood pressure, not to mention dizziness, drowziness, and fatigue. If the doctor prescribes an antipsychotic agent, the middle-ager should follow directions to the letter, resisting the urge to "take just one extra" when anxiety strikes.

● The **antidepressants** help lead the patient from the valley of despair. We'll talk more about depression in Chapter 6. The drugs important in treating this disabling emotional drain are imipramine (Tofranil), antitriptyline (Elavil), doxepin (Sinequan), protriptyline (Vivactil), and others. The drugs work slowly, and often favorable results follow a lag of several weeks. The depressed patient is always a suicide risk and doctors usually dispense these drugs in small quantities as well as offering psychotherapy and occasionally electroconvulsive therapy in selected individuals. Side effects? These include dry mouth, urinary retention, jaundice, sedation, and more. The antidepressants can be lifesavers for the patient who feels "Life isn't worth the effort" but only when taken under the direction of his personal physician.

    ●   **Analgesics** are painkillers. Most middle-agers lack access to the narcotic analgesics such as morphine, meperidine (Demerol), or codeine, but overuse of the nonnarcotic analgesics including propoxyphene (Darvon), phenacetin, APC, and aspirin is a medical and social reality. To a lesser or greater degree all analgesics share the potential to cause nausea, abdominal distress, dizziness, impaired consciousness, coma, and even death. Well we know that narcotic drugs can cause addiction, but we sometimes forget that the use of milder analgesics can establish harmful habit patterns. Special problems include kidney damage following overuse of phenacetin (found in APC tablets) and massive bleeding from the stomach can be the penalty for aspirin abuse. As with other medications in this chapter, the analgesics can be loyal friends when taken according to the doctor's directions, but harsh masters when they gain the upper hand.

    ●   **The sedative-hypnotic** agents reduce anxiety and promote restful sleep. In this group we find the barbiturates such as phenobarbital, amobarbital (Amytal), butabarbital (Butisol), and pentobarbital (Nembutal). Old-fashioned phenobarbital was the prototype, and about 1 million pounds of barbiturates—roughly 4½ billion doses—are consumed each year. Added to the list are the more recently developed ethchlorvynol (Placidyl), glutethimide (Doriden), and methaqualone (Sopor).

    What are the problems? One danger is oversedation, with drowziness, lethargy, and sometimes a morning hangover, particularly hazardous when hypnotic-sedatives are mixed with alcohol, tranquilizers, antihistamines, and some antihypertensive drugs. These drugs are favorites of potentially suicidal patients, who yearn for the permanent repose that overdosage can cause.

●   Diet pills in common use today are first cousins to the amphetamines. Although federal regulations limit the availability of amphetamine (Benzedrine) and dextroamphetamine (Dexedrine), millions of prescriptions are written each year for chlorphentermine (Pre-Sate), diethylpropion (Tenuate), phenmetrazine (Preludin), and phentermine (Ionamin). Taken once daily in the morning or perhaps before each meal, these drugs exert some small influence on the appetite. A jittery feeling is common, and if the middle-ager finds he or she is taking the drug for the "lift" it gives, it's time to stop. Side effects are dose-related and include agitation, slurred speech, tremors, and rapid heartbeat. If prescribed by the doctor, diet pills should be taken only during a period of controlled weight loss, with their use discontinued as soon as excess pounds have been shed.

The hard-core heroin addict is not the only drug abuser. In his own ways, the middle-ager sometimes abuses drugs. The first step in eliminating drug abuse is to recognize the problem. Discuss medication use with the physician, and follow his advice. Clean out the medicine cabinet, being careful to discard outdated and potentially harmful medications.

Then resolve: "These are my prime years! I want a clear head, without the blur of drugs in my system."

Martin H. Fisher had the final word on drugs: "Half the modern drugs could well be thrown out the window, except that the birds might eat them."

The Work Compulsion

Oscar Johnson owns a clothing store. It's not hard work, but he's there to open the door each morning at nine, eats a brown-bag lunch in the stockroom, and dashes back from dinner to greet customers in the evening. Six days a week, he measures waists, plans advertising, and frets about overhead. Sundays? Oscar pours over catalogs, balancing his present inventory against next season's fashions. His last vacation? That was 3 years ago—a weekend sales convention in Chicago. "Who has time for vacations when there's a business to run?"

The work addict can't find time to relax. To him, life is a duty and a chore. He keeps lists of projects to be completed and before one list is finished, he's started on another.

Inactivity gives the compulsive worker acute guilt pangs. "I feel

I should be doing something, getting something accomplished." Exactly what really doesn't matter, and when important work is finished, he tackles trivia. The thought of just loafing for an afternoon is intolerable.

Not all in their prime suffer the work compulsion, but many do. Most susceptible, paradoxically, are those whose lives are unfettered by the time clock:

The self-employed—the mom and pop business enterprise is a haven for the work addict. Solo ventures comprise the bulk of business failures, and to keep his head above water, the small-time entrepreneur often must devote many more hours to work than his corporate colleagues. Take a vacation? Who would mind the store?

Executives—they're in day-to-day competition with other companies and with younger men eyeing their positions. That means a briefcase full of work in the evening, weekends at the desk, and "working vacations."

Professional people—there's no telling when the phone will ring with a medical emergency, legal entanglement, throbbing toothache, or accounting crisis. Often the worst work addicts, we doctors should take a little of our own advice.

Working wives—they really have two jobs. After 8 hours at the desk, there's a house to clean and family to feed. Even at vacation time, there are meals to cook, clothes to wash, and children to mind. The working wife seems to be always on duty.

The clubwoman—she just can't say "No!" No one can handle the cancer drive, the library fair, or country club dance as well as she. It's as much work as pounding a typewriter, and drains her energy as surely as an 8-hour day in the office. Give up? The compulsive clubwoman can no more abandon her work than the executive can reject a promotion.

OFF DUTY

Mark Twain wrote in *Tom Sawyer,* "Work consists of whatever a body is obliged to do, and play consists of whatever a body is not obliged to do." The work addict needs to throw away his list once in a while. What's needed are some nonobligatory activities.

It takes some soul-searching, recognizing the value of creative leisure to rest the mind, recharge batteries, and use muscles otherwise inactive. The work addict is an orderly individual, and it's often best to bring order to leisure. This means allotting time for relaxation—

each day and each weekend—planning hours that have no label to them. Take Sunday: let's plan nothing and see what happens. Perhaps it will be a nice day for golf, or even a family picnic. Or maybe the urge to trim the hedge will be overwhelming. Wash the car, walk the dog, or lie in the sun. By budgeting time for relaxation, vital recreation won't be short-changed.

Longer time slots should be red-penciled on the calender. A 3-day weekend each month is a real shot-in-the-arm. Pick a new spot, perhaps a campground or resort hotel. Take the kids—or instead leave them at home and have a real vacation.

A week or two away from home each year should be mandatory. That's the way to return to the job really refreshed.

Recreation has its rewards—greater vitality, renewed interest in the family and job, and the zest for life that often is submerged in the day-by-day welter of trivia. Sure, it takes planning, but if the compulsive worker maps his recreation with the same zeal that he brings to his job, there can only be success.

Don't let all work and no play make a dull person out of *you*.

Rest for Your Life

Just as it needs food, drink, and exercise, the body needs rest. Most middle-agers need 6 to 8 hours of sleep each night, some less, a few more. Lingering too long at the party or staying awake to see the end of the Late-Late Show will take its toll in stamina tomorrow.

The best test of how much sleep you need is how you feel. Some middle-agers feel alert and peppy after 5 or 6 hours of slumber, and further loitering between the sheets only causes a groggy overslept feeling. For others, 8 hours are mandatory, and even 30 minutes less sleep results in a lethargy that lasts all day long.

Two problems arise. For some, rest won't come; and for others, there's not enough time in the schedule for needed sleep. Victims of both must pay the penalty imposed by a debt of sleep.

Worry is an archenemy of rest. Sleep eludes the individual whose mind is crowded with financial woes, job pressures, and family conflict. "How will I possibly get all my paperwork finished on time?" "How can we ever scrape together the money for this month's mortgage payment?"

For others, sleeplessness accompanies mental depression. Dog-tired, they drag through the day, only to toss and turn until well past midnight, then up to read a book, perhaps gobble a nocturnal snack or wander from room to room. Finally, after a few hours of fitful sleep, they awaken with the birds, unable to fall asleep again.

For others still, there's a physical discomfort. Perhaps it's the urgent summons of an inflamed bladder or prostate, or maybe the pain of arthritis, or the nasal roadblock of allergy or a common cold.

For these individuals, restful sleep will only follow resolution of the cause—abolishing worry, treating depression, or seeking medical treatment of disease.

Then there's the one with the too-full schedule. He works past midnight, laboring at his desk until the weight of drooping eyelids bring a halt to his labors. For others, it's meetings, dickering and debating until fatigue overcomes even the most determined committee member.

The moonlighter is the special problem. In my medical office, I've told many two-job iron men, "The money you earn on the second job is likely to be spent for doctor and hospital bills. Your body can stand 40, maybe 50 hours of work a week. After that, the muscles and mind rebel and will find some means to get rest. Maybe it will be flu, or an ulcer, or a heart attack. Who knows? But a double shift, particularly 6 or even 7 days a week, is a surefire way to ruin health, and fast."

Without question, cumulative sleep loss causes anxiety and often physical symptoms. The sleep debt may build up gradually, a half hour to an hour each night, and after a few weeks of short-changing the sandman, mental acuity suffers and physical vitality wanes. Decisions aren't as sharp, detail loses precision, and sloppiness creeps in. Colleagues begin to mutter, "It's hard to get along with Jim anymore. He always seems tired and cranky."

There is only one answer—a full ration of rest!

SLEEP FOR THE SLEEPLESS

How to get to sleep when sleep won't come? Mark this page in the book, and the next time sleep is as elusive as a leprechaun, reread the following six guides to healthful sleep:

1. Avoid daytime naps, a common cause of nighttime wakefulness.

2. Exercise regularly, priming the muscles for restful sleep.

3. Resolve conflicts—somehow—facing problems squarely and working out the best solutions possible. Then quit fretting!

4. Wind down beginning an hour or two before bedtime. Clear the desk, avoiding concentrated effort and tension at the day's end.

5. Establish a bedtime ritual—perhaps a half hour of quiet television viewing, maybe a warm shower, or how about a glass of warm milk as you read a favorite novel.

6. Use sedatives only as a last resort, and only on the advice of a physician.

EXCESSIVE REST

How about the other side of the coin? "There is weariness even in too much sleep," said Homer. Oversleeping can cause an all-day dragged-out feeling and may be followed by restlessness the next night. Many of the world's most successful people are early risers, explaining that the dawning hours are their most creative time.

Rest in bed alters body physiology. When I was in medical school, one professor there was fond of posing this question to new medical students on the ward: "Can you list ten ways that prolonged bed rest changes body function?" I may miss a few today, but here goes.

Too many hours in bed can:

Slow the pulse,
Lower the blood pressure,
Diminish respiration,
Slow movement of the bowels,
Inhibit the passage of urine,
Cause muscle shrinkage,
Slow circulation, inviting blood clots in the veins,
Cause skin pressure at points of contact,
Decrease metabolism, and
Cause calcium loss from bones.

Vitality in middle age requires making time for sleep, and taking the necessary steps to ensure restful repose. Get the quota of sleep that's right for you, and wake up refreshed, ready for the challenges of the day.

Helping the Doctor Help You

Maintaining good health during the middle years is a partnership between you and your doctor. He stands ready to offer medical advice, whether to sustain your present good health, or guide recovery from an illness. A source of day-by-day counsel when minor health questions arise, the family doctor can be a lifesaver when disease strikes.

Choose your family doctor with care. Some day your life might depend upon his skill and dedication. He may be a family physician; if so, check his office wall for the diploma of the American Board of Family Practice, the mark of a physician who has proven his worth by taking extensive refresher courses plus a rigorous 2-day examination. For other middle-agers, the personal physician may be a specialist in internal medicine—a physician who treats the medical diseases of adulthood, leaving children to the pediatricians and forswearing surgery, however minor. Or perhaps for Mrs. Middle-age, it's her trusted gynecologist who fills the role of family doctor. Whatever his breed, the physician needs your help to keep you fit.

HOW TO HELP

Promptly reporting all symptoms gives the doctor a crack at disease before it reaches that dreaded "I-wish-you-had-come-to-see-me-sooner" stage. Pain, bleeding, itching, name your symptoms—unless it can be readily explained and resolved promptly, a worrisome medical complaint deserves consultation with the physician. If given a chance to act early, the physician can often head off many of the conditions we'll discuss in Chapter 5.

Give the doctor all the facts. Don't editorialize or delete some detail that may seem embarassing: "I'm not going to mention that sore that's you-know-where. I would die of embarassment."

Or how about the man who thinks, "If I had told the doctor about bleeding from the rectum, he would have insisted upon an examination." Keeping secrets from the doctor can be a dangerous game.

Helping the doctor help you means following directions. If he prescribes a bland diet, he means it—no coffee, alcohol, or pizza. Medicine prescribed to be taken thrice daily with meals means just that, not two a day or four, and not on an empty stomach at 3 o'clock in the afternoon.

Don't neglect recommended follow-up visits. "Oh, everything seems fine now. I'm going to call his office and cancel my appointment." Don't do it! When the doctor calls you for a recheck, there's a reason. He may plan further treatment, more tests, or even consultation with a specialist. Keep the recheck appointment and help the doctor follow your progress.

Helping the doctor includes reminding him of special problems. If you have an ulcer, or glaucoma, or diabetes, or other condition that might be thrown out of joint by a new medication, refresh his memory. If you're allergic to penicillin, and he's pondering which antibiotic to prescribe for a sore throat, remind him.

A big help to the doctor who may not know your medical history is the Medic Alert emblem. The Medic Alert bracelet or necklace speaks for those who can't speak for themselves—because of unconsciousness, delirium, shock, or other reasons. Founded in California in 1956 after a doctor's daughter nearly succumbed to a tiny dose of tetanus antitoxin, the Medic Alert Foundation is now endorsed by more than 100 organizations, including the prestigious American Academy of Family Physicians. The Foundation provides an emergency data file on each member, listing unusual diseases, allergies, the patient's private physician and nearest relative. Members receive an individually engraved emblem and a wallet-size card identifying the primary medical problem as well as the member's identification number and the 24-hour-a-day emergency telephone number. For more information, write Medic Alert, P.O. Box 1009, Turlock, Calif. 95380.

Finally, you help your doctor help you by having a thorough annual physical examination. It's your best health insurance policy. The next section discusses the comprehensive health survey.

Invest an Hour in Your Health

"I really have no special complaints, Doctor, but I would like a complete physical examination from head to toe. I think I've reached the age when an annual physical checkup is important."

Harry Kellerman, responsible head of his household, invests in common stock and savings bonds. He and his wife each have a will to guard the family assets. But Harry has just undertaken his most important investment of the year, a 1-hour investment of time in preventive health maintenance.

The annual physical examination is a vital part of the continued medical care of all individuals, from infants through senior citizens. The comprehensive physical examination, including chest x-ray, electrocardiogram, and laboratory tests, helps detect diseases before overt symptoms occur and often during the grace period before irrevocable complications develop. Conveniently performed on or near your birth date, the annual health survey allows comparison of data from year to year and provides the physician with baseline studies which may become all-important if disease strikes.

Who should perform the examination? The best bet is the family physician, the same doctor you would call in case of emergency. Or perhaps he will recommend a nearby specialist in internal medicine, a consultant who will provide the family doctor with the information vital to his continued care, while standing ready to assist the primary physician if future illness develops. A third choice is the "production line" medical center, offering a plethora of tests at modest cost thanks to automation, but lacking the personal physician's involvement in the patient's problem, and posing the singular disadvantage that vital data obtained at a distant center may be locked safely in the files when chest pain strikes at 3 A.M.

Since the comprehensive annual physical examination is an unhurried survey of your health, the appointment should be made for a time when there is no sense of urgency. Most doctors find their appointments for comprehensive physical examinations are booked several weeks ahead, and rarely should such evaluation be done in a time of crisis. You should allow an hour or two of your time, depending upon the thoroughness of the examination and the efficiency of the doctor's office routine.

The ritual varies with each physician. Your doctor may perform the tests in his office laboratory or may refer you to the hospital for blood and urine tests or x-rays. Sometimes a special appointment will be made for the electrocardiogram. Nevertheless, with minor variations, the physical examination and analysis of data will be similar in most physicians' offices, and as an example, I will describe the procedure followed in my family practice.

EXAMINATION DAY

The patient reports to the office at 9 A.M., able to pass urine and before eating breakfast. Upon arrival, a urine specimen is obtained and blood is drawn for laboratory tests, after which the patient is offered juice or coffee to sustain him through the examination.

The nurse-technician will test the blood for hemoglobin to detect possible anemia, for cholesterol to detect elevations of this atherogenic substance, for sugar to detect hidden diabetes, for urea nitrogen to unmask a possible hidden buildup of kidney wastes in the blood stream, and for other tests that the doctor may deem important. While the blood tests are in progress, the urine is analyzed for the presence of sugar, protein, bile, acetone, blood and pus cells.

Once the laboratory machinery has been set in motion, the nurse measures the patient's height and weight, checking the figure on the scales with the previous year's value. Increasing weight may go hand-in-hand with rising blood pressure or a jump in the blood sugar level. The addition of excess pounds will prompt the doctor to declare, "It's diet time."

Cover one eye and read the letters. Vision is tested both with and without glasses, and changing visual acuity during middle age often signals the onset of presbyopia—aging of the eye that impairs vision at close range, signaling the need for corrective lenses.

In a quiet room, hearing is tested with an audiometer which tests auditory acuity in low, middle, and high frequency tones. Impaired appreciation of high frequency notes is often discovered, a defect perhaps unrealized by the patient until tested. The cause? It may be presbycusis (impaired hearing ascribed to aging), or perhaps it's due to ear wax or exposure to loud noises at work.

After preliminary tests by the nurse and technician, the doctor begins the interview, asking if the patient has any special problems and recording details of each specific symptom. After discussing the chief complaint, the doctor "goes fishing" for other possible problems—sleeplessness, weight loss, fatigue, dizziness, headache, sore throat, cough, indigestion, constipation, or urinary symptoms. Next comes questions about the past medical history, including childhood illnesses, previous hospitalization, past surgery and injuries. Nor is the patient's family neglected, and there are queries about diseases of the individual's mother, father, and siblings. Medications the patient may be taking, either regularly or intermittently, are reviewed, and a note is made of the intake of alcohol, coffee, and tobacco. Reviewed too are the patient's job and daily activities, common sources of problem symptoms, with questions about attitudes toward employment, overtime hours, and work-related stresses.

The scene shifts from the consultation to the examination room, where the patient is completely disrobed and draped with a gown to facilitate inspection of all parts of the body. The vital signs—blood pressure, pulse, respiration, and temperature—are recorded and compared with the previous year's values. A rising blood pressure may reflect hardening of the arteries, increased tension at work, a gluttonous weight gain, and even excessive salt intake. The finger on the pulse tells its rate and regularity, both barometers of the heart action. The respiratory rate, the number of breaths per minute, is checked; if abnormal, it may be an early sign of heart or lung disease. An elevated temperature may signal an acute infection or might be a subtle early sign of a hidden disease.

The ears are examined for infection, wax, or abnormalities of the eardrum. If dry, packed wax blocks the ear canal, it may be removed by the physician. Sometimes an unexpected hole in the eardrum is discovered, prompting referral to an ear specialist.

The eyes are carefully scrutinized, including the pupils, the eye movements, and the lining coat of the eyelid. Next the doctor checks the retina of the eye in a darkened room, examining tiny blood vessels which may give clues about possible hardening of the arteries. With the eye anesthetized with a local anesthetic, the intraocular pressure is determined using an instrument called a tonometer to detect possible early glaucoma—an insidious thief of vision present in 2 percent of all individuals aged forty and over.

The nose and oral cavity are examined for evidence of inflammation, polyps, or cancer, and the state of dental repair is noted.

The neck is checked for enlarged lymph nodes, perhaps due to infection in the throat or ears, or occasionally an early sign of cancer in the lung, stomach, or lymph glands. Also in the neck is the thyroid gland, subject to enlargement or lumps.

The chest is observed for equal motion of both sides during breathing and thumped to detect areas of the lung which are not filled with air. Sounds heard through the stethoscope may alert the doctor to possible bronchitis, emphysema, or even lung cancer.

Both male and female breasts are checked for lumps or nipple discharge, and any abnormal growth will be referred to a surgeon for possible removal.

The doctor's hand on the chest wall tells the thrust of the heart beat, and a light fingertip tap helps him measure the heart's size. Next he listens, carefully and quietly, to detect heart murmurs or irregularities of rhythm.

The abdomen is examined for abnormalities of the liver, spleen, kidneys, stomach, or intestines, with notes made of enlargement, tenderness, or lumps in vital internal organs.

The male adult is checked for enlargement of the testicles, an abnormal mass in the scrotum, and—"Turn your head to the left and cough"—a possible hernia.

A pelvic examination, essential for the woman each year, is performed using a speculum to view the cervix (mouth of the womb), and a Pap test for cancer is dispatched to the laboratory. Internal palpation determines the size of the uterus and ovaries.

The all-important rectal examination comes next, detecting possible hemorrhoids, bleeding, or other abnormalities of the rectum, as well as revealing the prostate status of male patients. Often the doctor examines using a sigmoidoscope—a 10-inch lighted tube revealing the secret recesses of the rectum and lower large intestine.

The reflexes are tapped, and a sluggish response may hint of thyroid deficiency, diabetes, alcoholism, or pernicious anemia.

A fingertip touch detects the pulse in the feet, revealing possible hardening of the peripheral arteries. The skin of the feet is examined, as well as the skin on other areas of the body, offering vital clues to chronic dermatitis, infection, or nutritional deficiency.

Now take a deep breath and hold it. CLICK, and the chest x-ray is recorded. Prompt developing allows a "wet reading" within 15 minutes, revealing possible heart enlargement or lung abnormalities often too subtle for stethoscope detection.

While the nurse develops the chest x-ray, an electrocardiogram is recorded. The EKG traces the conduction of electrical current across the heart wall, detecting disorders of rate, rhythm, and conduction. An electrically inert area in the heart wall that detours the electrical impulse may be telltale evidence of a previous heart attack, and even the normal electrocardiogram can prove invaluable when compared with a suspected disorder at some later date.

SUMMING UP

The tests are complete. The patient is dressed, the x-ray developed, the electrocardiogram interpreted, and laboratory analyses recorded. Next the patient sits down with his doctor to review the findings.

Perhaps a potentially troublesome problem has been detected—a bulging waistline, borderline blood pressure, or mild blood cholesterol elevation. Treatment is advised, possibly including weight reduction, medication, or dietary restriction—and follow-up visits are planned to assess the results of treatment.

Occasionally the examination reveals a potentially serious condition, such as an enlarged liver or shadow on the chest x-ray. Further tests are arranged, and maybe there will be a consultation with a specialist.

But most who invest time in their health will receive the most rewarding of all dividends when the doctor says, "Harry, I've checked you completely and reviewed all your tests. You're in first-rate health and I can't find a thing wrong. Keep your weight where it is, don't forget to exercise daily, and see me for your annual physical examination next year."

5

DISEASES OF THE MIDDLE YEARS

Before thirty, men seek disease; after thirty, diseases seek men.

Chinese proverb

EACH AGE OF LIFE has its disease pitfalls. Sore throats and chicken pox are among the many ills of kids, young adults are prime targets of infectious mononucleosis and hepatitis, while strokes and senility plague the aged. In this chapter, we'll discuss seven disease entities, some more serious than others, but all sharing one common denominator—they're of prime importance during the middle years.

Call them the Diseases of Maturity. Most have a hereditary tendency, some are penalties for self-indulgence, and almost all can be postponed by enlightened prophylaxis.

These are the enemies, all the more fearful because they carry the threat of economic hardship. If the middle-aged wage earner is disabled, who meets the mortgage payment, finances the kids' college tuition, or funds the retirement program? With Mrs. Middle-age on the sick list, could the family budget stand the strain of a nurse or housekeeper? Then there would be the hospital bills, doctor bills, drugstore bills, and all the rest—with Medicare help years away.

Happily, the middle-ager usually suffers more worry than physical illness, and for most, the in-between years are a relatively disease-free time of life. The chances are you'll meet none of them, but it's best to know your enemies. The following are maladies lurking in wait for the unwary middle-ager.

The Diabetes Curse

Diabetes mellitus is the prototype of diseases of maturity—it's influenced by heredity, aggravated by intemperate eating, and attended by ominous complications.

The disease is as old as recorded history, and is described in Egyptian writings 3,500 years old. Ancient Hebrews called the disease "honey water" because the urine of afflicted individuals attracted flies. The Greeks gave us the word diabetes, meaning "siphon," and Romans added mellitus meaning "honey." The metabolic defect was a death sentence to most victims, until the epic discovery of insulin in 1921.

Today, it's estimated that close to ten million Americans have diabetes, up to 2 percent of the population. In half of these individuals, the disorder smolders quietly undetected, all the while fomenting its complications.

Furthermore, the incidence of diabetes in the United States will continue to increase for three reasons. First, our life style fosters obesity, bringing diabetes to the fore. Second, each year the life expectancy of Americans lengthens, giving added years for more and more individuals to develop the disease. And third, diabetics who would have been infertile or died of their disease in years past are now surviving to pass the gene to their children, thanks to modern diet therapy, oral medication, and insulin.

DEFINING DIABETES

Diabetes is a deficiency of insulin—a hormone produced in the pancreas that is responsible for transporting sugar from the bloodstream to cells. Sugar, unable to enter cells where it is needed for energy, crowds the bloodstream like commuters in rush hour. When the throng of carbohydrates becomes excessive, it exits via the kidney as sugar-laden urine.

The fasting blood sugar of a diabetic is usually elevated, and following a meal, it rises to a greater height and stays higher longer than that of a normal individual. The normal blood sugar level is about 100 mg of glucose. Diabetic levels exceed 110 mg and 2 hours after eating usually remain well above 120 mg of glucose. When blood sugar levels exceed 170 mg, sugar begins to appear in the urine.

Who develops diabetes? Four factors exert their influence:

1.   Heredity plays a decisive role, as the disease can be transmitted from generation to generation, along with other family traits. The individual with diabetic forebears may be doomed to develop

the disease if he lives long enough, but its onset can be delayed by minimizing carbohydrate consumption and maintaining ideal weight.

2. Sex seems to play a role. More women than men develop diabetes, and there's a curious increased incidence in mothers who have had large babies.

3. Obesity is a prime factor, with increased caloric consumption taxing a metabolic system already laboring under an insulin deficiency. Some folks literally eat themselves into overt diabetes.

4. Age increases the likelihood of developing diabetes, as insulin-producing pancreatic cells wear out. Yet there's a ray of hope for the oldster: diabetes acquired late in life is usually not as malicious as disease developed earlier, perhaps because there will be fewer years for complications to develop.

"How can I tell if I have diabetes?" Only the doctor can tell for sure, and often the disease is detected upon routine physical examination (much preferable to lapsing into undiagnosed diabetic coma during the course of a flu).

Yet, sometimes symptoms occur and may be helpful in pinpointing the diagnosis. Excessive thirst, frequent urination, and increased hunger are classical complaints, owing to the passage of huge quantities of sugar-laden urine and a shortage of energy-producing sugar in body cells. Skin infections and itching are common, as sugar accumulates in surface cells to provide a fertile breeding ground for bacteria. Eventually, fluid loss causes visual changes, and sugar-starved tissues beget fatigue and weight loss.

This list of complaints will prompt the doctor to order blood sugar tests, confirming the diagnosis of diabetes, following which he will prescribe a plan of therapy.

TREATING DIABETES

The assault on diabetes is a three-pronged attack. First there's diet. Before insulin, diet therapy was all we had; each ounce of food was weighed and measured, taking all the fun out of mealtime. Today's diabetic diet is often more liberal (but not always), allowing menu planning from Exchange Lists of basic food groups. When the patient, physician, and perhaps dietitian plan the diet prescription together, the result should be a palatable, yet nutritious, daily food selection, keyed to the individual's likes and dislikes.

It's all-important that the diabetic understand the twofold goals of diet therapy. First is the reduction of carbohydrates the body must handle, substituting protein and some fats. The other goal is weight control, attaining and holding the individual's ideal weight. To learn more about diabetic diet therapy and other aspects of the disease, the middle-ager can request information from The American Diabetes Association, Inc., 1 West 48th Street, New York, N.Y. 10020.

Next comes oral medication and insulin therapy. All-important insulin was isolated in 1921 by Canadian medical scientists Dr. Frederick G. Banting and Dr. Charles Best. Now available in both rapid-acting and long-acting forms, insulin is required by almost all childhood diabetics and by a fair number of those whose disease begins during middle age.

Oral medication allows many middle-agers to escape the insulin needle. The five major pills and capsules available are acetohexamide (Dymelor), chlorpropamide (Diabinese), tolazamide (Tolinase), tolbutamide (Orinase), and phenformin (DBI). All help lower blood sugar, yet share a low potential for serious side effects. Not advised for use by the individual with soaring blood sugar levels or a tendency to coma, the antidiabetic pills are best prescribed for the mild diabetic with stable blood sugar levels whose disease began during middle age or later.

The third thrust against diabetes concerns prevention and treatment of complications. Here lies the heart of the battle, since the complications are often more treacherous than the disease itself. What are the dangers and how can they be side-stepped?

Diabetic acidosis and coma follow prolonged blood sugar peaks, often linked with increased metabolic demands (such as flu or pneumonia) that accelerate protein and fat breakdown for fuel. Acid byproducts accumulate in the bloodstream, upsetting the metabolic chemistry. The treatment? Immediate insulin and fluid therapy to regain control of the blood sugar level.

Plummeting blood sugar levels follow insulin shock, an overdose of lifesaving insulin, occurring rapidly and posing a more instant danger than slowly-developing acidosis. The story usually goes like this: "My wife took her usual insulin dose this morning, but she didn't eat much breakfast and skipped lunch altogether. About 4 o'clock in the afternoon, she became jittery, sweaty, and shook all over before becoming unconscious." Here's an emergency! The blood glucose level has dropped out of sight, and needs boosting. Fruit juice laced with sugar works if the patient is still awake. If unconscious, an injection of Glucagon (suitable for home administration by the diabetic or his family) or intravenous glucose is needed.

Skin infections plague the diabetic. They're related to high sugar levels, and usually subside once the diabetes is controlled. A classic symptom of the disease, infections are often a vital clue leading the physician to the diagnosis.

Hardening of the arteries strikes the diabetic at a younger age and with greater ferocity than nondiabetic individuals. At special risk are the feet and legs, where impaired circulation may lead to intractable ulcers, infection, or even gangrene. Threatened too are other areas of the body, and the diabetic is in jeopardy from heart attacks and strokes.

Visual changes are a special problem of the disease. Fluid fluctuations in the lens are more nuisance than treacherous and are common whenever diabetes undergoes change. With advanced age, there's the danger of cataracts, but the most fearful eye complication is retinopathy—disease of tiny blood vessels of the retina which may culminate in premature blindness.

Finally, there's neuropathy—short-circuited nerves most common in the legs, causing numbness, tingling, perhaps an aching pain, or sometimes loss of balance with an awkward gait.

Because the best hope of avoiding diabetes' awesome complications lies in early detection and prompt aggressive therapy, it's important that all middle-agers have a blood sugar test once a year. If diabetes is detected, follow the doctor's instruction to the letter. If you have the disease or it's in your family, learn about the disorder. An intensive training program in diabetic management is available to patients attending the Joslin Clinic, One Joslin Place, Boston, Mass. 02215, and patients that I have referred to the Joslin Clinic return with a heightened insight into their disease.

Diabetes is a curse, demanding sacrifice under threat of complications. Yet, there's a silver lining to the cloud. The middle-aged diabetic who follows his diet, exercises regularly, and heeds his doctor's advice often outlives his contemporary who boasts, "I never get sick, never see the doctor."

How High the Blood Pressure?

Twenty-five million Americans have high blood pressure; some see their doctors regularly, while many are unaware of the disorder.

The total rises each year as more individuals survive to develop this disease of aging. While admittedly more common in senior citizens, hypertension poses a special threat to the middle generation since complications may significantly shorten the life expectancy.

Contributing to the epidemic of high blood pressure is the hectic tempo of our times. Blood pressure is one barometer of modern living, but as the sailor's barometer falls when the storms approach, the blood pressure rises as emotional squalls threaten. When tranquility prevails, the blood pressure gauge gives a low steady reading.

Yet, there's more to the story. Heredity plays its role, and in some families, generation after generation suffers hypertension. Then there's diet, with obesity producing miles of extra capillaries forcing the heart to pump at a greater pressure, and salt consumption swelling the fluid content of the blood and creating a greater demand on the heart pump. Hardened arteries lacking elasticity contribute to the high blood pressure of the aging, not to mention the rare adrenal tumor or blood clot in the kidney. Finally come the unknown factors, poorly understood and yet-to-be-discovered tumors, hormones, and other causes that force doctors to label most high blood pressure as essential hypertension— meaning "cause unknown."

While medical science may not yet have all the pieces in the hypertensive puzzle, there are loads of useful statistics available, many courtesy of life insurance companies whose actuarial tables can pinpoint the danger of rising blood pressure. The hypertensive individual has more than five times the risk of dying of a stroke when compared to a normal person, a four times greater risk of kidney disease, a two to three times greater incidence of heart disease, a 50 percent greater susceptibility to digestive disease, and even a one-third higher risk of developing influenza or pneumonia. While the death certificate may not read "high blood pressure," each year hypertension kills more than one million Americans as damaged arteries lead to stroke, heart attack, or kidney failure.

WHY HIGH BLOOD PRESSURE?

Hypertension comes from Greek words meaning high force. The push required to pump blood through the arteries is called the blood pressure. The doctor's sphygmomanometer measures two levels: the higher force records the pressure of the heart contractions, while the lower level denotes the pressure in the vessels between heartbeats. Measurements are defined as the force raising a column of mercury measured in millimeters. The ideal blood pressure during the middle years is about 120/80 with a gradual rise with age owing to hardened arteries. Blood pressures above 150/100 are abnormal and some doctors will argue for a lower figure, according to the patient's age.

"But why worry about blood pressure? I feel fine!" The unconcerned may say. Here's why: while hypertension may blush to cause its first symptom, it's quietly pounding away at blood vessels in the brain, heart, and kidneys, setting the stage for life-threatening complications.

When symptoms occur, there may be dizziness and a pounding back-of-the-skull headache, characteristically peaking early in the morning. Sometimes there is facial flushing, easy fatiguability, and shortness of breath. Yet the prudent adult won't wait for these symptoms but has his blood pressure checked at least once yearly.

MEDICAL CARE FOR HIGH BLOOD PRESSURE

Perhaps it's during a routine physical examination or even a visit for the flu. The doctor inflates the blood pressure cuff, the tight armband squeezes, then relaxes, and he says, "The pressure's higher than it should be." Next will come some tests to detect possible curative causes and incipient complications—urine analysis, blood chemistry determinations, electrocardiogram, and x-rays. And the physician will take another reading or two to determine that true hypertension is sustained.

Then comes treatment. First to diet: the ideal weight is calculated and a weight reduction program instituted if excess pounds are present. Weight loss reduces the miles of arteries and capillaries through which blood must be pumped.

Salt restriction helps lower blood pressure, by reducing the fluid content of blood. The heart and blood vessels are a hydraulic system containing blood pumped by contraction of the heart. If we reduce the fluid in the system, the heart can pump at a lower pressure— simple hydrodynamics.

Reducing anxiety helps. This means sidestepping emotional conflicts, avoiding family squabbles, and firmly saying "No" to committee chairmanships and extra work. The physician may prescribe a mild tranquilizer to mute jangled nerves.

For generations, these measures were all we had to combat hypertension. Then in 1955, the drug therapy of hypertension began with a medical report describing the blood pressure lowering properties of reserpine—a derivative of rauwolfia serpentina, known to Hindu medicine men for centuries as a remedy for snake bite and insanity. Later came the diuretics—"water pills"—that removed excess fluid from the bloodstream, reducing the need for rigid salt restriction in many individuals, and now the first choice drug of most physicians. Other antihypertensive drugs followed: hydralazine (Apresoline), relaxing spasms in small arteries; guanethidine (Ismelin), defusing nerves that boost blood pressure; methyldopa (Aldomet), blocking formation of body chemicals that raise blood pressure; and others.

Controlling hypertension requires regular visits to the doctor to check weight, adjust medication, spot complications early, and record the all-important blood pressure readings. Medications may be increased or decreased, and often drugs are prescribed in combination. Some hypertensives require four or five pills daily to keep blood pressure under control.

There are side effects of medication to consider. Today's potent antihypertensive medications can have significant adverse reactions, and sometimes it's hard to tell if symptoms are due to bounding blood pressure or medication daze. When in doubt, check with the physician.

The hypertensive dropout carries a time bomb in his arteries. He sticks to his regimen for a while, but because there are no troublesome symptoms, enthusiasm sometimes wanes. He adds a pinch of salt to food, regains lost pounds, neglects to refill his medication, and exclaims, "Why go back to the doctor? I'll know when my blood pressure is high again."

Hypertension is a lifelong disease—it doesn't go away. And the first sign may be a heart attack or stroke. Lifelong therapy is required, and treatment is an investment in the future. The known or suspected hypertensive should have regular physical checkups, follow the doctor's instructions faithfully, and never meddle with medication dosage. The reward for diligence will be a longer, healthier life, with less likelihood of complicating kidney disease, strokes, and heart attacks.

The Heart Attack Threat

A vise crushes the chest. Oppressive pain shoots to the shoulders and down the arms. Breathing is shallow and labored. Clothing drenched with sweat clings damply. There's overwhelming weakness, yet the urge to stand and "walk the pain away." Someone's crying, a voice whispers, "Hurry, hurry!" From the distance comes the wail of an approaching siren.

It all happened suddenly. You awoke at the usual time, and what the weatherman had promised as "possible scattered showers" lay in the driveway—a full ten inches of wet virgin snow.

"I'm late," was all you could think.

The heavy breakfast your wife prepared ("You'll need a hot meal on a cold day like this") sat like a bowling ball in the stomach, and made you later still.

Off you bounded to tackle the snow, rushing, angry, overfed, and out of condition. The morning chill froze beads of perspiration into icicles. Finally, as the car was almost freed from driveway snow, the pain struck!

The doctor was at the hospital when the ambulance arrived. "Rush him to the Coronary Care Unit, begin oxygen, get an IV going, and do a stat electrocardiogram."

You remember the hospital ceiling, overhead lights whizzing by as the stretcher hurdled down the hall.

Then into a waiting bed, electrodes clamped on the wrists, ankles, and chest. The relentless beep, beep, beep of the oscilloscope began announcing each heartbeat, as if with gratitude. The coronary care nurses scurried about, performing their chores, and the last memory was an injection of morphine, bringing blessed relief from the painful chest pressure.

WHY THE HEART ATTACK?

The heart attack strikes with the sudden impact of an arrow in flight, as likely to fell the "never-a-sick-day-in-my-life" he-man as the 97-pound weakling. Yet it's not caprice that selects the heart attack victim. The key is atherosclerosis, and many factors play roles.

First there's heredity, which influences so many of the disorders of middle age. Fortuitous parental selection is an unearned blessing, but attention to other contributing factors can offset a family predisposition to atherosclerosis.

Hypertension speeds hardening of the arteries and carries the ever-present danger of bursting a critical vessel, causing a heart attack or stroke. Unquestionably, the hypertensive individual suffers an extra risk of heart attack, but the danger can be minimized by conscientious antihypertensive therapy.

Sex is a factor. For example, during the fifth decade of life, coronary heart disease strikes men six times as often as women.

Cigarette smoking is a prime precursor of heart disease, as well as almost single-handed cause of emphysema and lung cancer. The cigarette smoker has a 70 percent greater chance of developing coronary heart disease when compared with the nonsmoker.

Anxiety adds its insult, increasing blood pressure, stimulating the heart, and apparently increasing hardening of the arteries. How often the acute heart attack follows a period of overwork and emotional upheaval!

Then there's obesity, straining the heart to service pounds of flab and lug added weight from place to place.

Tied to obesity is overindulgence in cholesterol and fats. The American Heart Association recommends a daily cholesterol intake of 300 mg or less, while the yolk of one large egg contains 250 mg of cholesterol. Eliminating unnecessary animal fats in the diet, as well as high-cholesterol eggs, butter, cheese, and lard (see Page 51), helps prevent hardening of the arteries. Autopsies performed on American and oriental servicemen during the Korean War showed that many young Americans suffered progressive atherosclerosis at an early age while their oriental counterparts had arteries smooth as a baby's bottom.

Finally, there's physical exercise, the favorite topic of the late heart specialist, Paul Dudley White. Regular physical exercise helps keep blood circulating and arteries open, and can help prevent heart attacks as revealed by a 9-year study of 575 pairs of Irish brothers. From each family, one brother had immigrated to America while the other remained in Ireland. The study confirmed what had been suspected; the American brother suffered a greater incidence of heart disease, hardening of the arteries, and deaths from heart attack than his sibling back home. Why? Carefully the doctors studied the various factors. Diet? Mutton, milk, cream, and other high fat foods were dietary staples of both groups. Brothers in America and Ireland smoked and consumed alcoholic beverages about equally. The difference seemed to be in exercise, with the brother back in Ireland leading a more vigorous life than his sedentary sibling in America. In a 1971 article in *Woman's Day,* the study director, Harvard Nutritionist Dr. Frederick J. Stare, concluded, "It's not the cholesterol intake that hurts the heart. It's letting the cholesterol build up. Physical activity gets rid of it, burns up the saturated fats. That's the big lesson the Irish have for us."

AFTER THE HEART ATTACK

You awaken with a start. "Where am I?" Then you remember—the Coronary Care Unit. Your last memory was the pain before the injection.

In comes the nurse with breakfast. Juice. Cereal. Toast. No eggs or coffee. The intravenous tubing in the left arm hampers eating, and in the corner the oscilloscope monitor beeps away.

Next comes the doctor: "I'm afraid it's a heart attack. All the symptoms point in that direction, and the blood tests are confirmatory. The electrocardiogram instead of being normal like this (Figure 10) is abnormal like this (Figure 11).

"We'll give you medicine as needed for the pain, there will be a special diet, and we'll help prevent blood clots by 'thinning' the blood with an anticoagulant. You'll be at bed rest for a week or more, followed by sitting in a chair, then gradual resumption of walking. We'll figure on about 3 or 4 weeks in the hospital and 3 or 4 months before returning to work.

"I know this is bad news, but look on the bright side. You survived the first hours of the heart attack—the most dangerous time of all—and now that you're in the hospital, everything should be all right.

"When this is all over, your heart should be virtually as strong as ever. Yes, it's true that you'll have a greater risk for future heart attacks than the man who has yet to have his first, but if you follow all the rules, you should be able to resume your life again, including almost all activities that you enjoyed previously.

"Why did you have the heart attack? Well, there are four things that adversely affect a heart whose blood supply is already precarious—cold weather, emotional tension, overeating, and unaccustomed exertion. You broke all the rules yesterday morning, and that's what landed you here."

LEARNING ABOUT HEART ATTACKS

A heart attack means that one of the tiny arteries carrying blood to the heart has been damaged—perhaps by a blood clot or fragment of fat and cholesterol from the wall of the vessel. The portion of heart muscles served by the artery loses its blood supply and cries out in pain. The weakened portion of the heart will receive some blood flow from nearby arteries and will be gradually

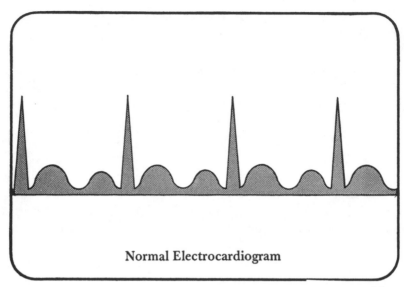

Normal Electrocardiogram

Figure 10

Figure 11

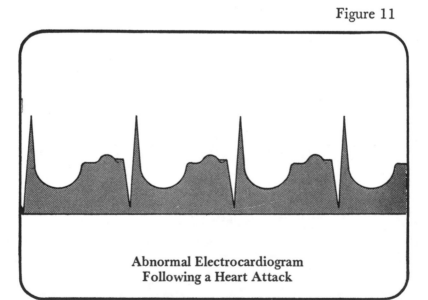

Abnormal Electrocardiogram
Following a Heart Attack

strengthened as scar tissue forms. But during the first few weeks and even months, it's important to reduce the heart's work by enforced rest, first in bed in the hospital and later at home.

Sometimes terms are confusing. The doctor may speak of a coronary occlusion, meaning blockage of the artery; or he may describe it as a myocardial infarction, denoting heart muscle lacking blood supply. It all means just one thing—a heart attack. You may hear the term angina; this describes chest pain caused by impaired circulation to the heart, but differs from a heart attack in being transitory and reversible, with no permanent damage to heart muscle.

Heart disease causes about 2 million deaths each year and is the leading killer during the middle years. The August, 1973 issue of *Physicians' World* tells us that "a male living in North America has approximately a one in five chance of developing clinical coronary artery disease before age sixty."

There's a wealth of information available about atherosclerosis and heart attacks. The American Heart Association, with national headquarters at 44 East 23rd Street, New York, N.Y. 10010, sponsors local programs offering information and educational services, working in conjunction with private physicians and cardiac clinics. The interested reader may write to the local American Heart Association chapter or national headquarters for information; particularly useful is the American Heart Association Cookbook with 400 heart-preserving recipes for everything from hors d'oeuvres to desserts.

Atherosclerosis is not simply a disease of the elderly. It begins in young adulthood, perhaps even in childhood, and is a major cause of death during the middle years due to heart attacks and other vascular calamities. Although some degree of arterial hardening is inevitable with age, its progress can be slowed by weight control, sensible dietary restrictions, regular physical exercise, avoiding smoking, and following the advice of your family physician.

Short of Breath

Some cigarettes give prizes. Smoke a pack a day for 30 years, from late teens until well into the middle years, and you've consumed 200,000 cigarettes, more than 2 million puffs. Your prize is likely to be chronic lung disease.

The American Review of Respiratory Diseases, May, 1973 issue, reported that "respiratory disease causes at least 10 percent of all deaths in the United States, and is the single most important cause of lost working time." These figures include pneumonia, common colds, and other acute respiratory infections. Yet, even when stuffy noses and once-in-a-decade chest infections are discounted, chronic lung disease afflicts more than 15 million Americans, making it one of the most common disorders of the middle years.

THROUGH THE RESPIRATORY TRACT

The lungs contains millions of tiny air sacs separated by paper-thin walls containing capillaries. Inhalation, a muscular movement elevating the rib and chest wall, creates a vacuum that sucks air into the tiny lung sacs. While in the lungs, air gives up its life-sustaining oxygen and receives carbon dioxide wastes from the tiny blood capillaries. Then, relaxation of the chest wall forces air from the lungs as exhalation.

Let's take a tour of the respiratory tract (Figure 12), that ingenious system of tubes and balloons where respiration takes place. Get ready! We're going in on the next breath. There, the chest muscles are rising.

Here we go!

It's in through the nose. Watch out, don't get snared by the nasal hairs; these help keep out larger dust particles.

Now a quick slide down the throat. We'll pass the larynx or voicebox—see the vocal cords on each side. Muscular tensing of the vocal cords allows resonance as exhaled air passes through, just as air passing through a trumpet produces musical tones.

Next into the trachea, with cartilage half-moons supporting the circular tube. As we enter the chest, the trachea branches into bronchial tubes which soon divide into tributaries serving the air sacs of the lungs.

Last, we're whooshed into the alveoli—the business area of the lungs where oxygen is extracted and carbon dioxide eliminated from the blood. Look fast, we won't be here long, because when the chest wall relaxes, we'll be whisked out as stale air is exhaled.

Here we go back up the respiratory tree—bronchi to trachea, through the larynx, up the throat, out the nose, and free.

The healthy lung has 750 million small alveolar air sacs, and everyday living uses only about one quarter of these. The remainder is held in reserve for bursts of exercise and as a hedge against disease.

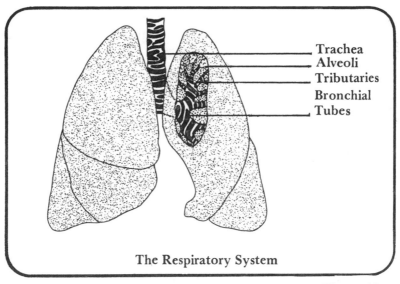

Trachea
Alveoli
Tributaries
Bronchial
Tubes

The Respiratory System

Figure 12

Figure 13

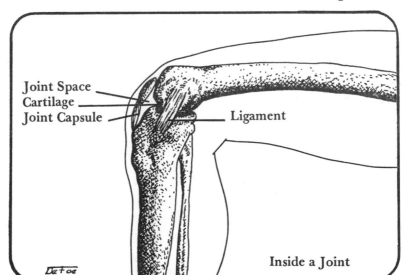

Joint Space
Cartilage
Joint Capsule

Ligament

Inside a Joint

CHRONIC LUNG DISEASE

Chronic lung disease includes chronic bronchitis and emphysema. Sure, there are other pulmonary maladies, such as asthma, tuberculosis, and histoplasmosis, but the significance of these is dwarfed by the magnitude of the bronchitis-emphysema problem in America today.

Chronic bronchitis follows the day-in day-out irritation of the bronchial tubes to the lung. The causes are legion, including bacterial infection, industrial pollution, exhaust fumes, house dust, air-borne pollens, and other respiratory irritants. A study performed in Great Britain showed that 10 to 15 percent of urban dwellers suffered chronic lung disease, compared with a 6 to 7 percent incidence in rural inhabitants.

Yet these factors all take a back seat to cigarette smoking, the most culpable culprit causing chronic bronchitis. The inhalation of toxic tars, perhaps added to the insult of airborne urban pollutants, causes a chronic irritation of bronchial lining walls.

Phlegm is produced by the bucketful, as bronchial cells respond to irritation by manufacturing mucus. Of course, there's only one way to eliminate phelgm—coughing. As chronic bronchitis progresses, arising from bed in the morning is attended by hacking and spitting to clear the nighttime accumulation of phlegm from the respiratory tract. With each cough, the walls of a few tiny air sacs burst, and small efficient alveoli are merged into a flabby large sac that exchanges oxygen and waste products poorly. Finally, month by month, cough by cough, chronic bronchitis blossoms into pulmonary emphysema.

Pulmonary emphysema, the smoker's grand prize, is the end result of years of bronchial irritation and coughing. Destruction of connecting walls between alveoli has diminished the lung surface available for oxygen exchange. The lungs' reserves are gone, the chest is held expanded as if attempting to gain a few more precious cubic inches of volume, and the patient complains of unremitting shortness of breath.

Shortness of breath—that's the hallmark of pulmonary emphysema. First there's difficulty breathing only with exertion, then it's puffing after walking across the room. In the end, the emphysema victim may be short of breath at rest, elbows braced on the table so his shoulder muscles can aid chest expansion, and sometimes his survival depends upon a home breathing apparatus.

Disability due to emphysema is often progressive. The irritated bronchial tube and emphysematous lung form a first-rate culture media for bacteria. The winter months are peppered with chest colds, often progressing into acute bronchial infections and perhaps pneumonia. Each acute episode causes further damage, and the victim may eventually become a respiratory cripple.

Emphysema can kill as well as cripple. As urban pollution and cigarette smoking have become widespread, the incidence of emphysema has skyrocketed. Between 1950 and 1964, the death rate for emphysema in males jumped tenfold. In 1950, 1.3 men per 100,000 died of emphysema compared with 12.6 per 100,000 in 1964. Today, emphysema is the fifth leading cause of death in males between ages fifty-five and seventy-four.

COMBATTING CHRONIC LUNG DISEASE

If your middle years are marred by chronic bronchitis and emphysema, there's much that can be done. General measures first. Very cold or very warm air should be avoided, as well as air in which humidity hangs like a wet blanket. Altitude may be a factor, and most chronic lung disease victims are most comfortable at 300 to 500 feet above sea level; motoring over mountains with rarified atmospheric oxygen may be dangerous. Climate? A change may help, but before moving the family, be sure to spend a prolonged vacation in your intended new home town. Don't expect magic—there are thousands of asthmatics living and wheezing in Arizona. And, of course, treat all colds or flu promptly.

The doctor may prescribe medication to open bronchial tubes and liquify mucus, possibly Tedral or Asbron. He'll probably advise drinking plenty of fluids to help dissolve thick, sticky phelgm.

Exercises help to remove stale air from diseased lungs. Here's one exercise that may improve breathing: sit in a straight-backed chair with the hands over the lower ribs and upper abdomen. Inhale deeply, feeling chest expansion push the hands out. Then exhale as completely as possible while compressing the chest wall from each side with the hands. The added hand pressure on the chest helps evacuate stale air from languishing lung cavities. For best results the chest compression exercise should be repeated ten times before each meal and at bedtime.

To drain accumulated mucus from the bronchial tubes and lungs, postural drainage is often recommended. A dose of expectorant medication such as glycerol guaiacolate followed by a glass of water helps loosen phelgm. Then lie with the hips on the bed and the chest inclined from the bed toward the floor, with elbows and forearms braced on the carpet. Inhale deeply and exhale completely, giving a few coughs with each exhalation. Turn first to the left, then to the right, draining accumulated phelgm from the cavities in each lung. If performed morning and night, postural drainage helps keep the lungs free of mucus.

Inhalation therapy is often helpful. The doctor may prescribe a hand inhaler to open bronchial passages, perhaps used before beginning postural drainage. More expensive and more potent is intermittent positive pressure breathing (IPPB), using rhythmic bursts of compressed air to assist breathing, carrying medication and expanding dormant lung cavities. Sometimes it's prescribed in the hospital, but the emphysema victim dependent upon IPPB soon finds a home unit well worth the investment.

Help is available for the chronic lung disease victim, and your local physician has much to offer. Yet, it's all doomed to failure if exposure to urban pollution persists and if the individual continues to smoke.

AVOIDING CHRONIC LUNG DISEASE

"How about me?" says Mr. Middle-age, "I smoke, and I guess I inhale my share of exhaust fumes. How can I tell if I'm developing chronic lung disease, and how can it be prevented?"

Chronic lung disease advances by inches. Developing at a snail's pace, its progress is scarcely noticed until one day you're mowing the lawn or playing basketball with the kids and realize, "I shouldn't be so short of breath."

Here's a home test to check lung function. Stop reading, put the book down, and try this test: light a match from an ordinary book and allow the initial flame to subside. Then hold the steadily burning match about twelve inches away from the mouth. Take a deep breath, count to twenty, then exhale forcefully with the mouth held open. Don't purse the lips. The person with normal lungs can easily extinguish the match, but the individual with chronic lung disease may huff and puff as the flame flickers contemptuously.

Of course, the best source of advice is the physician, and assessment of lung function should be part of the annual physical examination. Don't rely on the chest x-ray. Doctors know that by the time emphysema can be diagnosed on x-ray, the disease is already far advanced.

Chronic lung disease can be prevented—if tobacco smoke and other air-borne pollutants are avoided and if one exercises regularly, and seeks prompt medical care of all respiratory disorders.

Arthritis is a Mean Disease

Some unsung sage once told the arthritis story in five words—*arthritis is a mean disease.* He might have added that it's exceedingly common, medically expensive, and emotionally depressing.

Arthritis afflicts more than 22 million Americans, 5 million of these suffering rheumatoid arthritis, with the remaining individuals afflicted by osteoarthritis, gout, or one of a mixed bag of joint afflictions accompanying psoriasis, colitis, trauma, or infection.

The major forms of arthritis hit the middle-ager coming and going: first there's rheumatoid arthritis, which often begins during the young adult years or early middle age. Gouty arthritis may strike any time during the middle years, and as the senior years approach, osteoarthritis may emerge.

RHEUMATOID ARTHRITIS

Rheumatoid arthritis, also called arthritis deformans, is the potentially crippling joint disorder. Often beginning in the second, third, or fourth decade of life, the disease is two to three times more common in women than in men.

Here's what happens: the joint where two bones meet (see Figure 13) has a thin layer of cartilage cushioning each bone end and is enclosed within a thin-walled joint capsule. The joint space contains a thin film of fluid, providing lubrication. The entire joint structure is stabilized by thick fibrous ligaments joining bone to bone, and allowing motion only in the proper plane.

Rheumatoid arthritis causes an acute inflammation within the joint capsule. The joint responds by forming protective fluid and sometimes by thickening of the joint capsule—as if to protect against irritation. The joint becomes hot, red, and swollen. The pain is extreme, and attempts at joint motion cause severe discomfort. In time, inflammation takes its toll of delicate tissues, with destruction of cartilage and deformity of the knee, wrist, finger, or other joint.

Rheumatoid arthritis can strike any articulation. The knees, which bear the full body weight when walking, are often involved, but the wrists, ankles, and spine are also favorite targets. Characteristic hand deformities occur with fusiform swelling of the middle joints of the fingers, often linked with swelling and shifting of the knuckle joint, deviating the digits toward the fifth finger.

Like hemlines, arthritis has its ups and downs. It's worse in cold damp weather, better when sunny and dry. The joints stiffen when at rest, and become more mobile following moderate activity. Flare-ups of the disease may follow infection, fatigue, or emotional crisis—or the disease may become worse or better for no apparent reason.

Yes, arthritis is a pain in the neck—or virtually any joint in the body. It's the discomfort that makes arthritis mean—the aching, unremitting, 24-hour joint pain that plagues every motion. Rising from a chair becomes an aching effort, and a short walk to the kitchen is planned as a general would map a battle march.

For a while, the middle-aged arthritic can say, "It doesn't bother me too much. I can stand a lot of pain."

But in time, the stoic facade begins to crumble, and in despair, the arthritic may trudge from one doctor to the next, searching for the magic cure. None exists! Sure, relief may follow this medicine or that—perhaps due to the medication or merely because the natural rhythm of arthritis dictated improvement at this time.

Yet much can be done, and the victim of arthritis should place his care in the hands of a nearby compassionate physician with an interest in joint disease. How about the super-clinic in the Midwest or on the East Coast? Certainly, these doctors may have valid suggestions to modify treatment, but arthritis is a lifelong disorder requiring week-by-week and month-by-month therapeutic decisions. That means you'll need a local doctor who is as near as the telephone.

After all, despite their postgraduate degrees and specialists' pretentions, doctors have but several classes of medication to treat rheumatoid arthritis and these are available to all physicians:

●   **Aspirin** or one of its host of derivatives is still the mainstay of arthritis treatment. Many physicians prescribe up to 12 aspirin tablets daily (provided dizziness, ringing in the ears, and stomach distress do not occur), with other medication added to this base.

●   **Indomethacin (Indocin)** is another first-rate anti-arthritis drug. It seems strikingly beneficial to some individuals and offers little help to others. Its use is hampered by two chief side effects—abdominal cramps and lightheadedness.

- **Ibuprofen** (Motrin), **Fenoprofen** (Naflon), **Naproxen** (Naprosyn), **Tolemetin** (Toloctin). These medication and similar products that were released recently promise to be first-rate anti-arthritis drugs. Ibuprofen's clinical claim is a low incidence of nausea and other side effects, plus potent activity against arthritis.
- **Phenylbutazone** (Butazolidin) is a first-rate drug for a short-term use, and is a standard in treatment of the acute arthritic flare-up. Stomach irritation and blood disorders are among the hazards associated with long-term therapy.
- **Cortisone** comes as shots or pills and sometimes is injected into troublesome joints. Like phenylbutazone, its short-term benefit can be striking, and it's often used in intermittent courses of therapy. Peptic ulcers, fluid retention, and blood sugar elevations are the penalties for overuse.
- **Gold** injections are reserved for hard-core cases. The series of shots is relatively expensive, blood tests are needed to monitor gold's frequent side effects, and the therapeutic value is often less than what is hoped for.

Perhaps it's his use of physical therapy that distinguishes the truly arthritis-wise physician. Heat in all forms seems to help arthritis. At home a hot bath may bring relief, or hot packs may be applied to troublesome joints perhaps using a Hydrocollator. Or the physician may prescribe formal physical therapy including diathermy, ultrasound, or whirlpool treatments. For aching finger and hand joints, there's nothing like a hot paraffin bath.

If all else fails and progressive disease threatens to cause crippling, surgery may be the answer. Deformed hands can be reconstructed and damaged knees repaired in the operating room.

Rheumatoid arthritis is as mean a disease as ever, but modern medical therapy can do much to cushion its impact.

GOUT

We know what causes gouty arthritis; it's crystals of sodium urate deposited in joints. Uric acid is a bloodstream chemical produced by the breakdown of high protein foods. When the blood level is too high, joints collect sodium urate crystals which produce acute inflammation. Often the joint of the great toe is involved—hot, swollen, and intensely painful.

Once considered a disease of the wealthy (because only they could afford luxury high-protein foods), gout is now as likely to strike the laborer as the land baron, thanks to the rich American diet enjoyed by all social classes.

The doctor diagnoses gout upon examination of the painful joint, and more important, following determination of the blood uric acid level. The treatment of gout is a two-step process, directed at this pair of problems.

First comes attention to the painful joint, with a prescription for anti-inflammatory medication. Effective and useful in diagnosis since it relieves no disorder but gout, colchicine tablets may be taken at one- or two-hour intervals; dramatic improvement in the gouty joint follows about the first half dozen pills, often coincident with explosive intestinal cramps, vomiting, and diarrhea. A first choice drug is often phenylbutazone (Butazolidin), prescribed in doses greater than that taken for rheumatoid arthritis, and sometimes the physician will order indomethacin (Indocin) or cortisone to douse the flames of acute gout.

With the pain subdued, attention shifts to long-term therapy to avoid further flare-ups. Dietary restrictions are imposed, particularly eliminating organ foods such as liver, sweetbreads, kidney, or brains; small fish including anchovies or sardines; and excessive use of alcoholic beverages. Prescribed may be probenecid (Benemid) to help eliminate uric acid through the kidneys or allopurinol (Zyloprim) to lower uric acid by sabotaging its production.

Perhaps Benjamin Franklin had the best advice in preventing attacks of gout when he wrote in *Poor Richard's Almanack:*

Be temperate in wine, in eating, girls, and sloth,
Or the Gout will seize you and plague you both.

OSTEOARTHRITIS

Osteoarthritis is also called hypertrophic arthritis or degenerative arthritis, but perhaps it's not proper to call it arthritis at all. Really, it's the wear and tear of joints with age, grinding down the cartilage cushion so that bone ends grate painfully against one another, linked with the formation of bony spurs in the spine and peripheral joints.

The weight-bearing joints are commonly affected, notably the knees. Often involved are joints having suffered past damage—the knee injured in football or shoulder damaged while skiing years before. One feature of the disease is Heberden's nodes, a knobby enlargement of the last joint of the fingers, curiously more common in women than in men and showing a familial pattern.

Because osteoarthritis results from joint usage and age, it's most common after age fifty, and especially attacks weight-bearing joints of overweight individuals. There's little of the intense relentless inflammation of rheumatoid arthritis and hot, red joints occur seldom. Rather, there's the dull ache and sensation of grating when affected joints are moved, or perhaps the troublesome low back pain of spinal osteoarthritis.

Osteoarthritis therapy parallels that of rheumatoid arthritis. Heat is palliative, including warm baths, hot packs, and physical therapy for particularly troublesome joints. Rest may be helpful when a single articulation is severely inflamed, and weight reduction is advised for overweight individuals. Medication prescribed may include aspirin, indomethacin, phenylbutazone, and sometimes even cortisone.

The osteoarthritis victim can take comfort in knowing that, although painful at times, the disorder does not cause the crippling characteristic of rheumatoid arthritis.

The individual suffering arthritis of any type should learn about his problem. The physician is the best source of advice, and to supplement his care, The Arthritis Foundation, 3400 Peachtree Road, N.E., Atlanta, Ga. 30326, has a chapter near you, offering informative publications and perhaps sponsoring local clinics and home care programs.

Portrait of an Ulcer

A thing of beauty is the ulcer—crimson-toned and gracefully symmetrical. Located in the stomach or duodenum (first segment of the small intestine), the ulcer is framed by rolled edges, convoluted as though etched by a skilled craftsman. In the center is the crater, a hollow cavity chiseled into the stomach wall.

Look close! Through the ulcer opening, we can catch a glimpse of Mr. (or Mrs.) Ulcer. J.A.D. Anderson once described an ulcer as "the hole in a man's stomach through which he crawls to escape from his wife." Yet it's not so simple. The ulcer victim has a life style all his own, and his gastric defect accrues not from a desire to escape or as a mark of failure, but as a badge of selfless striving for achievement.

Mr. Ulcer works at top speed from dawn until dusk, gulping breakfast, dashing from appointment to meeting, rushing through lunch, then groaning at the three reports marked "URGENT" dropped on his desk at 4:15 in the afternoon. His briefcase bulges with work to keep him busy until midnight and through weekend afternoons. He's short on sleep, long on coffee, and fueled by nervous tension. When aggravation strikes, as it often does in his frantic day, the stomach churns out acid by the gallon.

Most likely to develop an ulcer is the executive or overcommitted socialite-mother, or even the lower-level foreman whose responsibilities exceed the tolerance of his stomach lining. Failures? They beget colitis, with cramps and diarrhea. The ulcer is the special reward of the high achiever.

UNDERSTANDING ULCERS

They're all called peptic ulcers, referring to pepsin and other stomach juices which digest food in the upper gastrointestinal tract. Yet, when in superabundance, these same peptic juices can nibble at the lining cells of the stomach or duodenum.

The stomach's lining has some natural resistance to peptic erosion not found in the duodenum portion of the small intestine. As acid outflow from the stomach bathes the duodenum, 70 percent of ulcers occur in this area. If an ulcer is inevitable, have yours in the duodenum, because cancerous change in this location is rare. The remaining three-tenths of peptic ulcers strike the stomach and these lesions are more worrisome since up to one in ten will eventually prove malignant.

The ulcer develops slowly, beginning with an irritation too small to cause symptoms. Gradually, as responsibility and aggravation approach the boiling point, the flow of acid quickens. A collar of protective thickening develops in the wall and the center gradually erodes into a painful and potentially dangerous ulcer.

What does Mr. Ulcer feel? Problems may begin during adolescence or the teenage years with stomach aches on school days. Later there's a sour stomach after a cup of coffee or indigestion following pizza.

In the middle years, heartburn may occur more often, following a few drinks or capping an aggravating day at the office. Milk cools the burning, and that works for a while. But eventually, usually in the spring or fall of the year (for some reason the worst seasons for ulcers), the burning pain becomes relentless, fired by even the blandest foods and overpowering all medication. At long last, there's time made in the schedule for a trip to the doctor, who orders an upper gastrointestinal x-ray series and finds the peptic ulcer.

Treatment is overdue.

OVERCOMING ULCERS

The doctor outlines an all-inclusive battle plan against the ulcer, beginning with dietary changes. While improper eating habits probably don't cause ulcers, dietary indiscretion can fan the flames of irritated lining cells. Say goodbye to spicy treats. First may come a super-bland diet—chiefly milk, cream, oatmeal, and creamed foods. Later, when the ulcer fires have been cooled, the menu is liberalized to include most common foods plus milk by the glassful, but still no coffee, tea, alcohol, pepperoni pizza, and overseasoned treats.

Antacids, like milk, neutralize acid peptic juices. They're taken following meals, between meals, and whenever acid heartburn threatens. No prescription is required, and a varied selection is available at the drugstore. Good choices include Riopan, Mylanta, or Gelusil.

To reduce acid peptic juice production, there are anticholinergic pills, derivatives of old-fashioned belladonna. Beside lowering acid levels, these medications slow bowel motility (and may cause constipation), reduce perspiration, dry saliva (and when the mouth feels a little dry, the dosage is just right), and may blur vision slightly.

Surgery? It's chiefly used for ulcer complications such as bleeding, perforation, or obstruction. The threat of hemorrhage hangs over the ulcer patient like the sword of Damocles, and may begin abruptly and painlessly, its presence signaled only by tarry-black feces and weakness owing to blood loss. Perforation—penetration of the ulcer through the stomach or duodenal wall and into the abdominal cavity—causes acute pain; heartburn changes to excruciating abdominal distress demanding instant medical attention. Obstruction occurs more gradually as ulcer scarring and swelling block the exodus of food from the stomach; vomiting begins and dehydration threatens.

The surgeon rushes to the rescue when these complications occur: hemorrhage may be managed by transfusions and diet, but the surgeon's knife is sometimes needed. More urgent is perforation, requiring immediate operative intervention. Obstruction may receive a trial of medical therapy, often followed by surgery.

Last, let's discuss the most important thrust of therapy. The ulcer developed due to a super-charged life style, and a change must come. Begin with less work, perhaps an extra afternoon or day off each week, time for gardening or reading. Reducing responsibility is vital, even when this means declining a coveted community post or rejecting a promotion. Vacations should be prescribed like medication, to be taken on a regular schedule without fail. In the last analysis, the overacid stomach will respond best to a change in temperament—beginning each new day with a zest for living, not with a list of urgent chores to be completed.

As the ulcer crater heals, we see framed not the tense face of Mr. Ulcer, but a pleasant portrait of Mr. Tranquility.

The Fear of Cancer

In 1926, Dr. Charles H. Mayo wrote in *The Annals of Surgery*, "While there are several chronic diseases more destructive of life than cancer, none is more feared." Today, almost 50 years later, the word cancer still strikes terror in the hearts of middle-aged men and women.

At least in part, it's fear of the unknown, since the origin of cancer is still a mystery. There's the dread of disfigurement, and the threat of a lingering death due to cancer—the number two killer during middle age, trailing only heart disease.

In the coming year, more than 650,000 new cases of cancer will be discovered, and 350,000 Americans will die of the disease. Experts predict 1.2 million new cancer cases annually in the United States by the year 2000, unless we can solve the cancer riddle.

THE RIDDLE OF CANCER

Cancer is the growth of cells gone wild. Beginning in a previously normal organ such as the lung or brain or even bone, cancer produces new mutant cells that reproduce like rabbits and soon overrun the normal tissues. Sometimes cancer works its mischief by causing pressure on nearby vital structures, while other tumors spread to distant parts of the body to begin satellite growths. Virtually any organ in the body can develop cancer, with symptoms, physical findings, and microscopic features peculiar to that tumor.

Nor are plants and animals free of cancer. Sunflowers and clover develop plant cancers, malignant neoplasms of the breast are common in dogs, and cancer is so common in mice that these rodents make excellent experimental subjects.

We know that malignant tumors cause death when untreated, and benign tumors may impair nearby organs, but without fatal termination.

We know a great deal about cancer, but we don't know the cause.

Yet, doctors have found may pieces to the puzzle, gleaned from observations made over centuries. The following are six factors that favor the development of cancer:

1.   **Heredity** is hard to control. Racial traits and family susceptibility account for the same cancer occurring in identical twins, and certain strains of mice predictably develop specific cancers in each generation. Blacks rarely suffer malignant melanoma of the skin, Caucasians develop cancer of the prostate nine times as often as Japanese, and Chinese individuals have a high incidence of cancer of the nasopharynx—all related to heredity, or perhaps to some factor as yet unknown.

2.   **Carcinogens**, substances that incite cancer, are factors that we can control. Potential carcinogens include tar, soot, hydrocarbon derivatives, coal dust, paraffin oil, aniline dyes, shale oil, cyclamates, asbestos, x-rays, and radioactive material. The carcinogenic properties of carbon soot were recognized as early as 1775 when Dr. Percival Pott linked chimney soot and the epidemic of scrotal cancer in young boys pressed into service as chimney sweeps. Later, doctors found that Scottish fishermen mending their nets with tarred twine held in the mouth had a sky-high incidence of lip cancer. Icelanders suffer a high frequency of stomach cancer, often occurring at an early age, probably related to a diet high in smoked meats and fish. Certain oils have carcinogenic properties and Bloody Mary in the musical "South Pacific" incurred a high risk of oral cancer from her devotion to chewing betel nuts.

More recently recognized influences include bladder cancer occurring in aniline dye workers 30 times more often than in the general population, and an incidence of leukemia in x-ray specialists ten times greater than in other individuals.

3.   **Viruses** may be the missing link in cancer, and in some tumors of chickens the evidence appears conclusive. Microorganisms

may be the answer to why early circumcision protects adult males from cancer of the penis and their wives from cervical cancer. Cross-cultural studies show that penile cancer among Moslems (who are usually circumcised between the third and fourteenth birthdays) approaches the level of the general population, while the incidence in Jews undergoing ritual infant circumcision approaches zero. The rarity of cervical cancer among elderly maiden ladies and nuns attests to the penile influence upon this tumor, perhaps (but not conclusively) related to microorganisms.

4. **Hormones** play a role in certain cancers, notably the breast and prostate, which both grow luxuriantly under hormonal stimulation.

5. **Pre-existing disease** is a common cancer prelude. Skin cancers are common in old burn scars, and the alcoholic is particularly at risk for cancer of the esophagus and larynx. Liver disease seems to invite cancer: the West African Bantu is prone to liver tumors owing to nutritional liver disease, while in the United States, more than half of all liver tumors (hepatomas) strike adults with cirrhosis of the liver.

6. **Unknown factors** are the missing pieces of the puzzle. Why do women who nurse their children rarely develop breast cancer? Why is breast cancer more common in women with thyroid deficiencies? Why do tumors of the thyroid and prostate grow very slowly, while lung and stomach cancers are rapidly lethal? Why does the previously healthy individual, the middle-ager to whom none of the above factors apply, develop cancer at all?

It's the caprice of cancer. Until the riddles are answered, we'll study the disease with statistics and treat with the best means at our disposal.

CANCER SITES

Perhaps we categorize and pigeonhole most diligently those diseases we are powerless to control. Cancer statistics have many facets including age distribution, tumor sites, survival rates, and mortality figures.

Statistics tell us that most cancers occur in individuals in their fifties and sixties. The reason is simple: this is the largest age group at risk. Deaths during later decades lower the number of cancer cases reported, as individuals who might have developed cancer succumb to heart attacks, strokes, and other diseases of old age. For the *individual,* however, the risk of developing most cancers increases with age.

Where and how often does cancer strike? Skin cancer is more common than generally realized, and how many people know that the breast is women's most common cancer site? Figures 14 and 15 illustrate where cancer strikes men and women of all ages.

Mortality due to cancers of various types is linked, not so much to the incidence of the tumor, but to its malignancy. Malignant tumors metastasize—spread from the original site to distant organs, often culminating in widespread secondary growths. Herein lies the lethal threat of cancer. The following are the most common causes of cancer deaths in males aged thirty-five to fifty-four:

1.   Lung cancer, the penality for excessive cigarette smoking, leads the list.

2.   Colon and rectum cancers, many detectable by physical and x-ray examinations, are curable if found early.

3.   Pancreas cancer, buried deep in the abdomen, is usually well advanced when first found.

4.   Brain cancer is malignant, and one of the most feared of all tumors.

5.   Stomach cancer, sometimes confused with peptic ulcer, is always highly malignant.

The middle years pose a special cancer threat to women from tumors of the breast and reproductive organs. Here are the five leading causes of female cancer deaths between ages thirty-five and fifty-four:

1.   Breast cancer is most common between ages forty-five and sixty-five, and uncommon after sixty-five, yet 17 percent of cases occur in women under forty years of age.

2.   Cancer of the uterus and cervix also strikes a younger age group than many other tumors. The tip-off is often a questionable Pap smear upon routine pelvic examination.

3.   Colon and rectum cancers, the most frequent internal "nonfeminine" tumors of middle-aged women, often cause rectal bleeding and changes in bowel habit.

4.   Lung cancer is on the rise in the "You've come a long way, Baby" smoking woman.

5.   Cancer of the ovary, nestled deep in the pelvis, often eludes detection until well advanced.

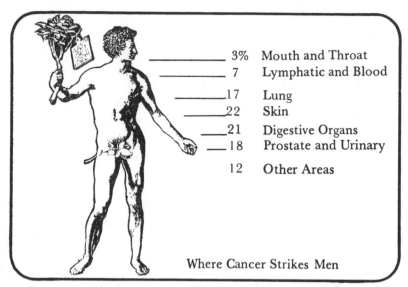

	3%	Mouth and Throat
	7	Lymphatic and Blood
	17	Lung
	22	Skin
	21	Digestive Organs
	18	Prostate and Urinary
	12	Other Areas

Where Cancer Strikes Men

Figure 14

Figure 15

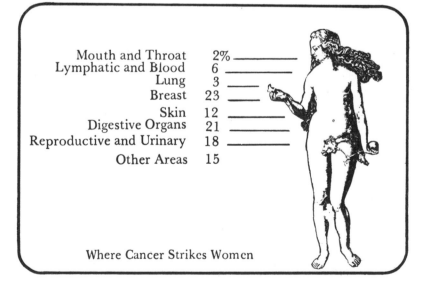

Mouth and Throat	2%	
Lymphatic and Blood	6	
Lung	3	
Breast	23	
Skin	12	
Digestive Organs	21	
Reproductive and Urinary	18	
Other Areas	15	

Where Cancer Strikes Women

DIAGNOSING CANCER

Until the riddle of cause and prevention is solved and until the doctor can offer a shot against cancer as he can against measles and mumps, our first defense is early diagnosis. Of prime importance is the periodic physical examination. Some doctors call it a cancer checkup, screening for malignancy in all organs of the body, and giving him a chance to detect tumors before the too-late-for-cure stage. At least half of all cancers are visible or can be palpated by the doctor, while another one quarter are accessible to instruments inserted into various body orifices. If you skipped over the last section in Chapter 4, reread it now, then plan to invest an hour in a comprehensive physical examination.

The doctor may order a CEA (carcinoembryonic antigen) test, searching for traces of cancer in the bloodstream. The carcinoembyronic antigen is a chemical substance present in embyros, cancer, and even some inflammatory diseases, but its most important use is in a new cancer screening test. Although the final results aren't in yet, it's apparent that the individual with elevated CEA levels often harbors a yet-undiscovered malignancy. As CEA values rise, the likelihood of malignancy skyrockets, and soaring values are found in individuals whose tumors have spread from the original locus to liver, bone, or other metastatic sites.

Symptoms are the clarion call of cancer, tempting the doctor to detect its presence. Physicians, working hand in hand with the American Cancer Society, have publicized eight cancer danger signals:

● A sore that does not heal, suggesting a tumor of the skin or mouth.

● A lump or thickening in the breast or elsewhere, a call for immediate medical evaluation.

● Unusual bleeding or discharge, symptoms that demand a thorough physical examination and perhaps x-rays.

● A change in a mole or wart, possibly signaling the onset of a malignant melanoma of the skin.

● Persistent indigestion or difficulty swallowing—possible signs of cancer of the throat, esophagus, or stomach.

● Lingering cough or hoarseness, suggesting a tumor of the larynx or lung; x-ray diagnosis is mandatory.

● A change in bowel habits, one early symptom of cancer of the colon or rectum.

- Unexplained weight loss or prolonged fever.

Of course, recognizing warning signs is only step one. Next comes the visit to the doctor—promptly, not 2 months from Tuesday. A physical examination and tests will follow, allowing exclusion of cancer or confirmation of the diagnosis.

If suspected cancer is confirmed, treatment begins at once.

TREATING CANCER

The assault on cancer includes surgery, irradiation, and chemotherapy. Choices vary according to the location of the tumor, age of the patient, stage of the disease, and up-to-date recommendations of specialists in cancer therapy.

In general, surgery is the treatment of choice. It implies a hope of cure, perhaps removing a segment of diseased colon, or a cancer-laden breast. It's the doctor's first choice when he thinks he can "get it all." Sometimes it's extensive, occasionally even disfiguring, but success on the operating table can mean life or death to the cancer patient.

Radiation therapy of cancer is coming into its own, as we learn more refined techniques and as better equipment becomes available. Radiation therapy includes deep x-ray therapy and radiocobalt for treatment of a number of susceptible tumors, plus radiophosphorus for polycythemia, radioactive iodine for thyroid cancer, and more. Often invoked as a last ditch effort, radiation treatment may be first choice therapy for some tumors (such as cancer of the cervix), and often is used in conjunction with surgery to "get the cells that might have been left behind." X-ray therapy can often shrink the incurable tumor, bringing blessed relief from pain when cancer involves the spine, and may add months or years to the life of the cancer victim.

Chemotherapy—chemical substances that combat cancer—is our newest weapon. The arsenal increases yearly as scientists develop new agents. Cancer chemotherapy comes to the fore in treatment of leukemia and multiple myeloma, while indispensable in therapy of tumors in many other areas. Critics may scoff, "Drugs don't cure cancer," but there have been many long-long-term survivals.

PREVENTING CANCER DURING THE MIDDLE YEARS

Writing in *Atlantic Monthly* in June, 1939, Henry E. Sigerist asserted, "Every child knows that prevention is not only better than cure, but also cheaper." When faced with a disease that is difficult to diagnose and harder to cure, prevention becomes paramount.

What can the adult do to prevent cancer? Certainly not all cancers are preventable, but the measures described in the following paragraphs may help to tip the scales in your favor.

Avoid exposure to carcinogens, at home or at work. The number one offender is tobacco, including cigarettes, cigars, and pipes. Review the list earlier in this section; if your work brings you in contact with any of these, check with your physician or local public health department.

Sun-bathe with care, since tanning rays age skin prematurely and can set the stage for skin cancers in later years. Avoid alcohol abuse, since alcoholism is a known factor in cancers of the larynx, esophagus, pancreas, and liver.

Use hormones cautiously, always asking the doctor if his hormone prescription might influence other organs.

Have male infants circumcised within the first week of life, increasing their chances of avoiding penile cancer and helping protect their future wives against cervical tumors.

See your doctor yearly for a thorough physical checkup including a chest x-ray, rectal examination, and for the ladies, a Papanicolaou smear.

Cancer is a prime threat to health in the middle years. It pays to learn about the enemy, and a good source is the American Cancer Society. Formed in 1913 by a group of ten physicians and five pioneering citizens, it is one of the oldest voluntary health groups in America. Its many chapters cooperate with private physicians and hospitals in bringing cancer information to the public and channeling funds into research and treatment. A wide variety of educational material is published, and a note to the American Cancer Society, 219 East 42nd Street, New York, N.Y. 10017, will bring informative material, along with the address of a local chapter near you.

Each year millions of dollars flow into cancer research. New surgical techniques, super-voltage x-ray machines, and exotic chemical compounds are the dividends. But, in my opinion, they're not really the answer. In the end, cancer will become as extinct as smallpox when we isolate the cause, allowing development of preventative measures, perhaps a vaccine. Who knows?

With adequate funding of research, the dedication of scientists, and perhaps a pinch of serendipity, medical historians of the twenty-first century may know cancer only from textbooks.

EMOTIONAL CHALLENGES OF THE MIDDLE YEARS

If there be a hell upon earth, it is to be found in a melancholy man's heart.
Robert Burton (1577-1640)
The Anatomy of Melancholy

NOT ALL MALADIES OF THE MIDDLE YEARS are physical. Some are mental—or, if you please, emotional—and are often more distressing than their somatic counterparts. My patients who have suffered both physical pain and mental anguish invariably insist they would choose pain if forced to endure one or the other.

Theories and therapy of emotional problems have a colorful history. Let's travel through time to ancient Babylonia, where psychiatric diagnosis was simple indeed: demons caused dementia. Simple as that. Sanity returned when the demons were banished.

Next a big jump to the Middle Ages, and we now recognize the demon as Satan himself. The treatment? Exorcism, with its elaborate trappings and rituals.

Let's pause in the sixteenth century at the Hospital of Saint Mary of Bethlehem, where the treatment of emotional disorders was pragmatic. The mentally ill were confined in chains, sequestering them from society and earning Bedlam a special niche in the English lexicon.

By the twentieth century, Adler, Jung, and Freud—the putative fathers of modern psychiatry—had broken the chains of Bedlam and returned the emotionally ill to the parlor, where a touch of eccentricity was respectable and sometimes even fashionable.

Today, we've come full circle in psychotherapy. The trappings are a notebook and couch, and the rituals are free association and analysis, as the therapist drives demonic symptoms from the psyche. This is not an accurate picture of psychotherapy—but reinforces the myth about it.

In this chapter, we'll discuss everyday emotional woes that plague middle-agers—the neuroses, if you prefer medical jargon. The psychoses, overwhelming derangements of mental function likely to land a Londoner in ancient Bedlam, are less common disorders found at all ages, and we'll leave them to the psychiatric textbooks. Here we'll discuss the common emotional problems generated by the unique physical and social events of the middle years.

When Anxiety Overwhelms

Anxiety is with us every day. It prods us out of bed in the morning, lest the day's chores go undone, and spurs us to keep working when we would rather nap or just go fishing. It gives the burst of energy to deal with danger, to slam the brakes when a child darts in front of the car, or rush for the door if fire threatens. Anxiety begets respectability, reliability, and productivity, yet sometimes causes symptoms as the body reacts to minor stresses with major defenses.

PROBING ANXIETY

Anxiety is a jittery feeling of impending disaster. The erudite Sir Bertrand Russell pinpointed the problem: "Our instinctive emotions are those we have inherited from a much more dangerous world and contain, therefore, a larger proportion of fear than they should." Anxiety is the sensation of swaying on a mountain cliff, swimming through shark-infested waters, or dodging traffic in the middle of the expressway—and it can last all day long. In generations past, the anxious individual needed a burst of epinephrine to fight or flee. Today he copes, but the pulse quickens, the blood pressure bounds, and nerves tense all the same.

Anxiety often reaches its peak in the middle years. Sometimes the cause is obvious: the decision to approach the boss, "I need a raise," the call to speak before the P.T.A., the news that mother-in-law plans to visit, or simply deciding what to have for dinner. Yet middle-aged anxiety is often less specific—free-floating it's sometimes called. Its origins are hard to identify, but may include imagined loss of youth and sexuality, financial insecurity, pressures on the job, and the problems of parenthood. Add to these the demanding pace of life in the 1970's, and it's little wonder that the mental machinery runs full speed from morning until night.

Apprehension during times of stress is normal. Anxiety becomes pathological when it is out of proportion to the cause (panic about party preparations), when it persists long after the precipitating event (fear of driving lasting months after an automobile accident), or when it compromises daily activities and physical health (as we'll see next).

You can spot the anxious individual at a party. Watch the eyes; the pupils may be slightly enlarged, and he'll blink at every second word. Shake hands, and feel the sweaty palm. Watch the fingers as they fumble with buttons and pencils and glasses, just as Captain Queeg (*The Caine Muntiny,* remember?) reached for his little steel balls when under stress. There'll be other body language too—picking at imaginary lint, tugging at cuffs, crossing and uncrossing the legs. It's all unproductive activity, discharging nervous impulses, but hampering the anxious individual's effective functioning.

There may be more troublesome physical symptoms. Most common is the tension headache, a dull throbbing in the temples at the end of the day, pounding like a chorus of tympani. For some, it's a shaking tremor of the hand that becomes worse at the most inopportune times. For others, high-tension anxiety increases stomach acid production that can foment ulcers, prods intestinal peristalsis that can trigger colitis, and can even send the individual scurrying frequently to the bathroom with a "nervous bladder." And let's not forget the harmful effects of too many cigarettes, highballs "to calm the nerves," and nights when sleep won't come.

Sometimes, like a short-circuited wire that blows a fuse, hysteria strikes. A common blown fuse is hyperventilation—the compulsive urge to take deep breaths. The call to the doctor usually sounds like this, "Doctor, I'm sorry to call you on a Saturday night, but we've been extra-busy at work, and I haven't had time to make an appointment. My breathing has seemed difficult for about 3 weeks, and tonight I've been working hard on reports. Suddenly, a half hour ago, I felt I was smothering. Right now, it's an effort to talk and I can't get a deep breath."

When the doctor examines this patient, he'll note repeated deep sighing breaths and a dramatic absence of physical abnormalities. The chest x-ray? It's as normal as ants at a picnic. The anxious over-worked caller is describing hyperventilation, and needs reassurance of the absence of physical illness plus a sharp cutback in his worries and responsibilities.

ALLEVIATING ANXIETY

When anxiety overwhelms, it's time to seek treatment. Mention anxiety to the doctor, and he often reflexly reaches for the prescription blank. For generations, the first choice drug was old-fashioned phenobarbital, now largely replaced by chlordiazepoxide (Librium), diazepam (Valium), and oxazepam (Serax)—offering more tranquility with less sedation. Initially, tranquilizers are often taken three or four times daily, until the crisis is past. Later, the knowledge that the bottle is as near as the medicine cabinet can be an effective security blanket when anxiety threatens. But don't be beguiled; tranquilizers are only one aspect of therapy, and their prime advantage is often in setting the stage for counseling.

It's time to sort out the stresses of everyday living, and relieve the pressures that make the pulse pound and the stomach burn. It's often more difficult to find a competent counselor than secure a proper tranquilizer prescription. Sometimes the best source of counsel is a wise family physician; other individuals turn to a psychotherapist, or perhaps to a religious advisor. If the causes are simple and straightforward, a few sessions may suffice, but if overwhelming anxiety stems from deep-seated conflicts, months of therapy may be needed. Always remember: anxiety is a symptom, not a disease. Cure of incapacitating anxiety follows not suppressing the symptom with tranquilizers, but identifying and removing the causes.

Avoidance is like the climate therapy sometimes prescribed for the incapacitated asthmatic who moves to Arizona. It won't cure the disease, but precipitating factors are minimized. Avoidance therapy includes declining the committee chairmanship that nine persons have probably already refused, saying "no" to the urge to work late at the office, skirting downtown rush hour traffic, and even shopping during hours when stores aren't crowded. Side-stepping anxiety-provoking situations is the goal, minimizing the wear and tear on already frayed nerves.

Avoiding anxiety includes sublimation—channeling nervous energy into creative outlets. Work is a good way to let off steam. Chopping wood, yanking weeds from the garden, or decapitating grass with a mower all help drain anxious impulses. Feel angry? Take it out on a tennis ball, or by swinging a golf club, but not by berating innocent family members, fretting about events beyond control, or engaging in purposeless, worry-bead activity.

Anxious energy is what provokes the housewife to create a gourmet meal, the engineer to construct a sturdy bridge, and writers like myself to keep scribbling when they could be playing golf. A pinch of tension adds zest to life. But when anxiety gets the upper hand, interferring with health and productivity, then the middle-ager should take stock of the stresses in his life, and seek professional guidance.

Neurasthenia

Neurasthenia is the stepchild of anxiety. The word means debility of the nerves and perhaps the original definition connoted poor transmission through nerve fibers; but in most cases, chronic anxiety is the villain.

Lethargy is the lot of the neurasthenic. He drags from bed exhausted, plods wearily through the day, and crumples in the evening. All energy is consumed by his neurotic disorder, with none left for work or fun.

A favorite site of neurasthenic symptoms is the heart: "My heart keeps pounding, Doctor. It skips beats and keeps me awake at night. I feel so weak I'm afraid I'm going to have a heart attack."

Or perhaps the symptom is simply fatigue: "Doctor, I'd like to do more for my family, but I never have the pep. I have about enough energy to fix breakfast and after that I drag through the day longing for a few extra hours of rest. My idea of a fun vacation is dozing 24 hours each day."

The doctor makes the diagnosis of neurasthenia reluctantly. He knows that diabetes, cancer, thyroid disease, and depression can all cause similar complaints—and it's up to him to prove that the neurasthenic is free of these disorders. There's no place for curbstone diagnoses here, and a thorough physical examination will be followed by laboratory tests, x-rays, and an electrocardiogram—all strikingly normal in the neurasthenic.

Once the diagnosis is secure, treatment is begun. The first task is finding why the neurasthenic has taken refuge in these particular symptoms at this time in his or her life. Symptoms may spring from patterns handed down by parents who escaped stress in the sickbed or in the doctor's office. Overwhelming, perhaps, are the stresses of the middle years—financial demands, marital woes, or children's lives in turmoil. Sometimes the cause is worry about real or fancied physical illness. I recall one middle-aged matron whose vitality went down the drain. "Why?" I wondered. Finally the cause came to light: Several years ago, a gynecologist had mentioned that she had a fibroid tumor of the uterus. The uterine fibroid is an all-but-harmless growth, but she hadn't heard that part of the explanation. All she heard was "tumor"—and that meant cancer. She had not returned to the gynecologist, had never mentioned the growth to her family, and had suffered progressively waning vitality while awaiting the inevitable spread of her "cancer."

Most causes are more elusive, but careful probing by the physician will often unearth the etiology of neurasthenia. Once found, the cause is confronted during counseling. Conflicts are resolved and energy is directed from somatic complaints into productive activity.

Medication? It's often prescribed as an adjunct to counseling, and may include vitamins, tranquilizers, psychic energizers, and tonics. Much of their value is more psychological than physical—the mental lift that derives from taking regular medication.

The neurasthenic's file can be closed when he awakens in the morning and exclaims, "What a great day! Let's get out of bed and get going."

Hypochondriasis

This section is for the middle-ager who has everything—from athlete's foot to Zulu fever. Give a pencil and paper to a neurasthenic, and you've made a hypochondriac. Known for their long, long lists of physical complaints, hypochondriacs crowd the waiting rooms of doctors around the world.

Middle-agers comprise more than their share of hypochondriacs. Perhaps it's panic at the thought of aging. "You're wearing out. You're falling apart," says the little voice inside, and inconsequential everyday aches and pains become magnified into maladies of monumental proportions. Multiple symptoms in many organs are the rule, and a wag once devised a do-it-yourself test for hypochondriasis: you know you've got it when you can't find anything right.

Sometimes we think that hypochondriasis is an affliction of the affluent, who have little to do with their time but dream up new ailments. In fact, it's a malady of all cultures and social classes. I wrote an article about hypochondriasis titled "Doctor, I Wrote it all

Down" (*Medical Insight,* July, 1972). The many letters received in response highlight the magnitude of the problem. One of the most colorful came from a physician describing an experience as a medical missionary in Africa: "While traveling on the Orashi River in Nigeria in a canoe, a young boy raced along the bank shouting at the top of his lungs, 'Doctor, Doctor!' We pulled the canoe into the bank where I was met by a teenage youngster with an anxiety-ridden face who told me in distraught terms that the air was flowing in one side of his nose faster than it was in the other."

Another reply to my hypochondriasis article came from a Texas physician who suggested that "the wild enumeration of symptoms on paper is good therapy for the patient and a great aid to him." Confronting his complaints helps the individual pinpoint problems and is certainly a more constructive outlet than popping pills or pining away in depression.

Sitting in the doctor's seat, I have no simple cure for the hypochondriac. Relieve him of his symptoms, and he'll develop others. Give him the handful of prescriptions that he seems to crave, and he may challenge the record of the all-time king of hypochondriacs, Samuel Jessup of Heckington, England, who is on record as having consumed 40,000 bottles of medication and 226,934 pills before his long-anticipated demise at age sixty-five.

Refer the hypochondriac to a specialist and he'll bounce back like a bad check. Send him to a psychiatrist and he's sure he's been rejected by his doctor.

The best efforts of the physician and family are those directed toward finding why the hypochondriac clings to his symptoms and what void they fill. Only then can the psychological defect be explored,and hopefully closed forever.

In the meantime, the doctor is confronted with a list of seventeen separate symptoms, while he knows that waiting patients are packed gluteus-to-gluteus, staring at the clock. Yet he examines each area of complaint, mindful that in the end, every hypochondriac will die of a physical disease.

The Empty Nest Syndrome

The empty nest syndrome—here's an emotional challenge peculiar to middle age. It's been propagated in folklore, dignified in psychiatric textbooks, and hurled like an epithet at generations of middle-aged women. In fact, the empty nest notion, like menopausal misconceptions, was probably a male invention constructed to confirm preconceived fantasies of female inadequacy.

The premise is simply this: with the husband buried in his work and children having flown the coop to school, job, or marriage, the lonely middle-aged housewife suffers fits of depression as the empty home echoes their absence. It's a facet of the postparental years that we'll discuss in Chapter 8, but it's a hurdle that can be side-stepped through proper planning and attitude adjustment.

The definitive book on the subject is *Living with Zest in an Empty Nest,* by author Jean Kinney, mother of six grown children. She writes, "Unhappily, when the nest empties, many women suddenly become aware that their old circle of friends has narrowed. Old school chums have moved away, business friends have transferred, a few older friends may have died," (quoted in *Modern Maturity,* April-May, 1971).

In prior years, what with chauffeuring kids; dutiful attendance at school plays, dance recitals, and football games; not to mention family evenings together and outings on weekends, the busy mother was scarcely aware of the attrition of her contemporaries. Suddenly it's as apparent as the empty place at the breakfast table.

The solution? New friends and new creative projects. As household duties diminish, there's time for new challenges. The busy ex-mother can rejoin the adult world, in church groups, discussion clubs, and even politics. At last there's time to travel without worrying about what the kids are up to at home. Husband and wife, for years joint arbitrators of childhood conflicts, can become reacquainted, and perhaps fall in love again.

Dr. Bernice Neugarten, Chairman of the University of Chicago's Graduate School Committee on Human Development, says, "Many of life's crises including menopause and the empty nest syndrome have been exaggerated. Menopause bothers very few women seriously. And most women are relieved and happy when their children leave home. Many marriages get better after this happens, because the parents are no longer fighting over the children."

No doubt the empty nest syndrome was a paramount problem in days gone by when woman's role was defined as wife and mother. But with emancipation of women from the kitchen, and their ever-increasing involvement in the world of commerce, politics, and art, freedom from household duties can only offer opportunities for self-expression.

Hopefully in years to come, the empty nest nonsense will vanish from psychiatric texts like other outmoded concepts.

The Weight of Depression

Depression is a different story; it's a mental illness of major importance to middle-agers, causing agonizing dejection, debilitating inertia, and occasional disastrous consequences.

The depressed individual fills the room with gloom: "Doctor, I feel so bad; if I were a building I'd be condemned." Despair hangs like a dark cloud, overshadowing all activities and pervading each waking hour.

Depression spares no social class, and many are the famous persons who have suffered what Rona and Laurence Cherry called "The Common Cold of Mental Ailments" (*New York Times Magazine,* November 25, 1973). Abraham Lincoln's political career was clouded by depression when he wrote, "If what I feel were equally distributed to the whole human family, there would not be one cheerful face on earth." A history of depression blocked the aspirations of Vice-Presidential Candidate Thomas Eagleton in 1972, and depression-related suicide ended the life of writer Ernest Hemingway in 1961.

THE MOST UNDERTREATED DISEASE

"Pull yourself together," family and friends advise. It's like recommending lifting himself by the proverbial bootstraps, and the depressed individual needs such counsel like a drowning man needs an anchor. "Snap-out-of-it" advice merely emphasizes his inadequacy.

More to the point is the medical therapy of depression, including medication, psychotherapy, and sometimes electroshock treatments. Speaking at the 1973 annual convention of the American Medical Association, Dr. Nathan S. Kline, Director of Research at New York's Rockland State Hospital, described depression as the most undertreated of any major disease, estimating that 15 percent of all individuals from late teens to early seventies may suffer depression during any calendar year—a total patient population of 20 million Americans.

With psychotherapists in short supply and potential patients approximating the population of California, it's not suprising that medication is the mainstay of therapy. Depression is an emotional disorder where drug therapy can be all-important . . . and perhaps lifesaving. In his discussion, Doctor Kline remarked that family physicians and similar nonpsychiatric practitioners accounted for more than half of all prescriptions for mood-alterating drugs. Yet, he lamented, only 8.1 percent of these new prescriptions were earmarked for depression.

What drugs can banish the dark clouds of depression? First choice of most physicians is one of the tricylic compounds including imipramine (Tofranil) and amitriptyline (Elavil), tried and true standbys whose effects may not be apparent until a week or two after beginning medication. Or perhaps the prescription will be nortriptyline (Aventyl) or doxepin (Sinequan or Adapin), more rapid acting medications that also help relieve anxiety. For the apathetic depressed individual, there's protriptyline (Vivactil), helping spark vitality while lifting depression.

Less commonly prescribed are the monoamine oxidase inhibitors: tranylcypromine (Parnate), phenelzine (Nardil) and others. The American Medical Association Drug Evaluations states that "the monoamine oxidase inhibitors are generally less effective and have potentially more serious adverse effects than the tricyclic compounds."

Occasionally, despair begets inertia and the doctor prescribes a stimulant such as methylphenidate (Ritalin) to lift the spirits and get the depressed individual back in action again. In other patients, lithium has been the treatment of choice.

Psychotherapy along with medication especially in suicidal people is advised when depression disrupts the patient's life. Two levels of psychiatric treatment are available: supportive psychotherapy, often available in the family physician's office or through a counselor, shores up the sagging ego and helps sustain the individual through his period of depression. It's giving the car a push until it runs again, without dismantling the engine for repairs.

Psychoanalysis is a thorough mental overhaul, long-term therapy aimed at uncovering emotional conflicts and hammering out a resolution. It's expensive, time-consuming, and reserved for those individuals overwhelmed by depression.

Electroshock therapy is the third possible treatment of depression, and although last choice for obvious reasons, it can blast depression from the psyches of selected individuals. It is especially effective in suicidal cases because of fast remission of depression and the suicide threat.

WHY BE DEPRESSED?

Depression strikes all ages, but is particularly prevalent during the middle years. What causes depression, with its distressing symptoms and formidable therapeutic alternatives?

A real or fancied loss situation is common and although perhaps not the sole cause, is often the fabled "last straw." Writing in the *Journal of Psychosomatic Research,* Dr. Thomas H. Holmes, Professor of Psychiatry and Behavioral Sciences at the University of Washington School of Medicine, described life events often associated with disease. The leading five were death of a spouse, divorce, marital separation, jail term, and death of a close family member—all involving loss of a loved one or personal freedom. These events and others like them, such as illness or injury, job loss, or financial debacle, may trigger depression. During a crisis, a "reactive depression" expresses grief and is usually short-lived. But when the loss situation accompanies a pre-existing depression or merely adds to the progressive erosion of the individual's dreams and security, the outlook is less rosy.

Since the historic report *Mourning and Melancholia* by Sigmund Freud in 1917 dignified the diagnosis of depression, we have learned a great deal. We know that in depression, a love-hate conflict often rages. The individual is often ambivalent toward his or her spouse, conscious of deficiencies, yearning for greener pastures, yet reluctant to abandon a relationship built upon decades of connubiality. Sometimes it's a love-hate ambivalence toward his children, to whom he's devoted, while disgusted by their antics. It may be the job, comfortable yet frustrating, while some women may love their home life while resenting its responsibilities.

Most depressed individuals share a self-critical attitude. From within, a demanding voice whispers, "You are not good enough, you've not tried as hard as you should have, and you'll never reach your goals. You're inadequate, unworthy, a failure."

All together—the sense of loss, the struggle of love and hate, and the self-disapproval—they add to form the weight of depression, dragging the individual down, down to the depth of despair.

LOOKING UP

What's the way out of the valley of depression? When all seems black, and life not worth living, what is there to look forward to?

The depressed individual clutches at threads of hope. Perhaps a new drug will work, or maybe a change at work or home suggested by the doctor. Of course, there's the return appointment with the doctor; maybe things will change by then.

Here are a few facts that may offer hope to the depressed:

- The younger the depressed individual, the better the prognosis for rapid and long-lasting recovery.
- A reactive depression related to a loss situation has a better outlook than chronic depression for which no cause is obvious.
- The earlier the treatment, the better. The depression of recent onset offers more hope than the despair already present for months or years.
- No matter how deep the depression and even if no treatment is received, the black mood will almost always pass with time.

Depression, like the stock market, is cyclic. Just as depression present now will fade, it may return again, and herein lies the lethal threat of the disease—suicide. While the apathetic individual in the depths of depression usually lacks the initiative to implement a self-destructive act, the person descending into or arising from the valley of despair may agree with the inner voice that "life isn't worth living" and decide upon suicide as a solution.

Suicide is No Solution

In a book devoted to the magnificence of the middle years, why discuss suicide? Here's why. It's a problem of the middle-ager who often faces divorce, the death of loved ones, emotional conflicts, and sometimes the awful realization that success has passed him by. Of all age groups, suicide has a special fancy for the middle generation.

Self-destruction is the sixth most common cause of death in middle-aged males, and the suicide death rate of males is three times that for women in the same age group. Nevertheless, middle-aged women make more suicide attempts than men, and the lower rate of consummation may indicate that many are mere gestures, or attest to women's ineptitude in violent acts.

Suicide is no stranger to civilized society. In ancient Greece, condemned criminals were permitted to end their own lives, and Socrates exemplified this tradition when he drank the hemlock.

Centuries later, the Catholic Church debated fiercely whether suicide, itself a mortal sin, was an acceptable alternative to rape.

Today, 13 of every 100,000 Americans commit suicide yearly. West Berlin, living under the Communist gun, leads the world with 41.7 suicides per 100,000, followed by Hungary with 34.9, East Germany with 28.7, Czechoslovakia with 24.5, and Finland with 23.3. At the bottom of the list is Mexico with a strong Roman Catholic conscience and a suicide rate of only 1.1 per 100,000.

The urban dweller is more likely to commit suicide than the rural resident, perhaps due to the hectic pace of city life—or perhaps the small-town inhabitant, well-known to all, is reluctant to tarnish his community image by self-destruction.

Divorced or widowed individuals are more suicide-prone than those who are married or even those who have never been to the altar. Certainly, the widowed and divorced have suffered losses, while the latter must be reluctant to leave their wives, children, or parents with the stigma of self-destruction.

Who commits suicide? Mr. Highrisk is a male in the middle years, divorced, separated, or perhaps widowed, suffering a recent physical or emotional problem. Death or desertion of a loved one may be the catalyst. He or she may have made past suicidal gestures, and one or more relatives may have, too. He is likely to be drinking, with alcohol eroding his fragile defenses. The crisis often comes on a bright, clear spring or autumn day, when Mr. Highrisk thinks, "Why must I be so miserable on such a lovely day?"

AN ACT OF ANGER

The suicidal act is an expression of anger, directed both toward loved ones and toward himself. In a sense, it's a heads-I-win, tails-you-lose bet: if a suicidal gesture succeeds, death punishes the family with grief and guilt. Yet if the individual survives the suicidal drama, he has accomplished his goal of inflicting remorse upon loved ones.

Three kinds of self-destructive individuals are found. First is the serious suicide. For reasons that seem compelling, he's planned the final act. There's attention to detail, perhaps including an attempt to conceal the fact of suicide or augment insurance payments to the family. He's chosen his method, often one that is painless, yet permanent. And he frequently succeeds.

Next there's the actor—master of the suicidal gesture. Often acting impulsively and with a flair, yet in deadly earnest, he subconsciously chooses suicidal methods doomed to failure. The wrists are slashed too lightly, the dose of sleeping pills too small. These individuals call the crisis lines in large cities and send their pleas for help to small-town physicians. In the suicidal gesture, they are attempting to communicate their despair to another human being. Do these suicidal gestures succeed? Sometimes they do, as luck runs out and rescue efforts fail.

The third is the silent suicide. He carries a death wish, a self-destruct mechanism. He's the wartime hero who receives his medals posthumously, he's the driver of the auto in the fatal accident without skid marks, and he's the individual who smokes and drinks himself to death despite medical advice. A suicide? Perhaps not technically, but it's self-destruction all the same.

How can we reduce suicides during the middle years? We must tune into the symptoms of depression, particularly when linked with loss, sensing when the death wish may burgeon to the surface. We must discuss the suicide problem openly, and face it as a real threat during middle age. Finally, medical care must be sought for all individuals whose actions seem to whisper, "Suicide."

Equanimity in the Middle Years

Some sail through the meridian years with scarcely an emotional cloud. For them, the middle years are decades of contentment, with equanimity the rule.

I believe the key to peace of mind is being content with one's lot; it's acceptance of the inevitabilities of the age. Contentment is saying, "I'm happy with my family. My children? We've done our best and now they are on their own. My wife (or husband)? I've years of love invested there. Now's the time to collect dividends, not trade for a new issue."

Contentment is saying, "I'm satisfied with my home; a few more mortgage payments and it's all mine. Buy a bigger one then? All I'll gain will be more lawn to mow and more monthly expenses."

Contentment is saying, "My job suits me. I'll never be president, but I don't think I want to be anyhow. My work gives me a sense of accomplishment, beside providing a good living for my family."

Equanimity means "getting your mind right." Youth should be critical and strive for change. But not the adult. It's his lot to defend the status quo, lest the forces of change overwhelm. In the middle years, dissatisfaction can only breed discontent, and peace of mind flies out the window.

It helps to understand emotional problems and mental health, particularly as they relate to our middle generation. Here are two topnotch sources of mental health information:

The Mental Health Association, Inc. 1800 North Kent Street, Rosslyn Station, Arlington, Va. 22209

The National Clearinghouse for Mental Health Information, 5600 Fishers Lane, Rockville, Md. 20857

The phone numbers are: (301) 443-4515 for public inquiries, and (301) 443-4517 for computer searches for professionals.

Is peace of mind a worthy goal in the middle years? I think so, and so did English Clergyman Charles Buck a century and a half ago, as he lauded the contended mind: "The excellence of equanimity is beyond all praise. One of this disposition is not dejected in adversity, nor elated in prosperity: he is affable to others, and contented to himself."

7

TRANQUILITY IN JEOPARDY:
THE THREATS TO HAPPINESS

Man is born unto trouble, as the sparks fly upward.
Job 5:7

DISEASE, DIVORCE, AND DEATH are not the only challenges of middle age. Some are more subtle—little traps that imperil peace of mind. Through their daily actions, many middle-agers weave nets that bind them to unnecessary responsibility, undue conflict, and needless mental anguish.

Here are seven snares that may imperil peace of mind during middle age.

The Challenge of Leisure Time

With increasing mechanization and the current rush toward early retirement, today's adult can look forward to the increasing luxury of leisure hours. The 50-hour week of toil was once all too common. Now it's 40 hours, and just around the corner is a gentlemenly 30-hour work week.

National holidays have been gerrymandered to create a spate of long weekends, educators enjoy 2-month summer holidays, anniversaries of minor political events seem to justify days off for millions, and industry is bending to labor's pleas for increasingly liberal vacation schedules.

How are the idle hours to be spent? How many middle-agers are guilty of murdering time, killing leisure hours in indolent lounging, gulping food, guzzling drink, chatting aimlessly, or blankly staring at the television tube? The digestion is assaulted, the senses imperiled, and physical fitness abandoned—all to dispose of leisure time.

PUTTING LEISURE TIME TO WORK

Benjamin Franklin warned, "Trouble springs from idleness, and grievous toil from needless ease." Leisure time is raw material. It's a lump of clay that can be molded into a useful vessel, or can remain an unformed ugly nuisance. It's time for work that can have meaning, or can be passed in idle grunts to lounging cronies.

A patient, let's call him Roland Burns, visited my office not too many months ago. His complaint? Fatigue dogged his every step: "Doctor, I don't know why I should be so tired. My job is easy; I sit at a desk all day. And I have more than my share of time off. I do nothing that would make me tired. The kids mow the lawn, my wife keeps the house clean, and my most strenuous exertion of the day is the trip from my television seat to the refrigerator."

What did Roland Burns need? Two things—interest and physical activity. My prescription included the restriction of television viewing to 1 hour in the evening, or perhaps an all-important sports event on weekends. Afternoon naps and snacks were out. And Roland's energies were channeled into new outlets. The choices are legion—gardening, hunting, fishing, collecting, politics, sports of every description, and many more.

"Roland, you must spend some time each day in active physical exercise." Chapter 4 outlines a first-rate fitness program, which should be supplemented by daily physical effort—trimming the hedges, sweeping the garage, washing the car, or bicycling with the family.

Last week Roland Burns returned to the office, 10 pounds lighter, tanned, and looking physically fit. "Doctor, I don't know how to thank you. I've not felt so well in years. I took your advice and traded television for trapshooting; it gets me outdoors and away from worries at the office. I'm helping my son with the yard work now; our home has never looked better, and working together has been a tonic for the father-son relationship. We've planned a trip to a baseball game next weekend—never did that before. Your advice did the trick, Doctor, it got me off my backside and back in the world again."

Leisure time is like physical exercise; energy invested pays dividends. Idle hours sowed idly will reap little gain, but the middle-ager who fills his leisure time with stimulating activities and physical exercise will harvest rich rewards.

The Volunteer Trap

People in their prime are the volunteer workers of America—serving selflessly in hospitals, libraries, churches, and community activities. There are service clubs, planning boards, civic committees, and fund-raising drives for every illness known to modern science. These groups share a constant need for willing workers to donate time and energy in volunteer service.

Yet what begins as a well-intentioned effort at community service can mushroom into an all-consuming series of commitments, as the middle-ager surrenders to the urge to say, "Yes, I'll do it," all too often. When this happens, he or she is caught in the volunteer trap.

CAUGHT IN THE TRAP

Men—whether members of the Rotary Club, Boy Scout leaders, or fund-raisers for the local library—may fall into the volunteer trap for business or personal reasons, leaving them with little free time for relaxation or family life.

Women are equally likely to be victims. When Mrs. Middle-age was young, women didn't work. Of course, there were a few—maiden schoolteachers and librarians, single salesgirls awaiting suitors, and the widow forced to earn her own bread and butter. But for the most part, father, and later husband, was the wage-earner. Women did woman's work and in many households, it hasn't changed.

Then the children leave, and idle hours hang heavily. Should she go to work? Mrs. Middle-age may soon find that she has no training and lacks skills needed in the world of business. What's open to her? Where can she feel needed?

Volunteer work!

Consider Mary Griffith. She's president of the Literary Club this year, secretary of the Garden Club, vice-president of the League of Women Voters, in charge of the Cancer Crusade and on the governing board of the Hospital Auxiliary. Mary confides to her friends, "I'm thinking of running for the school board next year. If only there were more hours in the day."

Everyone says, "Call Mary. She'll get the job done. She's unbelievably capable."

But Mary's family is less impressed with her achievements. A few years ago her young son drew a picture of Mommy with a telephone attached to one ear; he thought it was a permanent appendage. Her long-suffering husband is John Griffith, and the only warm meal he ever gets is a lonely TV dinner. He saw his wife a week ago Wednesday; they attended the same meeting.

Mary Griffith is caught in the volunteer trap.

The volunteer trap has always been a pitfall for the well-to-do. If Winifred Banks had spent less time crusading for women's rights and stayed home to care for Jane and Michael, there would have been no need for the Peripatetic nanny Mary Poppins.

Men, too, become ensnared. Harold Ferguson was Man-of-the-Year last year. All call him a dynamo: "He's got more energy than a litter of puppies." Harold runs Little League single-handedly, leading fund-raising and umpiring most of the games. As a volunteer fireman, he's usually first on the scene when the whistle blows. He belongs to Rotary, Kiwanis, and Lion's Clubs, and heads the Local League for Juvenile Decency.

Poor Harold Ferguson; while busy serving the youth of the community, his fourteen-year-old son has been arrested three times for delinquency. As the youth told police, "My Dad hasn't been home in the evening for so long that I forget what he looks like."

Harold Ferguson is caught in the volunteer trap.

How about you? Are you out at meetings more nights than not? Are you skipping dinner to chair committees? Or worse, dining while chatting on the telephone as the family eats in silence. Are your children beginning to say, "Why don't you ever stay home?"

Is your family suffering? And are you burning yourself out in a frenzy of feverish activity?

If the answer is yes, it's time to escape from the volunteer trap.

ESCAPE

How? First, the overcommitted volunteer must learn to delegate. The capable person, always selected as committee chairman, soon learns that jobs are best done by one, and shoulders the entire committee's responsibilities. But escaping from the volunteer trap demands delegation, and this means spreading duties to subordinates, leaving only the final coordination of individual efforts.

Resigning from volunteer groups is easier than you think. Blame your husband or wife: "John thinks I'm active in too many organizations." Or more to the point: "I've decided to limit my volunteer activities so that I can devote my best efforts to the one or two that really interest me." Then resign, withdraw, and let others shoulder their share of the load. The "irreplaceable" volunteer worker is often surprised to discover that the organization doesn't crumble in his or her absence.

Finally, decline new tasks. When asked to lead the Heart Fund this year, say, "No. I'm afraid I'm already overcommitted." When the P.T.A. offers you the presidency, respond, "No thanks, but I'll try to attend meetings just the same."

The volunteer trap is a self-made snare, and it's one the adult can escape—once he realizes that he's caught and resolves to cut entangling commitments.

The Urge to Own Things

As pernicious as the compulsion to volunteer can be the quest for acquisition. Here's how:

You're settled in the comfortable rut of adulthood. The children come and go; they have their own lives. The job? No problem there. And sex has become a routine that philandering could only disrupt. Then where, oh where, can the adult express his individuality? Some choose acquisitions—they suffer the urge to own things.

When Norton Bixby showed off his new Cadillac, neighbor Charles Harris countered with a Continental. Nort and Chuck—are they affluent executives or successful professional men? Nope, they're middle-income people, and neither could really afford the luxury automobile, which represented a huge outlay of dollars that perhaps should have been earmarked for retirement. Yet each felt compelled to proclaim through acquisitions, "Finally, I've arrived! I can afford the best car, the finest home, steak on the table, and a mink coat for my wife!"

House-poor. That's what it's called in real estate. Mr. and Mrs. Middle-age finally buy their dream home, draining savings and mortgaging their future. For them, the monthly payments mean moonlighting, backyard vacations, and casseroles for dinner. Of course, in their love affair with the new home, they gave scant thought to the expense of upkeep. Later, the whopping local tax bill arrives, giving their budget the knockout punch.

Once it was called "keeping up with the Joneses." But it's more than that. It's asking the world to admire your achievements, it's calling for outside confirmation of success and security, and it's quietly trying to reassure yourself that it won't all go up in smoke.

WHAT'S THE HARM?

The urge to own things is an innocent foible so long as the compulsion is confined to minor objects. The pedigreed pup, the garden tractor with twice the horsepower needed for the front lawn, the Paris gown for the Knights of Columbus dance—they're all harmless outlets for the acquisitive compulsions of the middle years.

But when the urge to own things moves to the budget-shattering big-ticket items—houses, cars, and boats—it's a different story. Folly here can spell financial ruin as the unwary are led down the primrose path by commission-hungry salesmen.

Yet if salesmen didn't beckon, these individuals would seek them out. Just as an addict must have his fix, the afflicted must buy and own things.

Why? For many, it reflects household attitudes of childhood when the Great Depression loomed, soup lines were seen on street corners, and cash was in short supply. For others, compulsive consumerism assuages feelings of inferiority, whether real or imagined. Then there are always the few who genuinely compete "to keep up with the Joneses."

Stifling the urge to own things is one step on the road to equanimity, contentment with your lot in life. It's saying, "Mine is not the biggest house or fanciest car in town, but they suit me. A boat? I need one like a pig needs a wallet. I buy what I need to live well and be comfortable, and that's enough for me. I'm satisfied, and that's what counts."

The Left-Behind Housewife

The left-behind housewife is a sorry lass. While her husband battled boredom in a college classroom, she waited tables and smiled for bigger tips. Then on to graduate school, where he improved his mind as she supported the family as a switchboard operator.

Finally, there was the Ph.D. For him a thesis, and for her a third child and a part-time typing job.

Now they've both reached the middle years. He's near the top of the executive ladder, hobnobbing with creative intellects and beautiful people. But his wife has been left behind. She hasn't read a book since Ivanhoe in high school, her clothes all look like rummage sale rejects, and her cocktail conversation runs out of gas once the topic leaves housework and children.

Mrs. Left-behind has only herself to blame. Given every opportunity for independence—an all-electric home, financial security, and freedom from the tyranny of the timeclock, she's forsaken her chance to become an individual. Instead, she's a parasite, and in her relationship with her husband, it's all take and no give. She has nothing to offer, except a rehash of his own ideas and a ragtag collection of trivia and gripes at day's end. Small wonder that the bright aggressive husband soon leaves her behind.

I recall one left-behind housewife whose chief problem was appearance. She looked bright and her eyes seemed to sparkle, but her clothes hung like old potato sacks ("I haven't bought a new dress in a year"). Her hair looked like an overgrown lawn ("My husband thinks the beauty parlor is a waste of time and money"), and her skin had never known the touch of make-up ("I always felt foolish wearing cosmetics").

Her feminine radar flashed warning signals when husband Ralph started eyeing the office cute young thing—smartly dressed, every hair in place, and made-up with an artist's flare. Her tale was sad, yet all too familiar.

There was only one way to win this battle. I prescribed a trip to the beautician, with a new hairstyle and a crash course in cosmetics. Next, some new with-it clothes—not expensive, but in style.

"But Ralph will insist we can't afford this," she said.

I replied, "Ralph's actions speak louder than words. He's told you that you're frumpy, and he's more attracted to the well-groomed woman. You can spend some money now on self-improvement, or would you and Ralph rather pay a divorce lawyer after you two have drifted farther and farther apart?

CATCHING UP

Can the left-behind housewife catch up?

Yes, she can, but it means she must stop living in her husband's shadow. She must cease parroting his ideas, and develop independent thinking. She must stop thinking of herself as a household drudge, and expand her role as wife, mistress, and lover. She must offer her husband some of the stimulation he finds in bright acquaintances at work.

The left-behind housewife, the intellectual freeloader, the

dutiful doormat, can catch up only by putting herself first. What's needed is a complete overhaul. Tops on the list should be a trip to the local fashion headquarters and a visit to the beautician. Get the works, a whole new image.

Then don't forget to refurbish the intellect: take an adult education course, join a study group, sign up for a book club. Choose a topic totally new to you, or perhaps a subject touching on your husband's work. Read and learn; then one morning bowl him over at the breakfast table with your new knowledge. When he comes home from work that evening, keep him off stride with a new idea, perhaps some thoughts about a book you've read, or some witticism from the discussion group.

The left-behind housewife can catch up, and pass her husband if she wishes. If you've been left behind in the backstretch, trim the chassis and overhaul the engine and get back in the race.

Women's Liberation Blues

In 1971, the Akron Beacon Journal reported a sign of the times in a florist shop window: "Support Women's Lib. Send HIM flowers."

Last week I was passed by a red sports car whose rear bumper carried the sticker: "Uppity Women, Unite." It's the clarion call of Women's Liberation.

Women's suffrage and hence the Women's Liberation Movement trace their roots to antislavery agitation. As Lucretia Mott reasoned in 1848, if we can fight for the rights of Negro slaves, how about the rights of free women! On July 19 of that year, the first Women's Rights Convention convened at the home of Elizabeth Cady Stanton in the quiet village of Seneca Falls, New York.

Baby, you've come a long way!

Yet by 1900, only New Zealand allowed women to vote in national elections. Voting rights for Russian women made their debut following the 1917 revolution, but it was not until 3 years later in 1920 that women could cast their votes for the President of the United States.

The final goal is worldwide women's suffrage, and in 1952, the United Nations Convention on the Political Rights of Women asserted that, "Women shall be entitled to vote in all elections on equal terms with men, without any discrimination."

Gaining the vote was only the beginning. Women entered the

business world, at first as secretaries and salesgirls, and before long they were climbing the executive ladder. Then came pantsuits, cigarettes "for women only," and soon soprano voices were heard in taverns and clubrooms that had been the male domain for decades.

In the end came the cry for true equality. Distinctions between the sexes became blurred as committees spawned chairpersons and small communities elected people wearing mini-skirts to the town council. Today there are more and more women doctors and male nurses, first grade school teachers may wear trousers and ties, and hair styles only add to the confusion.

Through it all, many middle-aged males shake their heads in bewilderment.

THE LIBERATION LAMENT

In Grandma's day, a woman needed to be married. Of course, not all succeeded in snaring a mate, but those who didn't were failures to be pitied. The woman needed marriage for simple economic survival. Otherwise who would feed and clothe this helpless soul when her parents passed away?

The Industrial Revolution and jobs for women, not to mention the liberation movement, have changed all this. Working women now thumb their noses at male dominance. They proclaim, "I don't need a husband to support me. I stay married because I like and love him, but I'm not dependent upon him. I'm more than capable of supporting myself—both economically and emotionally."

Well said! But is the male ready to accept his liberated wife? Reared in more traditional times, he often clings to the concept of male supremacy. Dishes, dusting, and lonely evenings are not his cup of tea. When his day's work is done, he expects a hot meal on the table and a devoted wife by the fireside. Instead, he may be faced with the liberated woman home from her equally grueling 8 hours of work, the house still in morning's disarray, with dinner still to be defrosted.

When confronted by a wife who signs her name Ms. and who thinks the household head should be a committee of two, how may he react? The husband often sees the liberated woman not only as challenging his manhood, but dumping in his lap "women's work"—household duties that have been women's responsibility all his life.

The redistribution of household duties and who will go where in the evenings are only symptoms of the household conflict fomented by Women's Liberation. The real battle is this: who will wear the pants of the house?

The struggle for equality often becomes a battle for supremacy.

Or worse. As the male soon finds the competition tiresome, he seeks less competitive alternatives. Soon he finds the woods are full of unattached females who have shunned Women's Liberation and make him feel like "the boss" again. Maybe it's a divorcee, a widow, or the bright young secretary with a yen for a man with experience. To the husband of the liberated woman, it's an escape from the drone of "I'm your equal."

COMMUNICATE AND COMPROMISE

What's the solution? How can the liberated woman fulfill her intellect and education and achieve a sense of self-worth without jeopardizing her marriage?

You need to realize that personal liberation for you can upset the basis of a marriage founded in years of habit. Unless you're ready to risk that marriage for the principles of Women's Liberation, go slow. The liberated woman is particularly lucky if her husband can accept aprons and dishpan hands. But wave the red flag of Women's Liberation before the old-fashioned male household head and provider, and you may be in for the fight of your life.

Of course, there's a solution. Each must give a little and strive for a lifestyle that is agreeable to both. Perhaps the individuals themselves can communicate openly enough to state feelings about the role each will assume in their relationship. Occasionally, professional counseling may allow them to understand each other's needs. Hopefully, the outcome will be a true compromise, with each more sensitive to the feelings of the other.

The woman who has the best of yesterday and today can say, "I have a happy home, a man who loves me, and the opportunity to pursue my interests. Who could be more liberated?"

The Failure Fantasy

Now that we've discussed challenges particularly pertinent to women in their middle years, let's turn to a problem that's the Waterloo of many males in the same age bracket.

Failure to attain goals is his special source of sorrow. "Oft expectation fails, and most oft where most it promises," wrote William Shakespeare. Two and a half centuries later we continue to grieve when efforts fall short of self-imposed (and often unrealistic) goals.

Last week Frank Newton confessed over his third martini, "I was sure I would be a vice president by age fifty. Now here I am, fifty-five and fading fast, and still in the second level of management. Young sharpshooters are leaving me in the dust as they grab challenging projects. I've got the experience and the know-how, but today these take a back seat to youthful enthusiasm and bright ideas. It's hard to admit that I've gone as far as I can go in the firm, and men my age just don't quit and look elsewhere. Unless a miracle happens, I'll rot at the same desk until retirement.

"When I left college, I was fired by ambition and dreams; now here I am in my middle years with retirement not too many years away, and I've just realized, 'I'm a failure!' "

Frank Newton—he's loved by his wife, respected by his coworkers, and admired in the community. His years have been productive and he has enriched the lives of those about him. Yet Frank's middle years are marred by the fantasy of failure.

Why?

NOT EVERY BOY CAN BE PRESIDENT

Perhaps Frank's childhood set the stage. We were reared in the last age of heroes. Love's first kiss turned the warty frog into a handsome prince who promptly married the princess (whose judgement in kissing frogs must be questioned) and lived happily ever after. Through quick wit and perserverance, the Hardy Boys and Nancy Drew solved their multiple dilemmas. Rudyard Kipling extolled the virtue of keeping one's head while others about are losing their's, Horace Greeley advised young men to open new frontiers, and countless movie heroes demonstrated that the good guy always wins in the end. These myths of childhood shared a single moral: with hard work, no goal is too high. Any boy can be President.

Graduates of the schools of fantasy of the 1930's and 1940's are the adults of today. Were they misled? Do they sense betrayal upon learning that not every American boy will live in the White House. Or be Vice-President. Or even have an office with carpeting.

Real life is not as rosy as the formula fantasies of childhood. Today reality is in vogue, and if today's with-it youth seem to lack the old-fashioned ambition of our generation, perhaps it's because they question the old goals. Today's young man sees success as an illusion, neither necessarily attainable nor desirable.

TURNING FAILURE INTO SUCCESS

Illusory also is the adult sense of failure, and when beguiled by the failure fantasy, it's time for some harsh words with the face in the magic mirror: "Stop sniveling, you self-deprecating so-and-so! So you think you're a failure. Well, let's take a close look at your life, and what you've accomplished so far. Maybe I can change your attitude and improve your self-image.

"First, list the goals you might have set at age twenty-one—a happy family in a comfortable home, a little money for a rainy day, a satisfying job, and a few luxuries to add spice to life. Although these perhaps aren't the dreams of today's youth, they're the goals that, whether you realized it or not, you set out to attain three-odd decades ago.

"How did you fare? The average adults in their middle years have attained most or all. Of course, some lack one or another, but most of us have won the race. We've attained the position and possessions we set out to acquire during more ambitious days."

Then why the feeling of failure?

Unrealistic goals are the answer. Most have triumphed beyond the dreams of previous generations or less affluent societies. So to help snap out of the "I'm a failure" doldrums, make your list of assets versus liabilities, wins versus losses, and shun the seduction of goals beyond your grasp.

A straight-from-the-shoulder confrontation, examining assets and abandoning unachievable goals, helps most find that failure was a fantasy after all. As American educator Amos B. Alcott said, "We mount to heaven mostly on the ruins of our cherished schemes, finding our failures were successes."

When Disaster Strikes

The middle years are a time of adversity, of trial, and often of disaster. Here we find the cold shocks that temper the mettle: During the middle years, aging parents have attained the age when death eyes them covetously; or it may be his or her health in jeopardy, disastrous when disability mars the productive years; and then there are the children, facing adult problems of drugs, legal encounters, sex, and courtship; finally, there's business, where failure can mean it's all been for nothing.

No one is ever really ready for death. A loved one may linger in a nursing home as the family awaits the final hour, or death may come as an unexpected visitor. Whatever the prelude, when life leaves a mother or father, spouse or child, it's a disaster of major proportions.

Aging parents are most at risk. It's the normal succession of generations, and the forty-eight-year-old individual probably has parents in their seventies. The demise of these senior citizens is an ever-present possibility, as is the lesser risk of an unexpected heart attack or accidental death of a spouse.

Disability can be a living death. The middle years are the productive decades when the rewards of education and training are harvested, all the more critical when several generations depend upon the earnings of the family head. In an instant, a drunken driver, a tiny ill-fated blood clot, or a wayward bacterium can confine him or her to the sickbed for months or years. The paycheck stops, and the family may first experience the indignity of welfare.

With the children, it's usually not the undeserved disaster, but a crisis created by their own actions. Our teenage children first experiment with drugs and alcohol, ill-equipped to control the urges these intoxicants release. Then there is the sexual revolution, with the parent's moral standards held in contempt by the aspiring generation. What we consider immoral may also be illegal, and many parents know the anguish of the midnight telephone call from a child who pleads, "Mother, I'm in jail. Can you help me?"

During these years, disaster can strike the business as well as the home. Unemployment is a calamity, as decades of training and experience become as obsolete as last year's fashions. The clerical worker, the skilled machinist, the long-time supervisor confident that only he knows the distribution of products or the routes of salesmen—they're all vulnerable to replacement, either by the bright young men schooled in modern methods or, what's worse, the machines which increasingly dominate American industry. Computers don't take 2-week vacations, they don't form unions or demand pay raises, and they rarely suffer illness.

Sometimes the fickle whims of change leave unemployment in their wake. Not too many years ago, the aerospace industry was king. Young men invested precious years in schooling, training for the industry of the future. Then interest waned, space exploration lost its glamour, and the aerospace industry slumped, with thousands of middle-aged engineers and technicians suddenly unemployed and competing for the handful of positions available. While they searched for jobs worthy of their education, these highly skilled engineers filled gas tanks, bagged groceries, or applied for welfare.

When fortunes fail, the young man can bounce back, but for people in their prime, it's a long fall from the pinnacle of success. They soon find it's an uphill fight to re-establish themselves in the world of commerce. "We don't hire anyone over fifty," decree personnel managers of many companies, forcing numerous job-hunters to swallow their pride, tighten their belts, and accept employment beneath their ability.

For others still, disaster means failure of the family business, usually the sole proprietorship—the corner grocery store next to the new supermarket, the gas station on the wrong corner, or the boutique in a town not ready for the latest fashions. Most business failures involve the solo ventures, and each year millions of middle-agers see their hopes dashed and savings trickle down the drain as customers fail to patronize their dream-shop, while creditors clamor for overdue payments. The finale? It's often bankruptcy, as expenses overwhelm receipts.

The middle-ager is no stranger to disaster at home or work. How can he cope with overwhelming adversity? What's the secret to sidestepping despondency?

DEALING WITH DISASTER

When catastrophe strikes, grief follows—and three distinct episodes occur. First comes the shock of realization—the recognition of death, disability, dashed hopes, or disastrous business dealings. It's a time of disbelief, of denial, and there may be numbness, weeping, or even agitation. Hands join and tears flow as family members realize that nightmare has become reality.

Next comes the stage of rumination. There's a painful longing, a stinging awareness of what might have been, and a preoccupation with details of the disaster. Guilt creeps in, attended by sleeplessness, impaired appetite, and despondency—classic symptoms of depression. Angry fingers may be pointed in accusation, and actions made at this time are often regretted. As events surrounding the disaster are rehashed and digested, it's a time for family members to support one another—offering a shoulder to the grief-stricken widow, the loan to a brother when his bankbook has run dry, a helping hand for the household overcome by illness, or telling your daughter, "I'll stick by you no matter what."

Stage three is assimilation. It begins weeks or months after the calamity, and brings a more detached view of the disaster. Death, disability, delinquency, or defeat is seen in perspective. Adversity is accepted and blessed resolution allows assimilation of the event into the fiber of being. Depressive symptoms disappear and life goes on.

The French author, Madame de Stael, once wrote, "Life often seems like a long shipwreck of which the debris are friendship, glory, and love. The shores of existence are strewn with them." The middle years brings both success and defeat, both joy and grief.

In the fertile garden of expectation grow the seeds of disappointment, and when disaster strikes there's naught to do but conquer grief, reassemble life's scattered pieces, and start to build again.

MARRIAGE, DIVORCE, AND COHABITATION

*I believe marriages would in general be as
happy, and often more so, if they were all made
by the Lord Chancellor, upon a due consideration
of the characters and circumstances, without
the parties having any choice in the matter.*
                              Samuel Johnson
                              March 22, 1776

"AND THEY LIVED HAPPILY EVER AFTER," end countless childhood fables, reenforcing the fairy tale that wedded bliss inevitably follows the marriage of hero and heroine. We adults know better. Making marriage work is a full-time job. Happy? Sure, but there will be tears, too—and anger, and remorse, and love.

Both parties know the ceremony merely launches the ship of marriage. Next comes the struggle to keep it afloat once the newness fades. Storms threaten, and many marriages end on the rocks of divorce, while others languish as the partners drift apart.

Making the Most of Marriage

Virtually all societies and even some animal species practice marriage—the more or less constant union of single male and female that establishes a family unit and provides for the care of offspring. The institution has been sanctified by the church, glorified in song, fantasized in fable, and deprecated by hedonists. Yet, of all the institutions of civilized people, marriage has prevailed—surviving through the centuries as the mortar holding society together.

Sometimes mortar cracks and chips, and keeping a marriage from crumbling calls for constant vigilance. All that's needed is the wisdom of a sage, the diplomacy of a prime minister, and the serenity of an oriental philosopher. With the average man first marrying at twenty-three and his female counterpart first taking the nuptial vows at twenty-one, it's no less than astounding that most marriages survive until the middle years.

The statistics are there for all to see. Of those individuals entering the fourth decade of life, three quarters will stay married to their present spouses through the middle years and into senior citizenship. It's during these years that marriage pays dividends.

The middle years are the time to make the most of marriage. The union surviving young adulthood has the odds in its favor. Oh, yes. There will be challenges, and we'll discuss them in this chapter. But this marriage has the clear-cut advantages—years of life together, of memories, the sense of oneness that can only grow with marriage, perhaps nurtured by the living bond of children. Most of all they have maturity, the detachment to see adversity in perspective, the ability to seek solutions rather than choose sides in divorce court.

They know that marriage is no more a lifelong honeymoon than every meal is a feast. After the strains of "I love you truly" fade, the marriage will mature only if other verbs are written into the scenario. *Respect* is required, just as it's important that married individuals *admire* one another. But perhaps the most vital verb is *like* because unless two individuals like one another, the marriage has no more future than a snowball in July.

A nine-year-old girl once described her relationship with the little boy next door, "Johnny and I aren't in love; we're in *like*." Probably no couple is truly in love if they don't like each other, respecting each other's appearance, intellect, and achievements. Sometimes the "like" relationship takes years of living together, exploring the hidden assets of the marriage partner.

But liking alone is not enough. Making the most of marriage takes effort. When your children seem over-burdened with school-work, you wisely advise, "The more you put into it, the more you'll get out of it." So it is with marriage. The spouse who gives his all to the relationship without thought of "getting" will reap rewards. It's the day-by-day little efforts—the "let-me-help" offer, sharing pride in small accomplishments, and the word of encouragement when spirits are low—that make a marriage bloom. The happiest marriages unite those individuals who share a special fondness as well as love, and are willing to merge their destinies, working together to create a family and home.

MAKING ONE MARRIAGE WORK

Marital bickering is as common as crabgrass. Sometimes it's beneficial; it clears the air. But other disagreements sow the seeds of discontent.

The success of the partnership may depend upon the adult's outlook. The thirty-five-year-old individual who laments, "My life is already half over," views the world through the gloom of pessimism, while the individual who asserts, "Half of my life is still ahead of me," sees life through rose-colored glasses. It's the same with marriage. Some spouses collect gripes as a squirrel hoards nuts, storing them in a secret cache for later enjoyment. There are dark days ahead for this marriage. But when the marital partners focus on the positive aspects, the good times, and the working together—then the marriage is more than halfway home.

Sometimes marital squabbles end in the doctor's office. When it became apparent that thirty-seven-year-old Martha Smith's physical complaints were triggered by marital discord, I called in Martha and her husband. She began: "We don't have a marriage. We never spend time together. Fred is always at the office or working at his desk at home. He hardly knows the children's names, and we haven't gone out together for months."

Fred countered: "The trouble is with Martha. She spends money like a sailor on shore leave and I work doubletime to pay the bills. Sure, I'd like to relax at home evenings with the family, but until I hide Martha's checkbook and credit cards, I can't see relief in sight."

A common problem? Yes, indeed, and often easily solved. Martha and Fred began making the most of their marriage when their outlooks changed. Their problem was not really the spendthrift wife or the husband with a work compulsion, but the relentless spotlight on marital flaws. The Smiths and I worked to change the focus. We talked about the happy times, the common goals, and the troubles they had shared. Together, we listed the good points and the gripes, and Fred and Martha found they had much to cherish. They began looking forward instead of back and the balance of the marriage changed from negative to positive. They looked ahead to half a lifetime together.

Make the most of your marriage during your middle years. Learn to like as well as love your mate, and make yourself both likeable and lovable. Respect his accomplishments, admire her appearance, and don't be afraid to say so. Tabulate your blessings when the blues threaten and never, never squirrel grudges away.

How to make the most of marriage was perhaps best said by the English essayist Joseph Addison more than 250 years ago: "Two persons who have chosen each other out of all the species, with the design to be each other's mutual comfort and entertainment, have, in that action, bound themselves to be good-humored, affable, discreet, forgiving, patient, and joyful, with respect to each other's frailties and perfections, to the end of their lives."

The Post-Parental Years

Much of the magnificence of middle-age marriage derives from the glorious state of post-parenthood. The man or woman in business may receive the obligatory gold watch and retirement dinner at age sixty-five, but the rigorous duties of parenthood end earlier.

For more than two decades, Mom and Dad have coped with baby sitters, Little League, a second mortgage to pay the orthodontist's bill, tears over acne pimples, and the multitude of other obligations that have led many middle-agers to conclude that the joys of parenthood are highly overrated. Then the last child leaves for college, work, or marriage.

They're gone! Of course, there are Thanksgiving and Christmas vacations with the kids at home again, and probably college tuition to pay, but the day-in day-out duties of child rearing have been lifted from tired middle-aged shoulders.

No more P.T.A. meetings, dance recitals, Boy and Girl Scout campouts, high school basketball games, and the countless other functions parents feel obliged to attend. No more dirty socks under the bed, raided refrigerators, and gym suits to wash. In the post parental years, cocktail conversation rises above toilet training, how much allowance is too much, and the abysmal performance of the high school football team. The recently retired parent may first taste the sweet wine of maturity, and in its heady glow, a love affair may bloom.

Once the children leave, they're not Mom and Dad any more—but Husband and Wife. There's a time of rediscovery—time to talk, or sit quietly with the television off. Without children to compete for attention, the warmth of intimacy is rekindled; as a friend said to me recently, "At last we are a couple again."

The joys of post-parenthood are the antidote for the empty nest syndrome. Weep not nostalgically for the cacophony of adolescence, and shed no tears for the turmoil of teenagers underfoot. Rather, welcome the new freedom and rejoice in the unaccustomed leisure, the beckoning opportunities, and fresh intimacy of the post-parental years. Say "no" to the empty nest and "yes" to life when the children are gone.

You may say, "That's okay in theory, but what do real people think of life in the post-parental years?"

In his book *Married Life in the Middle Years,* Irwin Deutscher tells of interviews with 49 middle-agers whose children had grown and departed. Of these individuals who had said "So long" to child rearing, almost half (22) rated the post parental years as the best time of life, and another 15 opted for "as good." The dissenters? Only 3 of the 49 interviewees lamented that the post-parental years were worse than the child-rearing era.

When the Husband Strays

Sometimes the marital foundation crumbles and the post-parental years reveal that children were the buttresses holding the marriage together. Intimacy yields to apathy, and finally discontent—until one partner feels the urge to stray.

Clarence Darrow once said, "Marriage is like going to a restaurant with friends. You order what you want, then you see what they ordered. And you wish you had ordered what they have."

The man in his middle years plagued by a nagging discontent with work and love and the lifestyle he has created, may find the urge to sample other pleasures overwhelming. For years, temptation is stifled, perhaps not by fidelity but by a lack of opportunity, until one evening the husband who 30 years ago blushed and said, "I do!", with three martinis in his bloodstream and a gleam in his eye, corners his best friend's wife in the hall and says, "Let's!"

The subtleties of marital fidelity vary around the world, often more attuned to the orderly propagation of the tribe than to ego-gratifying illusions of faithfulness. The Middle Eastern Moslem journeying on tribal business might undertake a short-term marriage contract during a prolonged stay in a distant city. When her tenure is terminated by the husband's departure, the wife is compensated for her service, with later-arriving offspring considered legal heirs of the "husband."

Mr. Eskimo faced with a trip in the frozen wastes yet encumbered by a pregnant spouse might exchange wives with a colleague remaining behind. When the wandering husband returns with his surrogate spouse, the original wives may be returned. Or maybe not.

In more affluent cultures where survival of the species is not subject to the whims of snow and sand, marital fidelity is governed by mores rather than necessity. Today, with the erosion of traditional morality and the abundance of opportunities for dalliance, statistics concerning male marital infidelity become outdated as soon as the ink on printed pages dries and are as unreliable as a wayward husband's protestations.

WHY HE CHEATS

Why do husbands cheat? Perhaps it's curlers on the pillow, or stockings in the shower, or dirty dishes in the sink. Often nagging sets the stage for unfaithfulness as our hero returns from the office grind to hear, "The drain is plugged again, and when are you going to mow the lawn? How about those shelves you were going to build in the hall closet? What's wrong with you anyhow? You never seem to want to do anything." He wants to do something, all right, but the law carries stiff penalties for mayhem. So he seeks a less violent outlet—the available airline stewardess or perhaps the willing wife next door.

The cause may be elusive as a whisper. There's a quiet moment at work. A secretary smiles—just friendly—and he realizes, "Work at the office is more fun than going home." It may not be long before he finds a home that's more fun to come home to.

What are the clues that the urge to stray has struck? It's overtime at work night after night. It's the out-of-town convention—no wives invited. Sometimes the symptom is heart-breaking rejection—spurning his wife's crowning culinary creation or even declining her invitation to bed. Worst of all, it may be silence—the maddening, demoralizing failure to communicate that seems to shout, "I won't waste breath on one too demented to comprehend."

Soon she learns he's communicating with a cocktail waitress, 20 years his junior, hot-pants and all. Or perhaps it's a receptionist, more tuned in to his 9-to-5 life than the wife who hasn't visited the office in years. A firm and youthful exuberance may camouflage the young contender's lack of maturity, yet to the straying middle-ager, she's the fulfillment of his sexual fantasies.

Friends may wonder, sometimes with envy, "What does the

young miss see in Mr. Middle-age?" To her, he's mature, worldly, experienced. He's affluent and can take her to exciting places beyond the means of her contemporaries. And most of all, he makes few demands. There's a brief encounter, a fond embrace, but no pleas for eternal fidelity.

Yet, the wayward husband does not always topple for the cute young thing. More and more, mature men seek liaisons with women their age . . . and older. Why? The mature woman has insight, patience, and experience that the mini-skirted miss will need 20 years to acquire. She's worldly and exciting and often beautiful. With creative cosmetology, helpful hormones, and even a surgical tuck here and there, it's not uncommon to see such a man sipping cocktails with a woman a few years his senior.

HOW TO HOLD THE STRAYING HUSBAND

Who's to blame when the husband strays? The contented husband can only consider an extramarital affair a bother and a threat to his continued happiness. When the husband strays, he is condemned as the transgressor, but his wife must share the blame. In some way, she's failing to fulfill the marital contract, and should ask herself, "How have I failed?" Maybe in the living room with a paucity of timely wit, perhaps in the kitchen with too many T.V. dinners; yet, it's most often in the bedroom, with ennui when there should be enthusiasm. When the urge to stray enters, the gate has often been unlatched from inside the home.

Bolt the door! There's just one way to hold the straying husband—or deter the tempted mate. It's not playing the wounded victim, which can only elicit sympathy from coffee-klatchers and the judge in divorce court. Mrs. Middle-age must turn on the charm when she feels her marriage threatened. Husbands don't stray from the cheerful home: no nagging, no matter how high the hedges grows or how many Sunday afternoon football games he watches. Try steak by candlelight, a little wine with dinner, then a new negligee. They all help. If all else fails, try vacation therapy—the ocean voyage or even a motel weekend—to convince him that you, not some simpering postadolescent or aging adventuress, are the woman of his dreams.

The Wayward Wife

Not only husbands stray. A generation ago, women fretted that their breadwinners might desert during the middle years, leaving them to manage the house and raise the children alone. Now the tables are turned. As the children depart one by one to seek their fortunes, today's woman finds that her energies are no longer dissipated by the demanding trivia of child rearing, and as she casts about for other outlets, sex, like knitting and painting, receives attention heretofore lavished on the children.

Hopefully, the awakening sexuality is shared with the husband, but all too often he is indifferent, perhaps mired in work, immobilized in front of the television, or lost in locker room sessions at the golf club. New attitudes toward sexuality, the explosion of menopausal myths, and the slogans of Women's Liberation have broken the traditional bonds of the married woman. Today's woman has been freed from much of the drudgery of housework and exudes new confidence in her femininity. And not uncommonly she celebrates her newfound freedom by undertaking an extramarital affair.

The mature woman rarely strays unless provoked by an unrewarding home life. Then, just to prove she is still youthful and attractive, she acts out her frustrations in liaison with a family friend, casual acquaintance, or even downy-chinned delivery boy.

WHO'S TO BLAME

What can provoke the middle-aged woman to risk marital disaster? It may be retaliation against the philandering husband—the prime ego insult. A demeaning mate, who rebuffs her efforts as homemaker and love-maker, may drive her to another's arms. It may be overwhelming boredom, a husband who's never home, grown children who never write, or the words of friends who terminate loveless marriages to boast of unwed bliss. Add to these the restless urge, the second adolescence that surges through the middle years—and the stage is set for the blunder of infidelity.

Perhaps women expect too much from marriage. In childhood fairy tales, prince married princess, and their lives thereafter were filled with happiness. Now we have television—gorgeous couples confronting the weekly comedy situation, emerging triumphant before the last commercial; they, too, live happily ever after. At least they do until the series is cancelled.

But when she takes the first step toward "cancelling the series," she finds she's entered a cloak and dagger world. "Where can I tell him I was tonight?" "Suppose somebody sees us?" "Don't you think it's dangerous going to your place?" She lives her days in danger of discovery.

Eventually, the family discovers. "The cuckold is the last that knows of it," wrote William Camden in 1636, yet in the end the husband learns the truth. Accusations follow, with tears, and retribution, and often separation. It's a sad outcome to what began as a lark.

As the straying husband's wife must share the blame, the husband with the horns must ask himself, "How did I let this happen?" Perhaps she has been taken for granted, or patronized, or ignored. Has he pulled the wings from the butterfly by censuring her greatest efforts and demeaning her intellect?

Yet all may not be lost.

In the female of the species, the nesting urge is strong. Sexual passions are less compelling than the promise of security and love. When she threatens to stray, there's one foolproof tactic: woo her with the ardor of a young suitor. Send flowers. Call her during the day. Plan a date—once each week or more. Praise her accomplishments and flatter her figure. And most important, pledge your love and trust as you did at the altar years ago.

The Ailing Marriage

Just as there are failing hearts and wheezing lungs, a marriage can become unhealthy. When this happens, it's the relationship that's ailing. Early symptoms may be subtle—the gentle rebuff, the bedtime headache, the unprovoked angry retort. But if ignored, these sentinel symptoms may develop into a full-blown case of marriagitis.

Marriagitis: it's the sick relationship between husband and wife that affects every thought and action. Each comment is examined for subtle significance, compliments are searched for sarcasm, and a peace offering of flowers provokes only suspicion.

It's a duet, with the two partners vying for the lead. At one minute, the husband plays the aggressor, and the wife the oppressed. An hour later, the roles are reversed. If one spouse relaxes his or her guard, the other leaps to the advantage. Day after day, debate rages on sans audience and sans conclusion.

The ailing marriage is a drama without end, the roles faithfully acted out by the opposing spouses. Each day dialogues like the following are heard in homes across the land. One is the money dialogue:

"What is this bill? Twenty six dollars for a new dress!"

"That's right, a new dress! I haven't had one in 2 years."

"What do you mean, you've got a whole closet full of clothes. You know we can't afford any luxuries right now."

"All right then, What about your new electric saw last month?"

"That's different. I need the saw to make things around here and save a little money, which is more than I can say for you. You handle money like a three-year-old."

"You're not any better—the way you're always picking up the check in restaurants to show off before your friends. And while we're at it, maybe we wouldn't have all these money problems if you earned a little more at that stupid job of yours."

"Well, at least I have a job and I bring home a paycheck every week. What about you? What do you do to help support this house?"

"I could work. There are a lot of good jobs open to women now. But I'll tell you one thing. If I take a job, it won't be to feed you and keep up this broken-down house."

"So the money I earn isn't good enough! If that's the way you feel, go to work—you and the rest of the nutty liberated women. But don't expect me to be cooking dinner when you get home in the evening. Because I won't be here at all."

"That's fine with me."

In other homes, it's the dirty-house dialogue:

"Mary, every ashtray in this house is full. When are you going to clean things up?"

"Clean them yourself. They're all your old cigar butts."

"It's not just the ashtrays I'm talking about. This house looks like the town garbage dump. There in the corner, there's tinsel from last Christmas. There's so much dust under the bed that even the roaches are sneezing, and your kitchen should be fumigated. It smells like something died out there."

"If you think it is so bad, why don't you help out? At least you could wash the dishes or fix that sink that's been half-plugged for 2 years."

"Look, I work hard 8 hours a day, and I'm entitled to some relaxation. What do you do? You sit on your backside watching television, getting fatter and fatter as the house gets dirtier and dirtier."

"If you don't like it, then why don't you live somewhere else!"

"Well, maybe I will!"

SLAM goes the door.

See how the dialogue escalated from a dirty ashtray to total calamity. Neither person planned the climax, but it's often the way the encounters end.

CAUSES OF THE AILING MARRIAGE

The causes of marital discord are legion. Rarely can one say, "This or that is the single reason." More often a multitude of small troubles combines to cause disaster. We've already discussed ill-spent leisure time, and the dangers of overvolunteering. Money woes can follow the ownership compulsion, and the left-behind housewife or super-liberated woman may soon be replaced. Disaster—fantasized or real—may cement the marriage or send it toppling.

The postparental readjustment can throw an unstable marriage into a tailspin: "I no longer have to stay with you for the children's sake. They're gone now, and I just may leave, too!" In some homes, middle-agers become reacquainted once the children depart, only to learn that they really don't like one another at all.

In other marriages, it's the failure to provide emotional support. Oliver Goldsmith once said, "All that a husband or wife really wants is to be pitied a little, praised a little, appreciated a little." But if these small boons are not forthcoming, trouble may follow in large measure. Many spouses treat their mates with arrogance, while chance acquaintances are greeted with courtesy and good cheer. It's not long before the aggrieved proclaims, "I won't bow to your tyranny any longer."

Other couples argue. Dear Abby (Abigail Van Buren) once wrote, "Show me a married couple who boast that they have never had an argument, and I'll show you a pair of lovebirds complete with bird brains." Yet, many abuse the honorable institution of the family argument. They stray from issues, inject biting personal invective, and sometimes punctuate their expletives with physical violence. Even worse, some hold grudges, passing day after day and night after night in stony silence, each waiting for the opponent to capitulate. Soon the topic of the argument is forgotten, and what survives is hostility and acrimony.

In still other marriages, the relationship deteriorates into a continuing confrontation. Partners become adversaries determined to dominate one another. The weapons? Sex, the weekly paycheck, or peace of mind become ammunition to gain a tenuous advantage.

The most common battleground is the marital bed. A divorce court judge once said, "When marriage fails, the cause is not usually found in the living room, kitchen, or even the checkbook; it's in the bedroom." Sometimes one spouse or the other has strayed, but the more common complaint is a loss of desire, a paucity of gusto, and the untimely assertion that the bedroom is for sleeping. Sex is dispensed as a reward for favors, given grudgingly if at all.

The weight of small insults builds year after year, until finally dry rot has gutted the marital relationship, as a cancer destroys vital organs. In the end, drastic therapy is needed if the marriage is to survive.

HEALING THE AILING MARRIAGE

There are three solutions to marital schism. You can endure the sick relationship; millions do, bearing the torment as though it were a badge of honor. After a few years, the ears become deaf to nagging, and the skin is no longer pierced by barbs. Spouses coexist in sullen apathy, each acting out a role without joy or passion.

Or the ailing marriage can be rejuvenated. This takes professional help, and partners seriously interested in revitalizing their union should seek a professional marriage counselor. Beware the self-appointed expert. Check credentials: many individuals with marginal qualifications have entered this field, offering advice as likely to be harmful as beneficial. In many cases, embattled couples turn to their spiritual leader or family physician who may, with aptitude and training, provide guidance on a par with the best marriage counselor. (If in a quandry, contact the American Association of Marriage and Family Counselors, 225 Yale Avenue, Claremont, Ca. 91711, for guidance.)

One-party marriage counseling is like waltzing alone. Don't waste your money and the counselor's time unless both husband and wife are interested in therapy. Single spouse marriage counseling simply doesn't work. Both partners must resolve to be honest, to see the sessions through, and to give offered advice a fair try—even if some suggestions seem a bit pedantic or a trifle foolish.

Marriage counseling doesn't always help, and sometimes foments discontent. Professional intervention can lead to guilt feelings: "Why can't I make a success of marriage on my own?" Problems arise if the marriage counselor attempts to impose his morality, religious beliefs, or personal prejudices upon the couple in counseling. When the marriage counselor is of a different generation, he may cling to yesterday's concepts of sexuality and male-female roles, waving these notions like a banner.

Marriage counseling perhaps fails more often than not, yet many unions have been saved by creative guidance, as the trip to the marriage counselor's office marked their first joint venture in years. Across the counselor's desk, the problem is confronted. The fact of marital discord is first admitted, and recognition of the problem is a small step toward solution.

Often the marriage counselor asks, "Why are you here? What do you really want from counseling? Do you think your marriage can be saved, should be saved, and why?" He knows that patched-up marriages have a poor prognosis, that not all marriages should be rescued, and that some relationships suffer so grievously that they should be put out of their misery promptly. That means divorce.

Divorce is the third solution to the ailing marriage. Montaigne wrote, "Marriage may be compared to a cage: the birds outside despair to get in and those within despair to get out." Divorce is getting out. Some see it as failure—the inability of two partners to sustain a viable marriage. But divorce is often constructive, and many once-married individuals agree that termination of the marriage was "the best move ever made." The next sections take a closer look at divorce during the middle years.

Who Wants a Divorce?

When decay weakens marriage bonds, or spouses stray, or life together becomes intolerable for reasons large and small, the middle-aged husband and wife often see their marriage end before the bench of a man we'll call Judge N. Frederick MacLaine. His is a divorce court, and last week we had a long conversation. I asked him, "Who wants a divorce?"

"Really, nobody," he replied. "Each day, in the justice office down the hall and in the church across the street, couples plight their troth and swear eternal love. Each assumes the union will last forever. Yet, as the years pass, the partners often drift apart. Sometimes the gulf is widened by physical abuse, mental cruelty, or blatant infidelity. But more often, the husband and wife grow from lovers to opponents. It doesn't happen overnight. Day by day, small disagreements escalate into continuing warfare, and soon the home becomes a battlefield. From time to time a truce is attempted, but hostilities soon break out again. In the end, the best solution is often divorce."

Judge MacLaine continued, "Sometimes I think of myself as a surgeon, severing the bonds of a sick union, relieving physical suffering and emotional distress. It's like separating Siamese twins. Yet, of course, the procedure is more legal than medical. Marriage is a contract, perhaps made in heaven, but signed on the dotted line like any other business agreement. Each partner brings to the bargaining table certain assets and not a few liabilities. Marriage merges the assets in hopes of mutual benefits, and the agreement is sealed in good faith. When and if it becomes evident that the union was a bad bargain for one or both parties, the law allows individuals to "buy out of the contract." That's what keeps my divorce court busy.

"Divorce courts in America do a booming business, and it's increasing every year. In 1960, there was one divorce for every four marriages, but by 1970, the ratio had increased to one in three. In 1975 there were 2,182,000 marriages and 987,000 divorces, with the total number of marriages declining and the total number of divorces increasing compared to previous years. (Source: *The World Almanac: 1977.*)

"State lawmakers and judges have asserted their individuality throughout American history, and each state has always had its own unique divorce requirements. Consequently, migratory divorce has long been popular, as consenting couples skip to liberal states to obtain the quickest, cheapest, least complicated divorces.

"In the early nineteenth century, Ohio was a favored divorce mill, and today, statistics would seem to indicate that Nevadans are poor marital risks, with the sparsely populated state recording a divorce rate of 21.4 divorces per 1,000 residents, compared with a national rate of only 4.0 per 1,000 individuals. The reason? The Nevada rate has been swelled by thousands of transient divorcees from states such as New York, which until 1967 allowed divorce only in the face of adultery, or from South Carolina, which until 1949 denied divorce to its residents for any reason.

"Yet, statistics tell a different story when the total number of divorces is considered. Leading the divorce derby is California with 129,144 divorces in 1975. Next comes sunny Texas with 77,438 and Florida with 63,267. New York State's still-tough divorce laws held its score to 55,502 while the grand total for

Nevada was only 9,906 divorces." (Source: *The World Almanac: 1977.*)

"How about divorce in other cultures?" I asked.

The Judge replied, "Religion has been a major deterrent to divorce throughout history, and even today in many countries where the Roman Catholic tradition prevails, marriage is terminated only by death of one of the parties.

"Under Islamic law, the Arab sheik can reject any of his wives by proclaiming, 'I divorce thee,' although in the male supremist tradition, wives are not granted the same easy exit from marriage.

"Minor children throw roadblocks in the path of couples considering divorce in the Soviet Union, where state policy discourages divorce when offspring are involved. On the other hand, childless Russian couples can dissolve their marital vows by joint notification of the local commissar.

"Perhaps anthropologist Margaret Mead has the best solution, which she discussed in the August-September, 1970 issue of *Modern Maturity*. Dr. Mead proposed what she called the two-step marriage. First would be the 'individual' or 'student' marriage, allowing young people to adjust to the give and take of cohabitation, but without the burden of children. If the union crumbles, there's no youngster trapped in the middle. Of course, the individual marriage sans children can succeed only in cultures where reliable contraception is available.

"Next comes what Doctor Mead called the 'parental' marriage, implying that the couple plan children. The parental marriage is a permanent contract, based on a mutual desire to raise a family. Divorce involving the parental marriage would be much more difficult than termination of the individual marriage, because it would break all-important parent-child bonds. As the article pointed out, Doctor Mead's two-step marriage proposal has brought a storm of disapproval, but it might calm the troubled waters of obligatory marriage, unwanted children, and one-parent families—and help clear my divorce court docket."

THE DIVORCE DECISION

Most middle-agers have divorce fantasies. In their dreams, they throw off the harness and live in unfettered bliss forever after. It reminds me of a book (whose title I have long forgotten), telling of a middle-aged Frenchman who despaired of business, society, and married life, and travelled half way around the world to seek peace and contentment. He was sure he had found paradise when in 1940 he moved to the quiet Pacific Island of Guadalcanal.

Yet despite the possible perils, many persons opt for divorce. "I want out," they say. The individuals coming before Judge MacLaine's divorce court fall into three groups:

The marital impossibles should never marry in the first place. Lester Hobart is one of these: At a party or a chance meeting on the street, he's the paragon of affability—witty, charming, and terribly interested in what you have to say. But close relationships terrify Lester, and when communication threatens to progress beyond banalities, he becomes hostile and aggressive. When Lester drinks, which is almost every night, verbal and physical abuse often follow. Chance acquaintances think he's wonderful, but his present wife (his third) knows better, and she's secretly packing for a quick trip to Mexico.

The mismated might have made a go of marriage with other partners. They say that opposites attract, but that doesn't mean they can succeed in life together. Take Ronald and Jane for example, his idea of a fun evening is Monday Night Football on television; she loves dancing. He's a fresh air sleep-with-the-window-wide-open enthusiast; she likes hot-house living. He's addicted to cigars; smoke makes her sneeze. She's an ashtray emptier; he tosses yesterday's underwear in a corner. They're Felix and Oscar, but nobody laughs.

The discontented are tired of marriage. They're also tired of work, of life, and of each other. The discontented think divorce will solve their problems. It won't. In this group are most straying husbands and wayward wives, busily manufacturing grounds for divorce where no other good reason exists. Eventually, the discontented act out their freedom fantasies, swelling the bank accounts of divorce lawyers.

Individuals considering divorce should choose their lawyers with care. Some are paper shufflers; others are true counselors-at-law. Keep in mind that just as the surgeon doesn't receive his big surgical payment unless he removes the gallbladder, the whopping legal fee follows bringing the divorce to completion, not saving the union. The divorce lawyer has a vested financial interest in dissolution of the marriage.

Parenthetically, it has been my experience that the attorney who is divorced or separated is more likely to recommend termination of the marriage than the barrister who lives in wedded bliss. All other things being equal, the couple who truly wish to save their marriage should seek out a happily married lawyer.

IS DIVORCE FOR YOU?

Courts permit termination of a marriage only for valid reasons—grounds for divorce. It's really not enough that he and she have grown tired of each other. One or more of the following seven grievances are cited in most divorce actions:

1.   **Cruelty**, mental or physical, leads the list in most states. It's the systematic attack on the partner's emotional well-being and physical health. Not all states allow divorce for mental cruelty, but repeated physical abuse is a universal justification for ending a marriage.

2.   **Adultery** was long the sole grounds for divorce in some states, prompting cooperating attorneys and their clients to stage elaborate and well-documented, but false liaisons, with all parties, often including the judge, privy to the hoax, Today, such deception is rarely practiced.

3.   **Desertion** should end the marriage by itself, yet most states require that 1 or more years pass before divorce is granted, with the abandoned spouse living in limbo in the meantime.

4.   **Failure to provide** allows the wife to break her marital bonds with the Saturday-night-husband or the big spender who dissipates his paycheck before arriving home on Friday night.

5.   **Habitual drunkenness** is a factor in thousands of divorces, and with an estimated 9 million overt or closet alcoholics in America, it's indeed a wonder that alcoholism is not the downfall of more marriages.

6.   **Imprisonment of a spouse**, often found hand-in-hand with failure to provide, allows freedom to the wife left behind. Waiting periods vary, and the fact of imprisonment is often the proverbial final straw that crushes an ill-fated marriage.

7.   **Insanity** justifies divorce in 24 states, following an average waiting period of five years.

Should there be tears at a divorce? Only sometimes. A few years ago, I attended a divorce party. It wasn't a marriage reception or anniversary celebration, but an old-fashioned wing-ding commemorating a divorce. A fine party it was, too. We celebrated not the end of a marriage but the beginning of a new life for two good friends who had agreed to go their separate ways. Judge MacLaine had presided, and that evening he told his wife, "I did a good job today. The operation was a success. I freed two patients from a marriage that was smothering them both. I trust I'll never see either in my court again."

Next case.

The Wonderful World of the Once-Married

To the middle-ager contemplating divorce, Oscar Wilde must seem to have possessed divine wisdom when he wrote, "Divorces are made in heaven." The mind, that great deceiver, comprehends only escape and adventure—escape from the bonds of a less than ideal marriage and the adventure that must surely come with freedom. Yet, those who live in the world of the once-married soon learn that the delicious independence may be an illusion.

To be sure, there's freedom. There are new places to see, new friends to meet, and new experiences to savor. There's the thrill of availability and the sudden realization of single status.

The telephone rings: no longer is it a nuisance, but rather the lifeline to the social world. Who's on the line? Another single? Perhaps a date? Or a new love affair?

To the once-married, life takes on new meaning. There's a rebirth of awareness—of subtle glances, of body language, of relationships between male and female. "The man in the elevator smiled today, and I'm sure he noticed me as I left," she thinks. Perhaps. Or maybe he was planning his strategy at a coming conference.

Soon the once-married feels the new longing. For years there has been the one-to-one relationship, he and she, man and woman, husband and wife. The urge for a new "someone special" is strong. Where to find the right one? How to avoid the overly anxious, the misfit, the predator?

Unless the void is soon filled, longing breeds loneliness. Solitary breakfasts, evenings with the television, and all the while trying to be both mom and dad to the kids—they all fan the flames of loneliness.

Old friends? They try for a while. But they're couples and you're a single—a threat! Maybe the divorce germ is catching. The single life may seem too enticing, and perhaps the married lass now sees her once-married friend as a competitor. For reasons often obscure, the once-married sees old friends drift away.

To find new acquaintances, it's back to the dating game. How many years has it been? You have almost forgotten how to start. The game plan has changed since we were young. Remember the church group, the Saturday night dance and community picnics of our youth? They departed with the jitterbug and pleated pants. Today there are singles bars, singles weekends at resorts, and even apartment complexes for the swinging singles. But there's the same old desperation, and the old openers are still there: "Do you come here often?" "Haven't we met before, maybe in Miami?" And even the time-honored, "What's a nice girl like you doing in a place like this?"

Don't despair. They must be here somewhere—the real people, the lovely lasses and dashing young men ready for a meaningful relationship. It's with them that the divorced middle-ager feels a kinship. Of course, he's more mature, actually a little older, and she's a little worried about the new baby sitter at home.

Look around. How many swinging singles have a touch of gray, saddlebags on the hips, and support hose? There's the hackneyed phrase, last year's funny story, and laughter just a little too late. It's a sad discovery—that the world of the once-married is not necessarily populated with beautiful people, but by slightly used individuals just like you and me.

The glamour fades, the phone doesn't ring. Maybe it's out of order. Computer dating short-circuits, solitary dining brings indigestion, and television shows become repeats.

You become restless, and perhaps regret a little. "It wasn't supposed to be like this at all. Whatever happened to the wonderful world of the once-married?"

A One-Parent Family

A real victim of divorce is not the deserted, the cuckold, or even the middle-ager who sees his dreams of single sensuality shattered. It's the children who suffer most when marriage ends. A child, whether toddling in the nursery or bounding off to college, is the fruit of a marriage, the product of love between two individuals. Whatever his age, the child knows this. When love crumbles and the marriage collapses, all the child can see is failure. Mother and Father have failed him, and he has failed to hold them together.

"But the children understand," insists the divorcée. Sure, the child understands. He understands that home as he knew it is gone, that his future is in turmoil, and his mother and father no longer love one another.

Children never really understand a divorce. They learn of it, accept it, and make the necessary adjustments. But they never understand.

One day the divorce is final. One parent's clothes are gone. One side of the bed is empty. The living room doesn't smell of his pipe or her perfume any more. Of course, the absent parent will send money, and perhaps visit every other Sunday. But from now on it's a one-parent family.

For all its apparent disadvantages,—the one-parent family is often a spectacular success. A family court judge once explained why: "A loving, happy one-parent household offers a better climate for child-rearing than the home in which parents fight like cats and dogs."

Any child will tell you: it's better to be happy with one parent than live in tears with two bickering adults.

Sometimes the child first comes to really know his parents after the divorce is final. While they lived together, the parents' energies were consumed by hostility, and they presented a dismal countenance to the children. "Mommy and Daddy were always mean and angry." Once divorced and physically separated from one another, mismated parents became tolerably kind and moderately cheerful—realizing the full potential of their personalities, a potential heretofore stifled by marital discord.

Help is available for the one-parent family. There are day care centers for childern so that the single parent can work. Scouting and sports bring boys and girls needed role models to help replace the missing Mother or Dad. And there are counselors to help youngsters cope with the realities and fantasies of parental separation.

Offering a helping hand to all one-parent families is Parents Without Partners, which strives to develop healthy family relationships within the single-parent framework. Picnic outings, family dinners, and hayrides with the children are all part of the fun, yet what is amusement for the children is a serious parental effort at preserving family unity and pride. Parents Without Partners says: "You're not alone. Come join us." A note to Parents Without Partners, Inc., 7910 Woodmont Avenue, Washington, D.C. 20014, will bring a reply telling of the chapter nearest you. A monthly magazine, *The Single Parent,* is also available.

As the glitter of single independence tarnishes, and as one-parent families pool their resources in joint activities, it's not surprising that the once-married swinger often abandons his hard won freedom and the single parent succumbs to the urge to wed again.

The Second Time Around

"Four of every five divorced persons get married again. Obviously their divorces had not signaled disenchantment with marriage as an institution. They were trying again, in the hope of doing better the second time around," wrote Lester Velie in the February, 1973 issue of *Readers Digest* ("The Myth of the Vanishing Family"). When we add the many once-marrieds cohabiting without benefit of clergy, the percentage of divorced individuals establishing one-to-one male-female relationships is high indeed.

Why remarry? Once singed by the fires of marital holocaust, the victim might be expected to avoid future danger. Yet, the marital fireside can give comfort and warmth, and despite the risks, the once-married is often drawn again to the warm companionship of marriage.

Most are middle-aged, and although first-time marriages among middle-agers account for only about one percent of all nuptials, a full one-fourth of individuals marrying for the second time are middle-agers.

THE RISKS OF REMARRIAGE

Of course, remarriage has its special problems. The once-married is a unique individual. No longer a bachelor or bachelorette, the divorcée (or widower) forsook his never-married status at the altar. His thinking, his way of life changed by the first marriage, he can never again return to the dewy-eyed innocence of the never-married.

Some middle-aged once-married hesitate. They ponder: "Will remarriage blight my relationship with the children? Will we lose our special parent-child bond if another adult joins the household?" Certainly, remarriage will change the daily give and take of parent and child, but it's usually for the better as the youngster gains a father figure or new mother, while the overworked single parent acquires an extra pair of helping hands. Sometimes families merge when graduates of Parents Without Partners pool their parental responsibilities and opt out of the organization.

Remarriage may muddle finances, especially if attempted

without enlightened legal advice. For the divorcée, there are alimony and child support payments to consider. The widow and widower face potential estate problems: upon the death of the remarried individual, should the estate go to children of the first marriage or the mate of the second? A wise attorney anticipates problems, and may insist upon a premarital agreement, spelling out all financial contingencies, with the agreement signed and sealed before the marital vows are taken.

With premature heart attacks claiming more and more middle-aged males, many a woman finds herself a widow long before her senior years. And the widow of any age faces a special problem. For some reason, perhaps as a self-imposed penance, there's the notion that the state of widowhood should be celibate in honor of the departed spouse. It's an anachronism, as up-to-date as the widow flinging herself onto her husband's funeral pyre. Yet the prejudice prevails, and the widowed once-married sometimes finds her remarriage plans stymied by family opinion and by misguided loyalty to the departed spouse.

Finally, there's the notion that second marriages are seldom successful. Yet, the opposite is true, probably because mature individuals are indeed discriminating in their choice of marital partners the second time around. After one divorce, there'll be no risking freedom on a fleeting infatuation. The myth of second marriage mishaps was exploded by Walter C. McKain, Professor of Sociology at the University of Connecticut, who studied 100 couples remarrying at age sixty or over. When interviewed after 5 years of marriage, only 6 couples of the 100 said their marriages were on the rocks. A full 74 couples rated their remarriages as successful.

Nevertheless, catastrophic second marriages occur, and perhaps could be avoided by premarital counseling. Marriage counselors earn their living dealing with unhappy unions, and all but the most insensitive develop a nose for those marriages that are destined to succeed and those doomed to failure. If contemplating remarriage during middle age, wouldn't it be a good idea to spend a few hours with a marriage counselor before saying "I do?" Tell her of your plans, listen to her comments, and ask, "Do you think this marriage will work?"

The second-time-around marriage is often better than the first. Middle-agers learn from their mistakes, and enter remarriage with wisdom acquired in battles past. Yet success is not inevitable, and second marriages are no less demanding than first unions. Marriage—whether first, second, or last—calls for devotion, sacrifice, and old-fashioned hard work if it's to be successful.

HOME HARMONY AND DISCORD

> *To be happy at home is the ultimate result of all ambition; the end to which every enterprise and labor tends, and of which every desire prompts the prosecution.*
> *Samuel Johnson (1709-1784)*

MARRIAGE AND THE HOME were favorite topics of the intrepid Doctor Johnson. He knew that home harmony fosters emotional tranquility, while household discord can only cause jangled nerves and vexing discontent.

Home harmony is what makes it all worthwhile. A man can endure complaining customers, and a demanding boss, and his job's many small annoyances—if only he can look forward to a happy home when the day's work's done. Slippers by the fire. Dinner on the table. A smiling wife and children to make a father proud.

Dreams! It's all an illusion. A childhood fantasy. Today's wife often works, the house is as she left it in the morning, and if she's home first after work, she'll defrost dinner. If not, well, there's always pizza.

The children, if they're home at all, may be less than quiet and well-mannered. What today's youngster lacks in timidity he makes up for in bravado. He knows! He knows that truth is relative, that virginity is as obsolete as bustles, and that hard work is for those not clever enough to know better.

Mercifully, not all middle-agers encounter these problems. The melody of most homes has but an occasional sour note. Yet when the household fugue adds a distraught husband, harried housewife, and tempestuous teenager, it can build to a cacophonous crescendo.

To find how harmony can be salvaged from the remnants of dissonance, read on.

A Gaggle of Gaps

In our rapidly changing world, the gulf separating the generations grows as each decade passes. In a slower, more gentle era a century ago, tradition dictated and propriety proclaimed. Not so today, with ideas speeding from new to obsolete, and young people questioning the traditions of generations past.

Between today's generations lies much more than several decades. Parent and child are separated by ideological gaps—chasms excavated in discontent and eroded in oratory—not time or distance, but thoughts, ideas, words, and values. I call them a gaggle of gaps.

Between father and son, mother and daughter, lies the nostalgia gap, and the dialogue often begins, "When I was your age . . . " Father walked a mile to school; his son rides three blocks. Mother washed the dishes each night and cleaned the house on Saturday; her daughter rarely makes her bed. Today's parent recalls being allowed to drive the family Ford, perhaps on Saturday night, as a reward for good behavior. Today's youngster wants his own new Mustang the day his driver's license arrives in the mail. For better or worse, times have changed, and those who can't keep up emotionally will see the gulf widen between his children and himself.

The morality gap may be the most distressing. To the middle-ager reared in days when sexy movies were for stag parties and nice girls were home by midnight, it's hard to comprehend frontal nudity on the screen, birth control clinics at high school doorsteps, and coed college dormitories. Ernest Hemingway wrote in *Death in The Afternoon,* "What is moral is what you feel good after and what is immoral is what you feel bad after." Today's young people seem to feel bad after practically nothing, but the new morality is distressing to most of today's parents, forming a gap between them and their children.

Then there's the reliability gap. In a weak moment, father promised Shelley a Sunday tennis match. But the weekend rolls around, and an unexpected client pops into town, and father must spend Sunday at his desk: 'Shelley, you understand, don't you?"

Shelley doesn't understand. Not really. All she knows is father failed to come through. He let her down! Kids without responsibility can't comprehend the responsibility of a parent to work or community commitments. When the unexpected forces a change in plans, the youngster can only see it as a promise broken. Childish selfishness? Sure! But the feeling that Mom and Dad are unreliable widens the gap between them.

The cultural gap is often more humorous than harmful. Remember when your parents implored, "Please turn down the radio. How can you stand to listen to that noise? Don't you get tired of listening to Jack Armstrong, Tom Mix, and the Lone Ranger night after night?" Remember when you stood in line to see Frank Sinatra in person, when he was skinny and had wavy hair? Or you spent your last two bits for the Andrews Sisters' record of "Don't Sit Under the Apple Tree"?

Now the shoe is on the other foot, and it's you who are saying, turn down the music. We lament, "Today's music is just noise— there's no melody or harmony as there used to be." To the parent, today's poetry is as comprehensible as calculus, and movies made for the modern teenager are beyond the parent's mentality. It's the cultural gap, growing wider every year, but Mom and Dad might be more tolerant if they reflect upon their one-time devotion to Gene Krupa, Bill Haley, and what we used to call modern progressive jazz.

The credibility gap extends beyond Washington, D.C. The modern parent often misstates a child's age to save on airline fares ("The airlines have plenty of money, and the plane will be making that trip anyhow"), drives a little above the speed limit ("They always let you have an extra 5 miles per hour"), and claims a few equivocal income tax deductions ("Everybody does it. It's part of the game"). These parents wonder why children question their veracity, and why they sometimes grow up to be less honest than George Washington.

Sometimes, the credibility gap between generations can be a vast abyss: "Frankly, Johnny, I can't believe anything you tell me any more." Actually, Johnny doesn't lie to his parents, but he communicates facts selectively, perhaps adding a little subjective coloring. Why? Like a good son, he's following his father's example, emulating techniques he has overheard for years. His motive? Simple self-preservation, since truthful admissions in his household are often met with hostility.

The values gap is perhaps the widest of all, as today's youngsters abandon traditional goals. A white collar job, a split level home in the suburbs, the snug pension plan—they're no longer prized by young persons. Satiated by luxuries lavished upon them by hard-working parents, today's youngsters reject material gains and strive for abstract attainments. Truth, reality, beauty, and freedom to do one's own thing—that's what counts today. There's the tacit assumption that others will supply the sweat and toil to keep society solvent, while the young individual contemplates eternal verities. Perhaps it will take a generation of poverty to return youth to traditions of frugality and hard work. Or maybe youth is right, and we middle-agers have, getting and spending, truly laid waste our souls.

Benjamin Wolman, Professor of Clinical Psychology at Long Island University, commented: "We are living in times of existential crisis. The old values, religious, traditional, moral standards have disappeared, and we haven't created anything new. Parents don't convey values to their children because they are not backed up by society."

Somewhere between the 60-hour-a-week ulcer-ridden executive and turned-on hippie, between the church-each-morning guilt-ridden religious zealot and the adamant atheist, and between the sexually repressed undress-in-the-bathroom adult and sleep-around teeny-bopper, there must be a common ground. Somehow the gaps must be bridged.

There's only one way—communication. Young people call it establishing a dialogue. It's the give and take, the exchange of ideas that can iron out differences. Dad may never become a rock music fan, and his daughter may never learn to waltz, but communication can allow a sharing of ideas. Prejudice must be put aside, and hostility abandoned. A truce. Then face-to-face communication can overcome rhetoric and bridge the gaps between the generations.

Why Don't My Children Talk to Me?

Talking with teenage children can be like pulling teeth. Sometimes I think I might as well write my side of the conversation on a sheet of paper, fold it into an airplane, and sail it out the window—for all the response I get. I'm not alone. Parents around the globe lament the reluctance of their offspring to communicate with the middle generation. Let's listen in on an everyday parent-child conversation as fourteen-year-old Mary Turner bursts through the kitchen door after school:

"Hi, Mom!"

"Hello, Mary, what did you do in school today."

"Oh, nothing." Mary drops her books, gulps a glass of Coke and starts for the door.

"Where are you going, Mary?"

"Nowhere."

"Who are you going with?"

"Nobody."

"What time will you be home?"

"Later," and the door slams behind her.

"Why don't my children talk to me?"

Why can't Mary and her mother communicate? Two reasons overshadow all others. First, Mary is in the throes of teenage rebellion, when she must assert her individuality if she is to become an independent adult rather than remain under parental domination. It's a trying time for parents and child alike, but necessary. During this time, the child may be uncommunicative, even hostile, and efforts at conversation are met with, "You don't understand!"

Second, Mary's mother used all the wrong conversational gambits. She interrogated her daughter, who in turn, responded like a police suspect: anything she said might be used against her. Let's try again, changing the dialogue:

"Hi, Mom!"

"Hi, Mary, I was just going to have a glass of Coke. You're welcome to join me."

"Thanks, I'd like that. My throat is parched from shouting at the basketball game today."

"How was the game?"

"It was really close, but we won in the last 30 seconds. Thanks for the Coke. I'm going out," and Mary races for the door.

"If Bill calls, what shall I tell him?"

"Oh, tell him I went to Sue's house. He can call me there or I'll be home about 5 o'clock." and the door slams behind her.

The conversation was more rewarding when Mary's mother showed interest without prying, when she was concerned rather than inquisitive. But conversational ploys won't solve all child-parent communication problems.

I asked my thirteen-year-old daughter why children don't talk to parents. Her reply? "When we say something, parents often don't understand. Sometimes they contradict or argue with you. So it's easier not to say anything."

"Well," I asked, "Not talking to people is a putdown. Do you do that to your friends?"

"Of course not," she replied, "I like my friends."

What she meant was this: I can be rude and disagreeable and sassy to parents—they have to love me. I can take parents for granted, but not my friends. Rudeness to a schoolmate can mean a friend lost.

Still other parent-child communication problems begin as adults berate their offspring unmercifully. They demand and shout, and threaten physical abuse. It's not likely they would address another adult in such a manner. As invective stings the child, he withdraws behind a wall of silence—and meaningful communication ceases.

Communication suffers when parents engage in a favorite sport—jamming their opinions down the throats of younger people. Certainly, it's the duty of parents to protect their offspring from folly, and only mature wisdom can temper youthful excesses. Yet, advice must be timely and tempered with diplomacy.

"Boys with long hair look like sissies." The remark bristles with prejudice and hostility, and is often counterproductive as junior reacts by growing even longer tresses.

Couldn't the parent better express his opinion by saying, "The new short hair styles for men are certainly an improvement over the crewcut and D.A. I remember from high school, and look much neater than long hair." The parent has stated a preference, giving direction as duty demands. Yet, he's not condemned the teenager who fails to follow his advice, as many will fail to do.

LEARNING TO COMMUNICATE

Today's kids have what Dr. Martin Symonds calls psychological sunburn. You say, "Hello," and they respond, "Don't bother me!"

Yet, if civilization is to survive, there must be dialogue between the generations. Here are six steps to help improve parent-child communication:

● Adults must state their positions on issues. Children yearn for adult guidance even when they seem consciously to act in opposition. Mary's mother says, "I think girls look best wearing skirts to school." And Mary? Slacks will be her uniform except on prom night. Yet, Mary gets the message: her mother cares—about her appearance and about her. When Mary is a mother a generation from now, what will she tell her daughter? You guessed it! "Girls look better in skirts."

• Parents must listen to the child's side. Today's children read, and listen to television commentary; and most of all, they think. When their views conflict with parental opinion, the child is sometimes right. It takes a parent with a strong ego to admit being wrong, but it is sometimes the only honest way. Never, never should the child's opinion be dismissed without giving him a hearing.

• The parents should agree. The parent-child conversational calamities are really a search for limits and a test of values. When Mom and Dad disagree, chaos rules. Savvy parents back one another's decisions, and reserve judgment on major issues until they have conferred.

• Avoid conversational confrontations. Discussions sometimes escalate into arguments; that's inevitable. But what's unnecessary is the final ultimatum: "Mary, you apologize to your mother or else!" Mary will grunt, "I'm sorry," but she'll nurse a grudge—and whatever the disagreement was, it's far from over. How much better to say, "Mary, you and your mother have cleared the air. Now let's all be friends again." Family harmony is restored and Mary saves face.

• Treat the youngster with respect. To parents their offspring will always be their babies, even though the "baby" is eighteen years old and packing for college. As the child grows older, the parent must suppress parental preaching and converse with his offspring as adult to adult. Show the maturing youngster the same respect you expect from him or would demand from one of your contemporaries. Remember, there's nothing in the rule book that says the parent is always right.

• Seek professional help when communications break down. Sometimes hostilities erupt, and angry words are followed by silence—day after day. The breakfast table becomes a battlefield, and the living room is chilled with silence. Counseling is often needed to bring a truce. A note to the Family Service Association of America, 44 East 23rd Street, New York, N.Y. 10010, should bring useful information and perhaps a recommendation on where professional help is available in your area.

Rare are those who don't sooner or later ask, "Where did we go, wrong as parents?" Over the years, each parent makes some decisions that are brilliant, offers some advice that is merely correct, and does some things that are overtly harmful. But remorse won't help and guilt erodes confidence.

I advise parents: analyze past mistakes if you must, but don't dwell on them. What's important is now and tomorrow. Few teenagers are beyond salvation, and the responsible parent begins *today* to be the best parent he can. His most vital job? Giving his offspring sound values to guide them during adult life, and the temerity to challenge dogma. One philosopher called it giving the child roots and wings. The key is communication, learning to talk not *to* your children, but *with* them.

Daughters: From Dolls to Dating

The relationship between father and daughter is something special, a bond to be treasured. Euripides told Hellinic parents, "To a father waxing old nothing is dearer than a daughter. Sons have spirits of higher pitch, but less inclined to sweet, endearing fondness." She's his baby, his Electra, and all is rosy until sometime 'twixt twelve and twenty, when her interests switch from dolls to dating.

Also unique is the bond between mother and daughter. It's girl to girl, woman to woman; and perhaps it's the best of both. It's sharing joys, and confidences, and tears. It's suffering together the anguish of adolescence and the pangs of puberty, but the true test comes when the daughter discovers boys.

Some parents cope constructively, melding smoothly into the new role as sponsors and guardians of the local lovely. Father is the object of her special fondness, a strong shoulder to cry on, and Mother is the bedrock of her moral strength. No problem here.

But Mom and Dad sometimes equate dating and debauchery, seeing legions of young men leading their baby to perdition. Dad remembers his boyhood days—oh, does he remember! To him, her suitors may be pimpled adolescents, hirsute hippies, or jive-talking junkies, but they all lust for his daughter's maidenhood.

Middle-aged mothers dated too—in their day. Sock hops in the school gym, double dates at the drive-in movie—and the organdy up-until-dawn excitement of prom night. Remember? Mothers recall and smile.

Yet, Mom and Dad are acutely aware of the moral changes since their dating days. They know that Planned Parenthood clinics, now found in most larger communities, are bringing birth control information and contraception to teenage girls—with or without parental knowledge and approval. And not a minute too soon, since more than half of America's teenagers engage in premarital sexual activity, more or less regularly, and often without the benefit of birth control devices. Perhaps Mom and Dad read the *McCall's* September, 1973 article by Shelley Steinmann List telling of the 50 high school girls in Westport, Connecticut, who had had abortions the previous year.

The prospect of their daughter's amorous adventures is too much for some parents to bear. Restrictions come first, then accusations, then finally ultimatums. The gulf widens and communication ceases. Stalemate.

They're on a collision course—parents and daughter—one that could end with a runaway child and distraught parents. There's only one hope to avoid disaster. Dad and Mom must bring their thinking up to date, and reopen lines of communication.

The chances are that today's daughter will know the thrill of sexual union long before she tries on her wedding gown. Obligatory virginity is a fine old tradition, admired by many but practiced by few. Parents can only hope that their daughter's premarital sexual liaisons will be meaningful, if not lasting, and that she'll be prudent, not pregnant.

For the daughter as well as the parent, it will be a time of crisis. Her values will be tested—values acquired from her parents by words and actions during the years since infancy. It's a time when she must demonstrate respect for her family and for herself.

When daughter first discovers boys and love and all the rest, parents must take a back seat. They've had well over a decade to mold her character. Now she's on her own, responsible for words and deeds. If Dad and Mom have been successful—if she's learned the value of integrity, responsibility, and self-respect—then their daughter will pass from dolls to dating without disaster.

I Remember When I Was Your Age, Son

When an old gentleman waggles his head and says: 'Ah, so I thought when I was your age,' it is not thought an answer at all if the young man retorts: 'My venerable sir, so shall I most probably think when I am yours.' And yet the one is as good as the other.

R. L. Stevenson
Crabbed Age and Youth

Young men bring energy to commerce, vigor to decaying institutions, and youthful integrity to government. Our sons, and our daughters, are our living link with immortality. They are our heirs, to whom someday we will bequeath society and the earth.

Are we, as middle-agers, preparing our sons for their destiny? When their time comes, can we look them in the eye and say, "Son, I've done the best I can. Now it's up to you."

Growing up today is not as it was in the 1940's. In those days, we bought savings stamps, cheered the flag, and loved our country—right or wrong. Remember collecting milkweed pods to make lifejackets for "Our Boys" in Europe. Each youngster's dream was an after school job—$.50 an hour was top money.

Today's young man is more likely to hoist a picket sign than a flag. He criticizes his government and cries for change. Savings? Why save? There may not be a tomorrow. Work? He has all he wants without working.

We—you and I, middle-aged Mom and Dad—are in danger of producing a generation of indolent offspring. Pampered, effete, overfed, and chauffeured from place to place, our sons sometimes seem devoid of all vestiges of manhood. Shoulder-length hair, high-heeled shoes, and unisex clothes blur the image. Sports, student government, and the countless other games in which young men pitted their brains and brawn in years gone by—today they're dying from disinterest. Where, oh where, are the young men of yesteryear? To the tune "I want my son to have everything I didn't have," we've built a monster—overgrown and slothful—that threatens to rule our lives. What will happen when society, as it must, passes to the next generation?

WHEN WE PASS THE TORCH

I believe that the next generation will rise to the challenge, just as youth throughout history has shouldered responsibility whenever it was thrust upon them. I may be wrong, but I don't think so. For generations, parents have despaired of childish antics and predicted disaster for youth. Shakespeare wrote, "I would that there were no age between sixteen and three-and-twenty, or that youth would sleep out the rest, for there is nothing in the between but getting wenches with child, wronging the ancientry, stealing, fighting."

And Samuel Johnson wrote of "the growing depravity of the

world, of the petulance and insolence of the rising generation." Yet that rising generation held the world on course and passed it to the next.

So will the youth of today. Somehow, while we have been allowing our sons their lethargy and financing their follies, they have been acquiring values that will do them credit in their mature years. No, they're not exactly the traditional values. Lacking Great Depression memories, today's youth is more likely to risk capital than hoard it in a bank. Seeing the high price paid in physical health and emotional tension by his overworked parents, young men of today prize peace of mind above success in business. Disillusioned with the perfidy of leaders in high places, our sons will be true to themselves rather than blindly loyal to state or flag.

With confidence, the middle-ager can say, "Things are not as they were when I was your age, son. They've changed, and so has what we hold valuable. But maybe youth really isn't much different; your generation is, like mine was, frivolous, restless, and often foolhardy. But when the crisis comes, as it surely must, you will don the cloak of manhood and make old men proud, as you fulfill your destiny."

What to Do with Mom and Dad

What to do with Mom and Dad can be a helluva problem. When the oldster in some primitive Indian tribes became too infirm to keep up the migratory pace, he or she was given a few days' food and left by the wayside. Cruel? Maybe so, but it solved a problem for the tribe whose survival depended upon quick movement from one hunting ground to another.

Today our solution to the problem of superannuated parents is less expedient, and sometimes less humane. The problem falls to the in-between generation, responsible for rearing the young while pondering what to do with Mom and Dad.

During the middle years each marriage carries up to four time bombs—the parents of the partners. Failing health of one or more can drain the family finances, throw the home into a tailspin, and place the marriage in jeopardy. Your mother-in-law doesn't want to be a burden, but when she's all alone, with arthritis aching so that she can hardly turn a doorknob, and the doctor says she needs someone with her around the clock, what can the daughter and son-in-law do?

Suppose you were the senior citizen? What would you like your children to do about you?

Visits are great. Grandma and Grandpa come with suitcase in hand. There are old family recipes, tales of when Mommy or Daddy was young, and family camaraderie at its best. For the spry oldster who can live alone "most of the time," it's a first-rate solution. In fact, if prolific in younger years, senior citizens with many offspring can visit from one household to the next indefinitely.

Sometimes the visit becomes permanent. Many three-generation households run smooth as butter, at least on the surface. But the mixture of children, parents, and grandchildren can be explosive—dynamite with a short fuse. The glow of family togetherness soon fades, and the relentless presence of Grandma or Grandpa becomes vexing. Eventually, there's hour-by-hour in-law conflict, with barbed jobs and sullen hostility.

"Why can't you keep your mother out of my kitchen? She is always meddling and never puts anything away."

"When is your father going to get off the porch and help a little around the house? I don't see why we have to support him when your brothers and sisters never chip in a dime."

Storm clouds are gathering under that roof, yet in other households, the addition of one or more senior members may help relieve financial woes as a pension check supplements the family income, or perhaps an extra hand with household chores frees a middle-aged daughter to look for a job. Sometimes the presence of an in-law can stabilize a shaky marriage, as husband and wife unite to solve the dilemma of what to do about the other generation.

When health is good, the outlets for senior citizens are endless, and sparking the oldster's interest in a project may be what's needed to improve family harmony. Service organizations get senior citizens away from the television and out of the house—and give purpose to life again. Here are three such organizations:

The Foster Grandparent Program is limited to individuals sixty years of age and over. These volunteers work with children who are emotionally disturbed, retarded, neglected, or institutionalized for a variety of reasons. At present more than 1,000 older Americans are involved, serving 28,000 children in child care institutions throughout the United States.

The Retired Senior Volunteer Program, with the engaging acronym RSVP, is the fastest growing volunteer program in America.

RSVP volunteers perform part-time clerical work, answer questions, act as messengers, and perform the hundred and one other nonprofessional jobs in hospitals and similar institutions across the country.

The Service Corps of Retired Executives has more than 4,000 volunteers—all graduates of the school of hard knocks in business. Members of SCORE (the organization's acronym) lend their knowledge and experience to owners of small businesses in need of good ideas and experienced counseling.

Information about the Foster Grandparent Program and RSVP can be obtained by writing to ACTION, Washington, D.C. 20525. Information about SCORE can be obtained by writing to SCORE National Office, Small Business Administration, 1441 L Street, N.W., Washington, D.C. 20005.

Often the problem is not filling idle hours for the senior family member, but rather deciding where he or she should live. A rest home or retirement village may be the answer. Most have minimum age requirements of fifty years or more; almost none permit children. In some retirement communities there are nursing homes or even health clinics caring for problems not requiring hospitalization. Careful planning makes allowance for the diminishing abilities of age. Needs are anticipated and life becomes simpler both for the senior citizen and for the family responsible for his or her well-being.

Eventually, a nursing home may be necessary. Across the country, senior citizens can choose from 22,000 nursing homes, ranging from converted Victorian mansions to spic and span new-as-tomorrow extended care facilities. The level of care varies with each institution, and a rough gauge is the cost. The minimum-charge institution may be fine for Aunt Tillie who needs only three meals a day and a little help in dressing, but might be woefully inadequate for Uncle Fred who requires tube feeding and upkeep of a urinary catheter. For information concerning nursing homes in your area, you can contact the American Health Care Association, 1200 15th Street, N.W., Washington, D.C. 20005.

Deciding where a parent should live can be agonizing, and often brings guilt feelings when the reluctant final judgment is a retirement village or nursing home. It's seldom a clear-cut choice, and the middle-ager must do his homework, explore all possibilities, and perhaps seek professional counsel, then conquer guilt fantasies and reach an objective decision as to what's right for the family, and for Mom and Dad.

10

THE REWARDS OF THE MIDDLE YEARS

You who are crossing forty may not know it,
but you are the luckiest generation ever.
Every day brings forth some new thing that adds
to the joy of life after forty. Work becomes easy
and brief. Play grows richer and longer. Leisure
lengthens. Life's afternoon is brighter, warmer,
fuller of song; and long before the shadows
stretch, every fruit grows ripe.
                                        Walter B. Pitkin

AT ABOUT THIS PAGE, the reader must begin to wonder, "So far I've struggled with nine chapters of challenges, muddled through the many woes of the in-between generation, and examined ways to cope. What's the purpose of it all? What are the goals—the rewards of middle age?"

Challenges and Rewards

Day after day, year after year, Mr. and Mrs. America joust with adversity and cross lances with misfortune. When the games are over and the banners have been struck, the triumphant claim their trophies.

In the nineteenth century, the English clergyman Charles Mildmay wrote, "Every duty brings its peculiar delight, every denial its appropriate compensation, every thought its recompense, every cross its crown; pay goes with performance as effect with cause."

What are the delights, the compensations, the pay of middle age?

First, there's the challenge of good and evil, right and left, Yin and Yang—the struggle between responsibility and revolution. If the adult can resolve the conflict without catastrophe, he reaps rewards of wisdom springing from experience.

The challenge of the "change of life" throws some for a loss, but the middle-ager who explodes the myths emerges with increased confidence in his or her sexuality.

Some call it vanity; to others, it's taking pride in appearance. It's the challenge of looking your best during middle age, neither juvenile nor prematurely aged. A wealth of help, both cosmetic and surgical, aids the middle-ager in attaining his or her goal—the look of maturity.

The temptation to overeat and underexercise can lure the middle-ager into a sad state of flab, and then there are alcohol, cigarettes, drugs, and overwork to drain vitality and sabotage health. By spurning these enticements, the middle-ager helps maintain a trim waistline, taut muscles, and the vitality to enjoy life.

Disease threatens during the middle years, often through no fault of the victim. Those who overcome illness or escape disease altogether, must give thanks for the most cherished prize of all—good health.

Good health implies freedom from anxiety, depression, and delusions of disease. Emotional problems face many middle-agers, and those triumphant are rewarded with priceless equanimity.

Contentment means avoiding the army of aggravations, large and small, that can plague the middle years: the spouse left in the lurch, the "I'm a failure" fantasy, marital woes, divorce difficulties, thankless sons and daughters, ailing oldsters, and all the rest. Here are life's everyday dilemmas, and the facility with which these challenges are met determines the quality of life in the middle years.

Years of Fulfillment

In youth you planted trees. At first they were little more than short sprouts in the ground, fighting for survival. Year after year, these saplings were buffeted by wind and rain, and blanketed with winter snow. But they grew with each passing season until, in the summer of life, they bear fruit sweeter than ripe cherries.

The middle years—the summer of life: it's the time when our youthful sins beget remorse and good deeds from the past pay dividends. This is the time when wishes are granted—if you've worked for your dreams the middle years are the season of fulfillment, if one will only reach for the brass ring, and dare to be bold.

The gods of Phrygia might have warned, "Be careful what you

wish for; you may receive it." King Midas learned a sad lesson. Examine your motives, update your goals, and be sure your wishes will bring you joy. For better or worse, the middle years are when you get what you've earned.

For those whose wishes find favor with the gods, there are special gifts bestowed. More treasured than gold in the middle years are:

● **Seasoned maturity** that comes only with on-the-job know-how and the "I've-been-there-too" expertise. You've worked hard for the knowledge; now enjoy it during middle age.

● **Personal respect** goes hand in hand with maturity, as others agree, "He always does a good job," or "She's tops in her field." It's having others seek your counsel and knowing that your opinion is valued.

● **Tranquility at home** follows years of life together. He's corrected all his wife's bad habits, or she's taught him not to leave dirty dishes in the sink. By the middle years, the marriage is well broken in, and the often turbulent "period of adjustment" is over.

● **Financial security** is the tangible reward for hard work and frugality, the monetary fruit borne by financial saplings planted during youth. During middle age, the mortgage is ceremoniously burned, and the retirement nest egg reaches maturity.

● **Creature comforts** come as affluence increases. The luxury car, the summer home, the dream trip to Europe—they're denied to struggling young adults with children underfoot, but within the means of middle-agers—if they but dream and save.

● **Personal freedom** is perhaps the most blessed gift of all, as middle-agers are freed from many of the strivings of youth and tiresome burdens of childrearing. There's time to live, and love, and plan. An afternoon on the golf course no longer causes pangs of guilt, and an evening movie no longer means paying a baby sitter. There's leisure time and energy to spare—and new horizons beckon, as we'll see shortly.

The middle years are when we collect dividends for past investments; it's coupon clipping time, as bonds bought in our youth pay off. And yet, it's not time to cash in all our chips, as new opportunities unfold.

New Horizons

The young man on the way up can't afford to come home from work at 4 P.M. and sit by the fire with his feet on the hassock; the man in his middle years can. The young housewife and mother hasn't time for community activities and the afternoon bridge club; the woman in her middle years does. During the middle years, days are no longer filled by frantic activity. Lessened responsibilities free extra hours, and there is time to explore new horizons.

To some, the middle years brings a new job. Too young to truly retire, the man with 20 or 25 years of service in the armed forces or as a policeman or a fireman may find he has acquired a hefty pension and free time to pursue a second career, hopefully less demanding than the first.

Free to seek a new career also is the woman in her middle years. Once the children are on their own, there's time to dust off old skills and return to work, perhaps resuming an interrupted clerical or professional career.

For others in the middle years, the new freedom means time to develop skills. Perhaps he is a golf enthusiast, or his tennis backhand needs practice. For others, the extra hours mean time to garden, arrange flowers, or tackle the redecoration scheme that had been planned for years.

Some try painting—it's fun, and there's little investment needed: some canvas or a piece of hardboard, an easel, oils, and a brush. And your imagination. Think you have no artistic talent? You'll never know if you don't try.

A few, like me, try writing. If you're fascinated by the flow of words, and feel the thrill of a well-turned phrase, then writing may be your creative outlet. How about a short story or a nonfiction article for publication in your field? Some persons take a short course in writing, reviewing composition, word choice, and other tools of the trade. It's a good hobby to take into the retirement years, as many middle-agers head for senior citizenship with the outline for their novel in the drawer, needing only time to put the words on paper.

Let's not forget books—which can stimulate your thinking and expand your horizons. Reading can heighten awareness during middle age; check the bibliography on Page 197 for an up-to-date list of recommended books. But don't stop there. Reading can open doors to new interests, and prepare the middle-ager for retirement years to come.

To some, a new career is too demanding, hobbies leave them cold, and reading causes restlessness. Yet, even for these people, there is an endless list of outlets for middle-aged creative energy: the American Red Cross, The League of Women Voters, the United Way, the Boy Scouts and Girl Scouts of America all rely on volunteer services for survival. Or how about hospital volunteer work, Sunday School teaching, or helping the local day care center?

For the more ambitious, there is VISTA—Volunteers in Service to America—offering those in the middle years the opportunity to serve the needy in cities and towns across the nation.

Those in the middle years with a special skill and a yen for travel may find the Peace Corps made to order. Following special training sessions, there's the opportunity for service in foreign lands, bringing American know-how to less developed countries. Want further information? Write ACTION, Washington, D.C. 20525.

The list goes on and on, increasing each year. As the sapling grows imperceptibly to become a stately oak, and the rushing mountain stream flows into the slowly moving river, so the leisure hours of middle age blend into the noble state of retirement.

On to Retirement

"I will be more than delighted when the time comes that I can retire to a cabin somewhere and take it easy and let others worry about budgets and all the other things that are constantly on my desk," wrote Dwight D. Eisenhower during his years as President.

During the middle years, calendars seem printed in disappearing ink and the hourglass of time flows with quicksand. The hands on the clock race round and round, and it seems you've scarcely packed away the New Year's Eve noisemakers when it's time to get them out again.

Like it or not, Mr. and Mrs. America are on the road to retirement. They're headed for the geriatric, or what more enthusiastic senior citizens call the geri*active* years.

Senior citizenship marks the end of the middle years, and brings its own special problems—money is often in short supply, health may fall prey to the degenerative diseases, or the inexorable progress of aging may bring the gloom of depression. They're all discussed in my book *Feeling Alive After 65* (Arlington House Publishers, Inc., 1973). But here, let's consider a special problem of the golden years, one that calls for advance planning during middle age: retirement.

Retirement—the word connotes withdrawal, removal, departure, escape, and even climbing into bed. But it must not be so, and the slothful retirement soon ends in stagnation, both mental and physical.

Remember high school graduation: you saw it as escape—finally free of Miss Jones and her book reports, and Mr. Hoffman's soporific lectures. Yet you wondered, because graduation was called "commencement." It was not an end, but a beginning.

Retirement, too, is a commencement. It's the start of a new and active phase of life. Retirement is not stopping; it's doing. A senior citizen with a twinkle in his eye once told me, "Retirement is doing those things that you always did, plus some you never had time for, and doing them because you enjoy them. And you can say 'No, thanks' to the rest."

WHY SIXTY-FIVE?

It's onset may be nebulous, but middle age seems to end abruptly at the sixty-fifth birthday, as federal agencies conspire to pigeonhole us all into handy categories.

> Happy Birthday to you!
> Happy Birthday to you!
> Here's your Medicare card,
> And your last paycheck too.

They're all guests at the sixty-fifth birthday party: the Social Security Agency, Medicare, the Pension Fund administrator, and legislators who decree, "It's all over at sixty-five." But it wasn't always so.

In the gay 1890's, 68 percent of males age sixty-five and over were employed, despite the shorter life expectancy eight decades ago. Employed oldersters shrank to 39 percent in 1954, and by 1963, only 24 percent of male senior citizens were on the job. The figure drops each year, and, although part-time jobs make fuzzy statistics, only about 5 to 10 percent of males over age sixty-five enjoy regular employment today.

It's a paradox—that the increased life expectancy and improved quality of health in the senior years should be linked to a progressive decline in meaningful employment. Why?

Mandated retirement is part of the answer. The Congressional decree that sixty-five is the beginning age for Social Security benefits for men helped marked that year as the "usual retirement age." Why sixty-five? Why not sixty-one or fifty-eight or seventy-two? How can a body of legislators, many well past sixty-five themselves, decide the very definitions of life?

Harken to a parallel problem: when oral contraceptives (birth control pills) were first released more than a decade ago, an unknown clerk in a federal agency reasoned, "But we can't allow doctors to prescribe these pills for women indefinitely," and a 2-year limit was slapped upon their use. Eventually, medical science triumphed over bureaucratic fiat, and the 2-year restriction was grudgingly advanced to 4 years, and then dropped altogether. Perhaps some day in the future, the age sixty-five mandate will be modified, allowing each middle-ager to plan his own retirement, scheduling his Social Security deposits and eventual benefits accordingly.

PLANNING FOR RETIREMENT

The American male celebrating his sixtieth birthday today has a life expectancy of about another 16 years; his female twin can expect to live another 20 years, more or less. There's a long time ahead, perhaps more years than you spent in school, or longer than you ever held a single job. Yet for this vital and hopefully golden age, there's often a paucity of planning. As Bernard E. Nash, Former Executive Director of the American Association of Retired Persons has written, "It is ironic that many Americans carefully plan every detail of a 2-week vacation, but do little or nothing to prepare for years of retirement living."

Planning: it's how bridge spans built from opposing shores can join precisely in the middle, it's how a smaller army can vanquish its numerically superior enemy, and it's the key to finding happiness in the senior years. The retirement blueprint is drawn during middle age, and three factors must be considered:

1.   **Planning where to live** can be the fun part, poring over brochures and visiting potential homesites. Florida, Colorado, Mexico, Spain—they all beckon. Climate is a consideration, as cold winter weather often brings frosty fingertips and frozen joints to oldsters. Taxes too must be pondered, particularly when contemplating life outside the United States. Of course, you will think about the family, and how easy or difficult it will be for them to visit your retirement paradise.

2.   **What you will do there** calls for forethought. The harassed middle-aged executive may snort and exclaim, "I'm going to rest, that's what!" But it's not enough. After the first few weeks of

indolence, joints will rust, and mental acuity withers if not put to use. Here's where the new horizons we discussed in the last section become vital. Middle age is the time to develop leisure interests— skills, hobbies, and avocations that will bring meaning to the retirement years.

    3.   **How you will pay for retirement** can be the thorniest problem of all and should be attacked early in middle age. Social Security helps, and the Social Security Act of 1935 marked the birth of federal pension plans in the United States. Annual reviews of the program have kept the level of pension payments for individuals at about one-third of covered earnings, but it may not be enough to overcome inflation. Private pension plans can add retirement dollars—whether provided by a benevolent employer, or from a professional corporation or the Keogh Plan available to all self-employed individuals. Other income sources include annuities, life insurance cash accumulations, and investments including stocks, bonds, and mutual funds.

    Most individuals in their middle years have but a nebulous idea of the income their investments will provide upon retirement, but it's not too hard to figure. An evening with pad, pencils, and policies, plus a note to the Social Security Administration, Baltimore, Maryland 21235 requesting a report of your Social Security earnings (don't forget to include your Social Security number) will give you a ballpark figure. If the projected retirement income seems too low, it's time to get busy.

    Fred Faassen, Former President of the American Association of Retired Persons, has written extensively about retirement and his articles in *Modern Maturity* should be required reading for all. In the April-May, 1971 issue, Mr. Faassen describes four ways to a happy retirement. First, life must have purpose and provide self-respect. Next, service to others is vital. Third, involvement with other human beings is the compass that holds the ship on course. And Mr. Faassen's fourth requirement for a happy retirement is personal recognition—the assurance by others that what we are doing is important.

    Mr. Faassen conducted a retirement planning course at his company. Initially, instruction was given to employees between ages sixty and sixty-five, but participants later remarked that the lectures would have been more valuable if offered 10 years before. Thus the Faassen Retirement Program opened its doors to employees fifty years of age and over, and soon began receiving requests from individuals in their forties.

The message is clear, and the American Association of Retired Persons has inaugurated a new division—Action for Independent Maturity (AIM). AIM is "designed to help younger people make a smooth and satisfying transition from their first career into retirement years without an abrupt change in lifestyle, standard of living, or self-fulfilling interest." Membership in AIM is opened to middle-agers between fifty and sixty-five years of age and may be obtained by writing to Action for Independent Maturity, Division of The American Association of Retired Persons, National Headquarters, 1909 K St., N.W., Washington, D.C. 20036

What's Ahead?

Today, most people can look forward to retirement, perhaps reluctantly, but with confidence if good plans have been made. But what lies ahead for today's teenager or young adult? What will be the quality of life in middle-age a quarter century from now?

Perhaps it's the pizza and milk at bedtime, or the aftermath of office aggravation, but we all dream when sleeping fitfully. Charles Churchill called dreams "children of the night, of indigestion bred." Let me tell you of one product of my somnolent rumination.

I stood alone in an empty room, dimly lit—and faced a giant television screen that dominated an entire wall. There were two chairs. I sat in one. Suddenly, without fanfare, a nondescript face face appeared on the screen:

"Good Evening. Here is the 11 o'clock news, this Friday, July 13, 1999.

"Congress today approved the Senate-proposed bill offering tax relief to all middle-income wage earners. Republican Congressman Eisenhower described the legislation as the first step to ease the heavy burden borne by hardworking middle-agers.

"The Museum of Natural History announced the purchase of 15 'like-new' specimens of automobiles from the 1970's. The automobile, once a major mode of transportation in the United States, will form a permanent museum display, adjacent to the ever-popular exhibit depicting the refining and uses of gasoline, fuel oil, and other obsolete fossil fuels.

"The President's task force to solve the energy crisis predicted another cold winter. As the chairman explained, 'Our once-promising atomic power plants have saturated all areas where nuclear wastes can be dumped. Radioactive emission already exceeds permissible levels in many areas of the country, and we have no alternative but to reduce power supplies until new energy sources can be found.'

"No-fault divorce legislation was signed into law by the Governor of New York State, making the Empire State the last in the nation to approve divorce by a written agreement of both parties. The Governor's mansion was picketed by dozens of angry lawyers protesting the loss of legal fees that will result.

"The recent American Medical Association announcement of an effective vaccine against cancer has brought cheers from around the world. As A.M.A. President Kildare remarked, 'Now if only we could find a cure for the common cold.'

"And this final word from Washington, D.C.: at present more than 500,000 young people from all over the United States are camping at the foot of Washington Monument and jamming traffic down Pennsylvania Avenue. The purpose of their demonstration, according to a spokesman, is 'to praise the parents of this nation for providing youth with food, shelter, education, and love—and to thank the middle-agers of the world for leaving the earth for the next generation a little better than they found it, with governments more responsive, medicines more effective, values more meaningful, and peace a little closer to reality.'"

I'll Take the Middle Years!

The future is empty pages in a history book—to be filled with print and pictures over the centuries to come. We know not whether any or all of the bulletins in my dream newscast will ever be reality. We can no more see into the future than relive yesterday.

The time is now and in this, the most affluent civilization the world has yet seen, the individual in the middle years is at the pinnacle. Jenkin Lloyd Jones, President of the Chamber of Commerce of the United States, had this to say about the mature years: "There is so much right and so little wrong with the middle-aged man, that the government doesn't even have a program for him. No social workers poke into his affairs; no age-group organizers incite his self-pity; politicians shrug him off and direct their promises to the old and the young. The happy fate of middle age is to be left alone."

Ask any mature person, "How would you like to be twenty years old again?" Few would answer "Yes." From the vantage point of maturity, youth is too demanding, too desperate. It seemed fun while we were there, but the youthful years of struggle were but stepping stones to the middle years.

Most would answer, "Be young again? Not me! The despair of dating, the adjustments of young marriage, changing diapers and pushing strollers, and rocking squalling infants in the middle of the night. I've served my time. I fought to get where I am in the community, in business, and in my home. Now I've made it. Repeat those years? Not on your life."

The mature adult: he has a reservoir of forty or fifty years of knowledge and experience. He's learned the subtleties of human intercourse, and how to cope with the ups and downs of everyday living. When the television commercial for that hair coloring compound whispers, "You're not getting *older,* you're getting better," he can smile and think, "How right you are!"

We started ten chapters ago to examine the quality of life in the middle years. How about it?

There's only one answer—it's terrific. Sure, there are trials, and obstacles, and challenges of all sorts, but they add gusto to living and somehow the middle-ager muddles through. And once the challenges have been met, the rewards are more than worth the effort. Youngsters and oldsters, shed no tears for the middle years. The quality of life here is the best ever.

And so, welcome to the adult generation. It's the establishment with a capital "E." It's a bulge at the waistline and a gusset in the slacks. It's remembering the Lindy, the Polka, and even the Bunnyhop. It's working from 9 to 5, it's a day's work for a day's pay, and it's delivering what's been promised. The middle years are responsible and rebellious, sedate and silly, with-it and out-of-it— and we wouldn't live it any other way.

BIBLIOGRAPHY

Some books are to be tasted, others to be swallowed, and some few to be chewed and digested.

Francis Bacon
Apothegms

HERE'S A LIST OF BOOKS for every taste, ranging from cooking to connubiality and rambling from mundane maladies to exotic customs, but all sharing a relevance to the middle years.

If the foregoing pages have whetted your appetite, you'll dash to your local library to sample one or two of these titles.

1. The American Heart Association Cookbook. New York, David McKay, Co., 1973.

"Eating," writes American Heart Association Medical Director, Dr. Campbell Moses, "is one of life's great pleasures." and to live long, we should eat not only well, but intelligently. The book details hundreds of recipes, both taste-tempting and healthful, from wake-up breakfast to bedtime snacks.

2. Arieti, Salvano. The Will to be Human. New York, Quadrangle Books, 1972.

The middle-ager, and indeed each individual, can control his or her life. What's needed is assertion of free will, breaking the bonds of conformity, futility, and oppressive mediocrity. Dr. Arieti urges his reader to tell the world, "It's my life, and I'll live it as I please." Strong stuff!

3 Bardwick, Judith M. Psychology of Women: A Study of Bio-Cultural Conflicts. New York, Harper & Row, 1971.

Freud was a man, and could never understand women anyhow. To really know why females do what they do, say what they say, and are what they are, one must follow the history of our culture, with its sex-determined roles. This 242-page book should give Mrs. Middle-age some insight into her identity, and Mr. Middle-age a deeper understanding of his wife's inner thoughts, conflicts, and goals.

4.   Bergler, Edmund. The Revolt of the Middle-Aged Man. New York, Grosset & Dunlap, 1957.
     "If only I could start over knowing what I know now." When the middle-aged male revolts—against his wife, his job, his children, and his way of life—he finds in the end that little has changed. He attempts to rearrange his life, but his unconscious needs lead him down familiar pathways to the same quicksand he hoped to escape. As the author writes, "He is licked at the start." The middle-aged male planning to chuck it all should spend a few hours with this book; it will be much less expensive than alimony.

5.   The Best of Life. New York/Boston, Time/Life, Little, Brown, 1973.
     It's a memory time for middle-agers, whose life span was chronicled by *Life* from 1936 to 1972. *Life* was always a picture magazine, with a few words reluctantly interposed. This book contains 680 photographs, and includes 100 color pages, detailing the 36 action-packed years of the magazine's existence.

6.   Brown, Harrison and Edward Hutchings, Jr. (Eds) Are Our Descendents Doomed? New York, Viking, 1972.
     Overpopulation, starvation, and exhaustion of our natural resources may be where we are headed. What can be done about these problems is discussed in this book. The articles presented are hardly light reading, but for the middle-ager concerned about the world his children will inherit, it is worth the effort.

7.   Butler, Robert N. and Myrna I. Lewis. Aging and Mental Health: Positive Psychosocial Approaches. St. Louis, C.V. Mosby Co., 1973.
     Here's a textbook written with style. Its focus is on the problems of old age, but it deals with challenges often faced by middle-agers—marital problems, sexual woes, guilt, loneliness, and depression—and gives the younger reader a preview of retirement. Sources of help and information are all listed in the Appendix. It's a topnotch book for the middle-ager who sees retirement on the horizon.

8.   Butterworth, Eric. Life is for Loving. New York, Harper & Row, 1973.
     Love can change our lives: that's the message of the

minister of Unity Center in New York City. This book is recommended for the middle-ager in need of a spiritual pick-me-up.

9. Choron, Jacques. Suicide. New York, Scribner's, 1972.
Why, who, when, and how, and is it really the right answer? What's the attempted suicide trying to say? The book explores the psychological aspects, while prevention centers try to cope with the suicidal crisis. Why include this book here? Because the middle years may also be the suicide years.

10. Clark, Linda A. Help Yourself to Health. New York, Pyramid, 1972.
Positive Thinking is the key to health, asserts Ms. Clark. Sweep out cerebral clutter, set your goals, then plunge into physical and spiritual contact with life about you. This is not your everyday health guide and will never replace the family physician, but it's worth reading.

11. Collins, Thomas. The Complete Guide to Retirement. Englewood Cliffs, Prentice-Hall, 1970.
This book should be required reading for all middle-agers. Topics include finances, selecting the dream home, and how to stay happy in retirement. There are scores of down-to-earth tips, including ways to increase your income, and how to avoid tax pitfalls. Written in a sparkling conversational style, The Complete Guide To Retirement is highly recommended.

12. Cooley, Leland F. and Lee M. Cooley. How to Avoid The Retirement Trap. New York, Popular Library, 1972.
Here's another first-rate retirement guide. Authoritatively written and well documented, the book helps "identify the most common difficulties we Americans face," and offers "specific, common sense easy-to-understand advice on how to avoid them." The authors underscore that middle age is when retirement plans must be laid.

13. Deutscher, Irwin. Married Life in the Middle Years: A Study of the Middle-Class Urban Postparental Couple. Kansas City, Mo., Community Studies Inc., 1959.
"What do we do now that the children are grown and on their own?" That's the question posed by this scholarly well researched monograph, based upon the author's doctoral dissertation. In-depth interviews are quoted at length, the spontaneity of the respondents' replies shining in glowing contrast to the author's plodding prose.

14. DuBrin, Andrew J. Women in Transition. Springfield, Illinois, Thomas, 1972.
Here's a book for Mrs. Middle-age, with facts and figures

gleaned from interviews with 600 women. The author dissects the housewife syndrome—including sexuality, communications, and responsibilities—and takes a penetrating look at women's reactions to these facets of their lives. Women's Lib is placed in perspective, with emphasis upon self-liberation with an enhanced self-image.

15. Fishbein, M. J. The Handy Home Medical Adviser and Concise Medical Encyclopedia. Garden City, N.Y., Doubleday, 1973.

Once called the Ernest Hemingway of the home health guides, Doctor Fishbein has authored a bookshelf full of first-rate medical reference sources. This 1973 edition seems the best buy for the money, discussing how symptoms lead to the diagnosis of disease, how common maladies are treated, and how they can be prevented in the first place. The first aid section can be a lifesaver, and there's a lucid explanation of many tongue-twisting terms used by doctors.

16. Franklin, Marshall, Martin Krauthamer, A. R. Tai, and Ann Pinchot. The Heart Doctor's Heart Book. New York, Grosset & Dunlap, 1974.

Heart disease remains the leading cause of death during middle age and the over-forty man (or woman) will benefit from reading this well written and informative book. A keynote is prevention, with advice concerning diet, exercise, and harmful habits, as well as specific recommendations for the cardiac patient. Put a star next to this book on your reading list.

17. Fraser, Stewart E. Sex, Schools, and Society: International Perspectives. Nashville, Aurora Publishers, 1972.

It's all here, Mom and Dad: what the kids are learning about sex, both in America and abroad. How about Sweden's *Handbook on Sex Instruction in the Schools,* Australia's *How Not to Be a Mummy,* or Masters and Johnson's *Playboy* interview? Wow! Remember when *The Moon is Blue* was banned in Boston?

18. Gaver, Jessyca R. The Complete Directory of Medical and Health Services. New York, Award Books, 1970.

Where can the middle-ager with arthritis, emphysema, diabetes, deafness, or a multitude of other ills find assistance? This book tells all, with specific recommendations and addresses. It's not much help to the healthy, but of inestimable value when chronic disease strikes.

19. Gray, Madeline. The Changing Years: Love After Forty. New York, New American Library, 1970.

Thirteen printings attest to the value of this timeless text on middle age. Written in a down-to-earth style and backed by authoritative quotes, the advice offered is timely for today's middle generation.

20. Hall, Ross Hume. Food for Nought: The Decline in Nutrition. Hagerstown, Harper & Row Publishers, 1974.

    Hall explores the global effects of modern food technology, including the medical, social, and technical problems faced by those who feed the world's population. The conclusion? There's much more to sound nutrition than calories, vitamin pills, and soybean hamburgers.

21. Harris, Thomas A. I'm O.K.—You're O.K. New York, Harper & Row, 1967.

    Here's the truth about Transactional Analysis—the study of how we give and get love and approval, rejection and disapproval. Don't skip the author's unique definitions of Parent, Adult, Child, O.K., and Games, or you'll wallow and sink in the pages that follow. Replete with quotes and footnotes, the book boasts sales of over a million hardcover copies, attesting to the enormous numbers of middle-age readers searching for meaning in their lives.

22. Hunt, Morton M. The World of the Formerly Married. New York, McGraw-Hill, 1966.

    First old friends fade away (they don't want to take sides), then there's the alienation and finally the loss of children ("but they understand"), next come the financial debacle of maintaining two households (and those lawyer's fees, Yow!), and last the certain knowledge of failure as a spouse. All in all, concludes the author, the life of the formerly married is not an idyllic carefree bash.

23. Israel, S. Leon. Diagnosis and Treatment of Menstrual Disorders and Sterility, 5th ed. Hagerstown, Harper & Row, 1967.

    Although I have quoted from it a few times, the reader should skip this technical text unless he or she has a professional degree. It's written for doctors, nurses, and other individuals privy to the secrets of the female reproductive organs. For them, it's an indispensable reference source.

24. Katchadourian, Herant A. and Donald T. Lunde. Fundamentals of Human Sexuality. New York, Holt, Rinehart, and Winston, 1972.

    Here are 514 pages of sexual facts and figures, covering everything from anatomy to morality, meotic to erotic. The book is a leading reference in a field of increasing interest to students of middle-age.

25. LeShan, Eda. The Wonderful Crisis of Middle Age. New York, David McKay, 1973.

    Eda LeShan takes us on a subjective journey through the

middle years. The premise is simple: It's about time to start doing what you've always wanted to. Examples highlight the text and there's much food for thought here.

26. Luce, Gay G. Body Time: Physiological Rhythms and Social Stress. New York, Pantheon, 1971.

Tick-tock tick-tock,
The sun goes up, the sun goes down,
The hands on the clock keep going around.
Schedules, rhythms, seasonal changes—they're all part of the body rhythm of man and animal. Keep in step if you can, and disrupt them at your peril. Here's the physical basis of jet lag and perhaps the key to a host of other mental and physical maladies.

27. Madsen, William. The American Alcoholic. Springfield, Ill., Charles C. Thomas Publishers, 1974.

Written by an anthropoligist, this profusely documented book attempts to synthesize the many diverse theories concerning alcoholism. A broad overview of the subject is presented, although the book might have been more worthwhile had a more systematic approach been undertaken.

28. Marine, Gene and Judith VanAllen. Food Pollution: The Violation of Our Inner Ecology. New York, Holt, Rinehart, and Winston, 1972.

This partisan presentation blasts flavored fluff and colored calories, particularly when we're not altogether sure of the consequences. And while we are at it, how about DDT? I might call this an anticookbook; there are enough facts and figures here to turn the middle-ager against eating altogether.

29. Martin, Clement G. How to Stay Young All Your Life. New York, Frederick Fell, 1966.

Here's a down-to-earth book, extolling the virtues of shadowboxing as exercise, calisthenics to the rhythm of "Prelude à l'Apres-midi d'un Faun," and the healthful boons of woodland strolls. While I don't agree with the author's assertion that "hot flashes are almost entirely emotional in origin" and a few other bromides of equivocal credibility, most advice offered is common sense and easily readable.

30. Masters, William H. and Virginia E. Johnson. Human Sexual Response. Boston, Little Brown, 1966.

Some say they started the sexual revolution, taking sex out of the bedroom and into the laboratory. Their scientific breakthrough, or sin, or what-have-you was not merely in structuring, measuring, and defining the horizons of sexual experience, but in bringing consenting adults together for that purpose.

31. Morgan, Elaine. The Descent of Woman. New York, Stein and Day, 1972.

    Female chauvinism is all the rage these days, and this book starts at the beginning—evolution. From here, the author skips through centuries and sophistries to arrive at the conclusion that, without men, even liberated women are doomed to extinction.

32. Neugarten, Bernice L. (Ed.) Middle Age and Aging: A Reader in Social Psychology. Chicago, The University of Chicago Press, 1968.

    Ms. Neugarten, acknowledged authority on the middle years, has compiled a collection of scholarly treatises covering the life and breadth of the middle years. Discussed are the dilemmas of "The Aging Leisure Participant," the "Quality of Postparental Life," "Aging Among the Highland Maya," and "Disenchantment in the Later Years of Marriage." The ubiquitous Doctors Masters and Johnson explore "The Human Sexual Response: The Aging Female and the Aging Male," and the editor co-authors "A Woman's Attitude Toward the Menopause."

33. Neugarten, Bernice L. and N. Datar. "The Middle Years," in Arietis (Ed.). American Handbook of Psychiatry, 2nd ed. New York, Basic Books, 1974.

    Again the spotlight is on Bernice Neugarten, who updates her concepts of middle age and deals with the concept of the mid-life "crisis."

34. Petersen, James A. Married Love in the Middle Years. New York, The Associated Press, 1968.

    Sensitive and meaningful—that's the best way to describe both love in the middle years and this fine book by Dr. Peterson of the University of Southern California. As passion wanes, married love becomes more meaningful. Recommended for the romantic.

35. Puner, Morton. To the Good Long Life: What We Know About Growing Old. New York, Universe Books, 1974.

    Chapter one begins, "We are in the midst of one of the quietest, least-heralded, most fruitful revolutions in history: the conquest of age as we have known and feared it." The book goes on to tell how we will all be growing older and liking it more and more. I must, however, take issue with the author's views of middle age: "Middle age, perhaps the worst of times, is often the time of greatest stress and anxiety. It is then that there is the rising sense of frustration, fear and defeat, and awareness that fame and fortune will never come, that the best of life is past." Not so! And I plan to send Mr. Puner a copy of *Welcome to the Middle Years.*

36. Quality of Life, Volume 2: The Middle Years. American Medical Association. Acton, Mass., 1974.

    This volume summarizes the 1973 American Medical Association Congress on the Quality of Life, and focuses on the years between twenty-five and sixty-five. The book is a series of reports and panel discussions concerning the chief challenges of our generation—job demands, marital woes, the woman's changing role, and the search for meaningful values in a changing world.

37. Small, Marvin. The Low Calorie Diet. New York, Simon and Schuster, 1971.

    In print since 1952, this cookbook contains taste-tempting, calorie-counting recipes for fatties of all ages. How about egg a la Florentine (160 calories), asparagus Milanaise (65 calories), or Norwegian jellied lamb chops (204 calories)? Included also are the usual diet book generalities and the obligatory calorie counter.

38. Taylor, Eric. Stay Thirty-Nine Forever. New York, Arco, 1972.

    Originally published in 1965 as *Fitness After Forty,* this compact book by the author of the *Official Royal Air Force Manual of Physical Fitness* touches on medical checkups, emotions, and self-medication, but the writer really gets the bit in his teeth when discussing exercise and diet. There is a "circuit training" exercise schedule, graphically illustrated, that would exhaust a Pittsburgh Steelers linebacker.

39. Taylor, Robert B. A Primer of Clinical Symptoms. Hagerstown, Md., Harper & Row, 1973.

    Symptoms are how diseases begin. Headache: tension or tumor? Cramps: constipation or cancer? This book discusses common symptoms in each area of the body, telling how the nature of the complaint plus associated signs and symptoms can help pinpoint the diagnosis. It helps answer the age-old question, "Should I call the doctor?"

40. Taylor, Robert B. Common Problems in Office Practice. Hagerstown, Md., Harper & Row, 1972.

    On your doctor's desk, you may spot this medical text which describes the diagnosis and treatment of the most common diseases encountered by the family physician. Written in a conversational style, this book gives you a peek at disease through the doctor's eyes, telling the diagnostic clues for which he searches, the tests he may order, and the therapeutic alternatives available.

41. Taylor, Robert B. Feeling Alive After 65. New Rochelle, N.Y., Arlington House Publishers, 1973.

   This book tells how to care for Mom and Dad, and explains how to stay healthy and feel alive after receiving your own Medicare card. There are timely tips on diet and exercise, instructions on home nursing procedures, details of diseases common after sixty-five, and the truth about Medicare payments. *Feeling Alive After 65* should be required reading for all middle-agers before entering the retirement years.

42. Taylor, Robert B. Doctor Taylor's Guide to Healthy Skin for All Ages. New Rochelle, N.Y., Arlington House Publishers, 1974.

   Here's a fun guide to skin care, as timely for the middle-ager as for the pimpled adolescent. There's a lively tour of skin by Freddy the Flea, a discussion of skin care at various ages (including the middle years), a peek at problem areas, an analysis of skin diseases, and the all-important seven steps to healthy skin. It's a light-hearted romp over the epidermis. Try it.

43. Terruwe, A.A. and C.W. Baars. Loving and Curing the Neurotic. New Rochelle, N.Y., Arlington House Publishers, 1972.

   In this 480-page text, the physician-authors relate the doctrines of Thomas Aquinas to jet age neuroses. There is a strong religious flavor throughout as extensive case histories illustrate the problems of repression, obsessive-compulsive neurosis, and other psychological entities. Middle-agers will find the section on frustration neurosis particularly timely.

44. Usdin, Gene (Ed.) The Psychiatric Forum. New York, Bruner, Mazel, 1972.

   Here's a potpourri of assertions and opinions on a variety of psychiatric topics. Particularly pertinent is Judd Marmor's discussion of the middle-age crisis, although at least one or two of the other topics are likely to spark some interest as well.

45. Valnet, Jean. Organic Garden Medicine: The Treatment of Illnesses Using Vegetables, Fruits, and Grains. New Paltz, N.Y., Erbonia Books, 1975.

   Linking folk remedies with modern scientific discoveries, Dr. Valnet tells how natural foods help prevent deficiency diseases and infectious disorders, as well as aiding recovery if illness strikes. The author lists the many vegetables, fruits, and grains—including principal known constituents, natural medical benefits, how the plants may be used medically, and how to prepare the juice, elixir, tea, poultice, oil, or other remedy. Dr. Valnet's book is a must for the health-conscious weekend-gardening middle-ager.

46. Wagman, Richard J. (Ed.). The New Concise Family Health and Medical Guide. Chicago, Ferguson, 1972.

It's a first-rate, well illustrated, complete guide to staying fit and avoiding diseases. Of the many home medical guides available, this must be one of the best.

47. Zane, Polly. The Jack Sprat Cookbook, or Good Eating on a Low-Cholesterol Diet. New York, Harper & Row. 1973.

Jack would have enjoyed his zero-fat diet more had he consulted Mrs. Zane's 497-page cookbook. The recipes are simple yet explicit, and seem certain to delight the palate of those engaged in the dietary assault on atherosclerosis.

INDEX

Robert B. Taylor, M.D. is a family physician in New Paltz, New York. He is a Charter Diplomate of the American Board of Family Practice and an editorial consultant to *Physician's Management*. Doctor Taylor's writing credits include *Feeling Alive After 65: The Complete Medical Guide For Senior Citizens and Their Families, Doctor Taylor's Guide to Healthy Skin for All Ages* and *Doctor Taylor's Self-help Medical Guide* (Arlington House Publishers), as well as a trio of medical textbooks—*Common Problems in Office Practice, The Practical Art of Medicine,* and *A Primer of Clinical Symptoms* (Harper & Row Publishers).